Policing Accounting Knowledge

IN LOVING MEMORY
OF A FRIEND AND COLLEAGUE

ANTHONY PUXTY

POLICING
ACCOUNTING
KNOWLEDGE:
The Market
For Excuses Affair

Tony Tinker
Professor of Accounting
Baruch College: City University of New York
and
Tony Puxty
Professor of Accounting and Finance
University of Strathclyde

Λ Markus Wiener Publishers
W Princeton

Paul Chapman Publishing Ltd.
P-CP London

For information write to:
Markus Wiener Publishers, 114 Jefferson Road, Princeton, NY 08540

For the United Kingdom and Continental Europe write to:
Paul Chapman Publishing Ltd., 144 Liverpool Rd., London N1 1LA

Library of Congress Cataloging-in-Publication Data

Tinker, Tony.
    Policing accounting knowledge : the market for excuses affair /
Tony Tinker and Anthony Puxty.
        (Critical accounting series)
    Includes bibliographical references.
    ISBN 1-55876-085-7
    1. Accounting.   2. Accounting—Research.   I. Puxty, Anthony G.
II. Title. III. Series.
HF5625.T48   1994
657—dc20   94-16676
                                                        CIP

British Library Cataloguing in Publication Data

Policing Accounting Knowledge: Market for
Excuses Affair.—(Critical Accounting
Series)
    I. Tinker, Tony   II. Puxty, Tony
    III. Series
    657

    ISBN 1-85396-265-1

Cover design by Cheryl Mirkin

Printed in the United States of America on acid-free paper.

Contents

Preface

The April, 1979 issue of *The Accounting Review* contained a paper by Ross L. Watts and Jerold L. Zimmerman of the University of Rochester. It was entitled "The Demand for and Supply of Accounting Theories: The Market for Excuses." The *Accounting Review* was then one of two journals that were accorded the highest ranking among US and international accounting academics. Almost all the papers it published tackled issues of relatively minor significance, applying statistical methodology in a flat, de-politicised and uncontroversial way. This paper stood out as being different. A paper by the same authors a year previously had attempted to cover new ground by applying its methods (which it labelled Positive Accounting Theory) to accounting choice in a challenging way. The 1979 paper was even more overtly controversial, since it purported to explain the whole process through which academic accounting ideas were produced. The resulting theory was most unflattering to academics themselves, since it depicted them as self-interested and opportunistic rather than scholarly, producing their ideas at the behest of those involved in the political process. Their motive in theorizing, according to the paper, was self-aggrandizement rather than disinterested inquiry.

Both before and after its publication, the paper stimulated controversy. The authors already had established international reputations, were publishing in a highly-regarded journal, and were from a major US school (the University of Rochester). Their paper attracted criticism and comment (in addition to tacit support) for both its central tenet and for the quality of argument and the evidence used to support that tenet. Nevertheless, despite much unpublished discussion and a number of textual comments submitted to the *Accounting Review* over the next few years, only one (by Charles Christenson of Harvard University) was published in that journal, followed by 1988 by a brief critical note by Ruth Hines. However other journals did publish critical comments on this paper specifically or on the Rochester programme of which this was a part (cf Tinker et al, 1982; Lowe et al, 1983; Peasnell and Williams, 198?; Williams, 1989; Whitley, 1988; Demski, 1988; Sterling, 1990; Kaplan and Ruland, 1991). Watts and Zimmerman themselves in their ten-year retrospect (1990) acknowledged that their reactions to submissions to the *Accounting Review* might have been too strongly worded, thus stifling debate and leading to misunderstanding.

Despite, or perhaps because of, this controversy, the paper was successful under at least two criteria: that it has won the *Notable Contribution to the Accounting Literature* award, and that it has stimulated debate, which according to the paper's own propositions constitutes a sign of success, since continued citation leads to an increasing reputation on the part of the original authors.

The appearance of the paper, despite the misgivings at the time of one of the referees (later revealed to be George Foster), is of considerable interest because it raises the question of the *policing of knowledge*. Put simply, those papers that get published in reputable journals—carrying the legitimacy that stems from the exigencies of the reviewing process—then become part of the accepted knowledge base of our discipline. They *are* knowledge, whereas that which is not published is not knowledge. This in turn raises the question: what is the nature of the review process which makes our knowledge base? Is it—indeed, can it be—disinterested, or are there social forces that lead to some claims to knowledge being accepted and other claims to knowledge being rejected? This is of the utmost importance, because the legitimacy of the knowledge depends on our faith in the propriety of the review process. Take away that propriety, and knowledge itself becomes political in a spiraling process, since what is accepted as an appropriate kind of method or philosophy of inquiry then affects any new claim to knowledge; and each new accretion carries with it the assumptions from the history of the knowledge process. To put this another way, once method X has become the accepted method, then any new paper that does not use method X will violate accepted norms and be rejected. In this way, method X becomes the only method leading to knowledge, and the method itself becomes immune from criticism.

Accounting knowledge is not exempt from this. Indeed, it is especially prone to it. As a result, information is needed on the policing of public accounting knowledge, since only in this way can we approach an understanding of how what we think we know came to be a part of knowledge, and how other knowledge might have been kept from us.

It is for this reason that we have produced this book. The Watts and Zimmerman paper we have selected is an especially appropriate vehicle for the process since the paper itself has profound political implications. There is thus an interplay between the politics within the paper and the politics of the acceptance of the paper. We are fortunate that the parties involved—the authors themselves, one of the reviewers and the editor—have generously agreed to allow the correspondence during the acceptance of the paper to be published, and that we are able to reproduce here further items: a previously unpublished response (by Boer and Moseley) to the original paper that was rejected by the same process that led to the acceptance of the original paper, and two responses (in earlier draft) that were subsequently published elsewhere in a modified form but were also rejected by that process (Lowe, Puxty and Laughlin, and Williams).

This book therefore consists of a prepublication draft of the paper itself; the correspondence that surrounded the original acceptance of the paper;

and the correspondence over various comments on the paper. We contextualize these documents in two original contributions. In the essay following this one, we consider the current status of positive accounting theory, which has reached a dominant position in (particularly US) academic accounting thought. In the final paper of this book, we examine the correspondence itself and analyze the processes at work in deciding what will or will not come to constitute knowledge.

We should once again like to thank the authors of these contributions—Germain Boer, George Foster, Richard Laughlin, Tony Lowe, Owen Moseley, Ross Watts, Paul Williams, Stephen Zeff, and Jerold Zimmerman—for their contributions to this book, and trust that it is helpful to the reader in understanding the processes of knowledge production in academic accounting.

Tony Tinker
Tony Puxty
June 1994

INTRODUCTION: THE RISE AND FALL OF POSITIVE ACCOUNTING THEORY

THE RISE AND FALL OF POSITIVE ACCOUNTING THEORY

TONY TINKER AND TONY PUXTY

1. Introduction

Review articles in accounting history sometimes err in pretentious ways. They often proceed on the assumption that, by delivering an exhaustive chronology of events, it is possible to convey a neutral and objective account of historical and theoretical affairs. There is rarely any explicit claim to objectivity in such writing; rather such "qualities" are left for readers to infer from the sheer preponderance of facts and detail, and the failure to mention the writer's subjective predispositions that predicate the whole enterprise.

A candid acknowledgment of the historian's role in reconstructing events—the subjective underpinnings of all historical accounts—is a prerequisite to beginning to evaluate one's own predispositions and claims. It is a truism to contend that all theoretical framings are subjective; it does not follow that all subjectivities are of equal validity. The willingness of writers to subject their own theoretical priors to critical self-examination is a necessary condition for enhancing theoretical validity. To do otherwise is to masquerade behind a spurious objectivity of empiricism and scientism.

This introduction attaches prime importance to the influence of (what Raymond Williams called) "Cultural Materialism" in shaping the shared subjectivities underlying scientific theoretical systems[1]. That scientific beliefs have a social genesis is not a new proposition, especially in economics (Dobb, 1973), management and organization theory (Braverman, 1974; Allen, 1975), physics (Ravetz, 1973; Baritz, 1960), astronomy (Kuhn, 1970), and other fields. However, such considerations have made little headway in the empiricist territories of accounting research, including that of accounting history.

The pertinence of this founding premise is evident from the controversies and disputes published in this volume. Most papers exhibit a fond affection for logocentricism and scholasticism in that, almost invariably, they appeal to epistemic standards to resolve the validity of their respective positions. Virtually no cognizance is taken of the indeterminacy of epistemic practice; that, for instance, incontestable empirical proof—or disproof—of a theory has never been delivered in the history of social science. Moreover, in contrast to this indeterminacy, there is little appreciation of the decisive influence of social and ideological forces in resolving academic debates. In short, in resolving disputes about theoretical truth, there is an unquestioned faith in "matters epistemic" and a near total neglect of extra-epistemic (social) factors.

The priority ascribed to cultural materialism underscores the social situatedness of ideas: that theories (paradigms) are creatures of particular social contexts. Several implications follow from this: First, it underlines the urgency of describing, in a coherent fashion, the various "socials" which different theoretical projects enact and reflect.[2] Second, it draws attention to the social origins of scientific theories; suggesting that the emergence and decline of theories follows neither an efficiency-technological frontier view of science (where "progress" is assured), or a fashion-and-fad model, or a pendulum model. In each of these cases, the social mechanism that animates movement is treated as inexplicable.

It follows from the above that we regard the rise and fall of theories as depending on their efficacy as social ideologies, and we situate the debates and controversies of the Watts and Zimmerman positive accounting research within this broad social context. We contend that the contributions and disputes included in this volume are manifestations of the wider ideological and social milieu, and that only by adequately apprehending this milieu can we begin to understand the successes and travails of the specific contributions. In short, the social context overshadows academic debate and preconditions its outcomes in fundamental ways, usually "behind the backs" of the protagonists. This review aims to show how theorizing may be conditioned and directed by forces that, as of necessity, escape the attention of the theorist. As Adorno argues in the *Negative Dialectics,* the social always exceeds our ability to comprehend it, and so epistemology is always provisional (Adorno, 1973).

Thus, section 2 of this review examines the etymological and intellectual origins of positive accounting theory, and proceeds rapidly to locate the paradigm in a wider social context. We attempt to show that, in the late 1960's and early 1970's, what later came to be known as positive accounting theory emerged to rescue the US profession from public outrage about the role of accounting in large takeovers and mergers. The victims in these wealth conflicts and wealth transfers were investors and powerful financial institutions; the benefactors were speculators, incumbent managers, and other powerful financial institutions. One consequence was the demise of the APB and the initiation of influential congressional investigations that threatened the profession's autonomy and self-regulatory status. Our contention is that positive accounting theory came to the rescue of a profession under siege.

Positive accounting theory has only been partially successful in performing a legitimizing and rationalizing role. We will argue that, in recent years, the paradigm has been "positive" in name only, and that, in substance, it has abandoned its original precepts, and has now assumed the form of a kind of parochial empiricism. This review posits an explanation of the rise and fall of positive accounting theory; it does so by focusing on the theory's inherent dialectical social contradictions.

In section 3, we explore the dialectics of positive theory—the rise and fall of its version of scientific truth—with regard to three variants of the theory: market studies, the theory of excuses, and (what we term) post-positive accounting theory. In each case we show that the theory emerges to provide a legitimizing role, yet ultimately fails in this apologetic function. This has led to the present situation where positive accounting as originally envisaged is extinct; its current practice vitiates its founding precepts, even by the admission of its leading exponents.[3]

Positive accounting is being replaced by a new paradigm; one that emphasizes usefulness, vocational training, practical application, etc. We argue in section 4 that while positive accounting theory has transformed itself to accommodate this new version of truth, it has nevertheless installed serious obstructions to its own transition and, more generally, the transformation of disciplinary practice. Thus, proponents of the New Order have become increasingly vociferous about the "costs" of positive accounting theory, in terms of educational retardation, intellectual obscurantism, and ethical instrumentalism.

These changes represent political opportunities for critical theorists to enable a dialectical transition from positivism, while seeking to avoid the trap of reformism. For this reason, in section 4, we sketch the emerging critique of positive accounting to acquaint researchers with useful political weapons. In this way, we finally return to the "objective" (social) conditions that confirm the substantive demise of positive accounting theory. Here we present evidence that underscores the contention that, as a social ideology, positive accounting is a spent force that no longer serves its apologetic function.

2. Positive Accounting Theory's Intellectual and Social Genesis

From its inception at the University of Chicago, positive accounting theory has fragmented into a series of factions and "schools". Rochester, Berkeley,

Stanford, Illinois, Texas, UCLA, NYU, and many others (a wag might call them the "chicagoettes") now compete for the title of "heir" to the True positive accounting research. Relations are so bad among the factions that some members no longer talk to others.

Despite the mutual disdain and theoretical incommensurability, research in the positive accounting field shares a common pedigree: a putative rejection of the theoretical canon that preceded it—normative accounting theory. Normative theory aspired to answer such questions as, "What are the expense, revenue, asset and liability amounts that should be reported in particular cases?" Deductive reasoning (not empirical and evidential analysis) was the modus operandi of normative researchers like Edwards and Bell (1961), Chambers (1966), Sterling (1970) in arriving at what "ought to" or "should" be done. Income theory, a derivative of neoclassical economic theory, is the theoretical rationale used by this paradigm. It was the idealistic character of normative theorizing, and the absence of any reference to "what accountants do", that attracted the criticisms of positive researchers.

Initially, this critique took the form of arguing that researchers need to understand "what is" before one might effect "what should be" (Dopuch, 1980; Nelson, 1973). However, this was rapidly extended to arguing that it was generally (logically) impossible to answer a normative question. Gonedes and Dopuch (1974) succinctly summarized the dilemma in terms of a choice between two assertions:

A1:   that stock prices can be used to assess the desirability of alternative accounting procedures or regulations;

A2:   that stock prices can be used to assess the effects of alternative accounting procedures or regulations;

These authors conclude that the first assertion is logically false (ibid., pp. 52) and that only the second assertion is valid: researchers can only evaluate the effects of accounting procedures and regulations. Notwithstanding their conclusions, Gonedes and Dopuch are queasy about totally abolishing "desirability" from their vocabulary, and thus they continued to use the word, quarantined in quotation marks, every time they used the word "effects." (ibid.) In the same vein, when Bill Beaver (1981) reminisces about the demise of normative accounting in his "Accounting Revolution" he also highlights words like "desirable," "ideal," "better," and "best" as though they carried a social disease.

Attempts to terminate the normative quest for answers to "ought" and "should" questions were particularly opportune. They occurred at a time when practicing accountants were under attack for their role in a number of takeover and merger scandals. Positive accounting offered them academic sanctuary from this barrage of public criticism by contending that, given the theoretical impossibility of distinguishing between good and bad accounting practices, the accounting industry could not be held liable for the financial debacles in the late 1960's and early 1970's.

In essence, the financial scandals condensed into major wealth expropriations between powerful sectors of the financial community. Accounting facilitated these expropriations in a variety of ways. National Student Marketing (NSM) for instance, overstated period income by manipulating revenue and expenses in order to produce the illusion of high income growth. With a stable price-earnings ration, higher income translated into an inflated stock price that management then used to make new share issues in a series of takeovers through share exchanges. When accounting manipulations—together with management's incompetence and extravagance—were discovered, NSM stock price dropped from $143 to $3.50. It thus transpired that investors who had acquired NSM shares, either via new issue, or through takeovers, had received, for their real assets, compensation with near worthless stock (Briloff, 1972; Tinker, 1985). In a similar manner, Reliance Insurance Company financed a series of acquisitions with stock inflated by fictitious accounting earnings. When this predator threatened the independence of the hallowed Chemical Bank however; the U.S. Congress threatened intervention (Briloff, 1972).

Comparable scandals involved Paramount Pictures and Gulf and Western, United Fruit and United Brands, and Penn Central. These and others incidents eventually prompted congressional investigations led by Senators Moss and Metcalfe. Congress discovered that eight large accounting firms controlled the entire mandated information flow of over 95% of the Fortune 500. This social context was the nursery of positive accounting theory (U.S. Congress, 1977a, 1976b).

3. Exemplars of Positive Accounting Research

How did positive accounting theory respond to the prevailing social context? What kind of legitimizing (ideological) role did it provide, and how did it manage to withstand the kind of withering criticism found in this volume? We explore these issues below in relation to market studies, the theory of excuses, and "modern" (post-positive) accounting research. We will see that the apparent truth of positive accounting was a temporary social truth, not an eternal epistemic one; and that its tenacity lay in its extra-intellectual resonance with an emerging ideological defense of a professional under attack. We shall also see that, as the attack on the profession subsided, so did the need for this ideological aid. Indeed, in the course of events, positive accounting ideology itself became an ideological embarrassment.

Market studies dramatize the ideological transitions of positive accounting (Dyckman et. al., 1985). Early investigators reasoned that the rapid speed with which stock markets impounded new information pertaining to a firm's business prospects implied that accounting information was inconsequential to stock price formation. Because accounting disclosure was based largely on historical (and already known) data, and because of the steady flow of (non-accounting) information, stock prices usually reflected this information long before the accounting disclosure. A fortiori, it followed that the accounting manipulations of NSM and Seven Flags over Texas, highlighted in the writing of Briloff, Chatov, Wyatt, and others, were irrelevant to the determination of stock prices. Hence, the profession could not be held liable in these disputes.

This line of reasoning carried with it an unwelcome implication that caused unease in both academia and in the profession: what was inconsequential was also worthless. In its extreme form therefore, the market studies argument becomes self-destructive in declaring the accounting enterprise irrelevant. For this reason, while informational efficiency arguments predominated in the early years when apologistic services were urgently needed, it never totally triumphed and as criticisms of the profession declined, so a growing number of researchers found the courage to "redeem" accounting disclosure by identifying circumstances where it made a "real" contribution.

Two areas of contribution were identified in the literature: First, in the signaling literature, where it was argued that management used financial reports to disclose new information about their policies and plans (Ross, 1979). In this framing, financial reports brought new and valuable information to the market. Notice that the taint of manipulation or bias are erased by this neoclassical re-construction: management are portrayed as earnest diligent advocates of stockholder interests, and markets are assumed to keep them honest. Managerial entrepreneurs diligently convey information about their plans, discoveries and innovations to the stock market through financial reports.

Second, there has emerged a literature on contracting where, accounting reports assume a significance in-and-of-themselves because they are used in agreements about compensation and income distribution among the corporation and bondholders, managers, banks, the IRS, and other corporate participants. This contracting research is still "positive" in that it explores the factors influencing management's choice of one accounting policy over others. The work is acknowledged as normative however in that it is "hoped" that the discovery of such relationships will be useful.

Today, among market study researchers, there is considerable dispute about the importance of signaling and contracting, and thus the importance of accounting disclosure. These disagreements only underscore the confusion about the apologetic function of research: how changing circumstances inevitably render scientific ideologies obsolete.

The saga over the theory for excuses—the topic of this volume—betrays lessons similar to those discussed above. Using a neoclassical supply and demand framework, Watts and Zimmerman explicitly target journalists, academics and other critics of the profession, who supply theoretical "excuses" in response to the demands from conflicting corporate stakeholders (Watts and Zimmerman, 1979, 1986, 1990; Bensten, 1979–80). In this view, all normative claims are a sham; theories are mere apologies supplied to advance the interests of one protagonist over others.

This thesis performs an even more spectacular "shot-through-the-foot" than that of market studies. Stigmatizing all theories as excuses is a logical (self-reflexive) boomerang: if all theories are excuses, then the theory of excuses is also an excuse.[4] Positive accounting research itself is also condemned as devoid of validity in this light. (Tinker, et. al, 1982). As a result of this internal contradiction, the theory of excuses plummeted like a stone soon after the initial euphoria.[5] Its onetime exponents now shuffle their theoretical feet with embarrassment when excuses theory is mentioned. We see, once again, that the nature of theoretical response to one era's ideological crisis ensures its eclipse in the next epoch.

However we cannot let the circumstances surrounding the paper's publication go without further comment. Watt's and Zimmerman's paper won the American Accounting Association's Distinguished Manuscript Award. Their peers adjudged the paper the best of its year. We might perhaps wonder how it is that a paper whose essential message was fairly shortly to be abandoned by its progenitors (though not without much of its argument being re-hashed in their 1986 book) was adjudged as being not merely good enough to get into a journal with such prestige as the *Accounting Review*, but to rise above all others in the dozens of academic accounting journals to be voted the outstanding manuscript of its year. At the very least, a charitable explanation might be that most research is so mind-numbingly boring and irrelevant to the real accounting problems of capitalism that the paper won votes because it was "interesting." Perhaps it was one of the few manuscripts in the "senior" journals that was not suffused with a arcane mathematical expressions, and thus permitted readers to understand it. But more seriously, perhaps the research community was perceptive enough to recognize the power of the dollar to buy power in a "democracy", and to reward a paper that exposed democracy's pretensions. Positive theorists may have subsequently tried to renounce their progeny, but by that time the community had already endorsed the paper's cynical view of the democratic process. Those who live by the sword die by the sword; and thus we were treated to the ironical spectacle of an elitist, self-congratulatory accounting academy presenting one of its ultimate accolades to a paper that undermined the foundations of the society it was so determined to sustain. Watts and Zimmerman (1990) now acknowledge the normative foundations of their positive accounting theory and, in this specific sense, have revoked their original anti-normative credentials. Their sponsorship of contracting research through their *Journal of Accounting and Economics* (and thus their tacit acceptance of the notion that research should be "useful") is further affirmation of this revocation.

Regrettably, this has not led them to reflect on "The Normative Origins of [their] Positive Theories". Rather, they unabashedly declare that, as the academic marketplace has judged their work to be superior, they must be right (Watts and Zimmerman, 1990). By their own theory-of-excuses reasoning, it also means that they have supplied the apology that has the broadest appeal to powerful vested interests.[6] For the reasons offered above, we must expect this ideology to lose its poignancy as circumstances change. In Watts and Zimmerman's own neoclassical vocabulary, technological obsolescence will eventually overtake their ideological commodity, and demand for it will decline.

4. Positivism and Dialectical Materialism

The primary contention of this introductory review is that theories are refuted, not by argument, but by circumstance. Specifically, theoretical systems are internally (dialectically) integral to a broader social system. The rise and fall of theories lies ultimately not merely in epistemic virtue, but in the mutual adaptation of ideological, social, cultural, political, economic (that is, "materialist") conditions (Tinker et. al., 1982; Tinker, 1985).

An examination of this broader context indicates that the "writing is on the wall" for the more primitive forms of positive accounting theory. First Executive, Lincoln Savings and Loans, ZZZZ Best, and many other audit failures have drawn public and congressional attention to the "quality" of auditing. "Quality" has become an urgency for large accounting firms.[7] Accordingly, education and "relevant research" have become much more pressing issues.

Ironically (although not in a dialectical sense) the obstacles to educational and research reform in the Academy arise from the very activities that the accounting firms bankrolled in earlier eras. The millions of dollars donated towards conferences, research projects, and chairs in positive accounting research has installed an antinormative bias in the educational system. University students are not instructed in the normative activity of reasoning out the "correct" expense, revenue, asset, or claim; rather, they are drilled in rote learning of FASB rules. In short, faithful to the positive accounting tradition, teaching has focused on, "what is", not "what should be." Indeed, the blind faith in "what the rules are" has displaced any conception of where the rules come from: so far as the average student needs to know, they might just as well have been handed down on tablets from Mount Olympus (or Mount Rushmore).

The reactionary legacy of positivism has impeded reform in the American Accounting Association itself. Finding the *Accounting Review* impossible to change, reformers eventually succeeded in introducing two new journals: The *Accounting Education Journal,* and a practitioner journal called *Accounting Horizons.* These initiatives were heavily contested at the time and the continued viability of the new journals is threatened by positivists who blame the new journals for the precarious financial condition of the Association.

Nevertheless, positivistic influences are receding (cf. Johnson and Kaplan, 1987; Johnson, 1992) and nowhere is this more pronounced than in education. The big 6 firms have donated $5 million dollars to the AAA to launch an Educational Change Commission, forcing the AAA to give top priority to education. In a highly symbolic motion, passed at the April 1991 AAA Council in Albuquerque in New Mexico, the objectives statement of the Association was changed to give pride of place to education, and a subsidiary role to research. In the proceedings of two recent meetings held at New York University, several leading positive accounting researchers "confessed" that their research over the last decade had produced little tangible benefit. (Ross Institute, 1991). Predictably, their colleagues in the AAA forgave them and invited them to a 1992 Harvard summit deliberate on what should be done next.

There are important methodological lessons from the above in examining the papers in this volume. "Truth" is ultimately a social construction, not an absolute, epistemic one. The persistence of positive accounting research in the face of the withering criticisms found in the debates below cannot be explained in intellectual terms alone; the social context must also be elucidated.

The table, CHRONOLOGY OF EVENTS: THE MARKET FOR EXCUSES AFFAIR, gives the reader an overview of the important stages in this historical episode. The first column recounts important precursors to the Excuses Theory in neoclassical economics; notably George Stigler's Captive Theory. Watts and Zimmerman's Excuses Theory followed exactly the same pattern as the earlier emergence and demise of George Stigler's Captive Theory. First, they both used economic reductionist arguments to devalue the status of noneconomic processes: Stigler reduced liberal democracy (political processes) to the effective demand of lobbies and powerful vested interests while Watts and Zimmerman subordinated social commentary and academic theorizing to market-driven excuses. Second, while these economically reductionist arguments follow "logically" from their positivistic (anti-normative) views of economics and accounting, they both contain the seeds of their own destruction. Thus Stigler's Captive Theory effectively

CHRONOLOGY OF EVENTS:
THE MARKET FOR EXCUSES AFFAIR

The Historical Antecedents in Neoclassical Economics:	"Market for Excuses Theory" in Accounting:	Direct Challenges to "Market for Excuses Theory"	Other Challenges to "Market for Excuses Theory"
1964: Stigler's Captive Theory of the State			
1976: Retraction of the Captive Theory via Peltzman			
1976: Jensen and Meckling theorize auditing & Accounting as monitoring commodities with positive marginal productivity.			
	1977: Watts and Zimmerman's (WZ's) "Demand for and Supply of Accounting Theories" submitted to THE ACCOUNTING REVIEW (TAR)		
	1979: WZ's paper published in TAR	**1980–1:** Boer & Moseley (BM) and Lowe, Puxty & Laughlin (LPL) submit critiques to WZ and TAR.	
		1981–2: BM and LPL critiques rejected by TAR.	**1982:** Tinker, Merino & Neimark's "Normative Origins of Positive Theories" published in ACCOUNTING, ORGANIZATIONS & SOCIETY (AOS)
		1983: LPL published in THE JOURNAL OF ACCOUNTING & PUBLIC POLICY	**1983:** Christenson's critique, "The Methodology of Positive Accounting" published in TAR
	1990: Watts & Zimmerman publish "Positive Accounting Theory: A Ten Year Perspective" in TAR.	**1987–9:** Williams' critique submitted & rejected by TAR; published in AOS.	**1986–91:** Peasnell & Williams (ABACUS), Whittington (ACCOUNTING & BUSINESS RESEARCH), Whitley (AOS), Hines (TAR), Sterling (ABACUS), Kaplan & Ruland (CRITICAL PERSPECTIVES ON ACCOUNTING)

declared liberal democracy—the "Will of the People"—to be driven by little more than the ability-to-pay; Watts and Zimmerman's Excuses Theory contends that academics are little more than apologists and paid hacks. The implications in the first case are that market processes and corporate activity are anti-democratic, in the second case, academic impartiality is viewed as a chimera. It was these socially dangerous implications of Captive Theory and the Excuses Theory that no doubt played a large part in their rapid demise.

The second column in the table notes the important milestones in the development of Watts and Zimmerman's opus. Column three details the chronology of research that directly challenges the Excuses Theory and attempted to do so initially through the mainstream *Accounting Review*. The last column details critiques of the Excuses Theory that appeared in less mainstream journal outlets.

Notes

1. We stress "cultural" materialism from the outset to avoid any vulgar reading of the kind of materialism we have in mind (see, for instance, Burchell et. al, 1985; Miller and O'Leary, 1987, 1993). As Raymond Williams correctly asserts, Marx's dialectical materialism cannot be reduced to "the economic," but embraces a material world that includes all "forms of life experience", including ideas and symbolic expression (hence the works of Benjamin, Adozzno, and others of the Frankfurt School). The emphasis on cultural materialism does not ignore economic, social, and political considerations, but focuses attention on the interplay between these elements, and symbolic factors, in understanding social processes (Tinker, 1985; Tinker et. al., 1982). We are faithful to this perspective in the way we associate the development of positive accounting theory with the financial crises and scandals of the 1960's and 1970's, and its subsequent decline with trends in the social context.

2. Declaring the importance of "the social" is no substitute for its systematic description, including the various forms it assumes, and the ways in which one form transforms into others. Neglecting such issues is especially pronounced in so called progressive accounting research that purportedly elevates "the social". Typically, this literature studiously ignores previous work that seeks to elucidate the social. (Marxism is the most conspicuous omission here, usually often for reasons of politically expediency.) Typically, this kind of progressive research proceeds, either by reducing "the social" to the symbolic (and by a kind of theoretical handwaiving, claiming that all else is inscribed in symbolism) or, by implying that the social is a kind of heterogeneous cacophony that defies precision. (Robson, 1993; Miller and O'Leary, 1987; Hines, 1988, 1989; Hoskin and Macve, 1986).

3. This point will be developed later. At this juncture we note that positive accounting researchers have finally candidly acknowledged their ultimately normative

concerns (cf. Christie, 1990; Watts and Zimmerman, 1990); what such researchers typically fail to grasp is the reasons why their paradigm has shifted towards reneging on its original canon. In short they lack a dialectical and reflective appreciation of their own situation.

4. Although initially implicitly claiming their own exemption from this as a nonnormative theory, Watts and Zimmerman have now acknowledged the normative origins of their own theorizing (Watts and Zimmerman, 1990).

5. As a striking example of the way that scholars who do not know their history are condemned to relive it, Watts and Zimmerman have virtually retrodden the same path as George Stigler some 25 years earlier (Stigler, 1964). Stigler's captive theory, like the excuses theory, contended that regulators were captured by the regulated; that in true supply and demand style, interest groups and lobbies bought votes, regulators, and regulations. The dangerous corollary of this thesis was that liberal democracy had been usurped by market capitalism's ability to pay. This kind of argument is not normally associated with budding Nobel Laureates; thus Stigler retracted his captive hypothesis (through Peltzman, 1976) and restored the chastity of Liberal Democracy.

6. For studies of the social production of academic theories, see Lehman (1993) and Lehman and Tinker (1987).

7. However it must be said that their quantophrenia has blinded them to the notion of quality (Allen, 1975; and Horkheimer, 1944). In particular, they have no notion of Quality. Quality cannot be measured—that makes it quantity. So their ethical blindness comes from an ideology of absence; the very negation of the "positive" that they venerate.

References

Adorno, Theodor W., and Max Horkheimer, *Dialectic of Enlightenment* (New York: Social Studies Association, 1944; reprinted, London: Verso, 1979).

——, *Negative Dialectics* (New York: Continuum Publishing Company, 1973).

Allen, V., *Social Analysis: A Marxist Critique and Alternative* (Harlow: Longman, 1975).

Baritz, Loren, *The Servants of Power: A History of the Use of Social Science in American Industry* (New York: John Wiley & Sons, 1960).

Beaver, William, *Financial Reporting: An Accounting Revolution* (Englewood Cliffs, New Jersey: Prentice Hall, 1981).

Bentson, G., "The Market for Public Accounting Services, Demand, Supply and Regulation," *The Accounting Journal,* Vol. 2, 1979–80, pp. 2–46.

Braverman, H., *Labor and Monopoly Capital* (New York: Monthly Review Press, 1974).

Briloff, A. J., *Unaccountable Accounting* (New York: Harper & Row, 1972).

Burchell, S., C. Clubb, and A. G. Hopwood, "Accounting in its Social Context: Towards a History of Value Added in the United Kingdom," *Accounting Organizations and Society,* 1985, pp. 381–414.

Chambers, R. J., *Accounting Evaluation and Economic Behavior* (Englewood Cliffs, New Jersey: Prentice Hall, 1966).

Christi, Andrew, A., "Aggregation of Test Statistics and Evaluation of the Evidence on Contracting and Size Hypothesis," *Journal of Accounting and Economics,* Vol. 12, January, 1990, pp. 15–36.

Dobb, Maurice, *Theories of Value and Income Distribution Since Adam Smith: Ideology and Economic Theory* (Cambridge: Cambridge University Press, 1973).

Dopuch, Nicholas, "Empirical vs. Non Empirical Research: Balancing Theory and Practice," *1979 Accounting Research Convention,* ed. Jonathan Davies (Tuscaloosa, Alabama: University of Alabama Press, 1980), pp. 67–83.

Dyckman, T. R., D. H. Downes, and R. P. Magee, *Efficient Capital Markets and Accounting: A Critical Analysis,* 2nd ed. (Englewood Cliffs, New Jersey, 1985).

Edwards, R. S. and P. Bell, *The Theory and Measurement of Business Income* (Berkeley: University of California Press, 1961).

Gonedes, N. and N. Dopuch, "Capital Market Equilibrium, Information Production, and Selecting Accounting Techniques: Theoretical Framework and Review of Empirical Work," *Studies on Financial Accounting Objectives, 1974 Supplement to the Journal of Accounting Research,* pp. 48–129.

Hines, R., "Financial Accounting Knowledge, Conceptual Framework Projects and the Social Construction of the Accounting Profession," *Accounting, Organizations and Society,* vol. 13, 1988, pp. 251–262.

Hoskin, K. W. and R. H. Macve, "Accounting and the Examination: A Genealogy of Disciplinary Power," *Accounting, Organizations and Society,* 1985, pp. 137–169.

Jensen, M. and W. H. Meckling, "Theory of the Firm: Managerial Behavior, Agency Costs and Ownership Structure," *Journal of Financial Economics,* 1976, October, pp. 305–60.

Johnson, T., *Relevance Regained: From Top-Down to Bottom-Up Management* (New York: The Free Press, 1992).

————, and R. Kaplan, *Relevance Lost: The Rise and Fall of Management Accounting* (Boston: HBS Press, 1987).

Kuhn, T. S., *The Structure of Scientific Revolutions,* 2nd ed. (Chicago: University of Chicago Press, 1970).

Lehman, C. and T. Tinker, "The Real Cultural Significance of Accounts," *Accounting, Organizations and Society,* 1987, pp. 503–522.

————, *Accounting's Changing Role in Social Conflict* (New York: Markus Wiener Publishing Co., 1993).

Miller, P. and T. O'Leary, "Accounting and the Construction of the Governable Person," *Accounting, Organizations and Society,* 1987, pp. 235–266.

————, and ————, "Accounting, Economic Citizenship and the Spatial *Re*ordering of Manufacture," *Accounting, Organization and Society,* forthcoming, 1993.

Nelson, Carl L., "A Priori Research in Accounting," *Accounting Research 1960–70: A Critical Evaluation,* N. Dopuch and L. Revsine eds. (Urbana: University of Illinois, 1973).

Peltzman, Sam, "Toward A More General Theory of Regulation," *The Journal of Law and Economics,* vol. XIX (2) August 1976, pp. 211–248.

Ravetz, J. R., *Scientific Knowledge and Its Social Problems* (Harmondsworth, U.K.: Penguin Books, 1973).

Robson, K., "Accounting Policy Making and "Interests": Accounting for Research and Development," *Critical Perspectives on Accounting*, vol. 4, no. 1, March 1933.

Ross Institute Annual Report, "The Economics of Financial Statement Analysis," 1991.

Ross, Stephen A., "Disclosure Regulation in the Financial Markets: Implications of Modern Finance Theory and Signalling Theory," *Issues in Financial Regulation* (New York: McGraw-Hill, 1979).

Sterling, R. R., *Theory of the Measurement of Enterprise Income* (Lawrenceville, Kansas: University of Kansas Press, 1970).

Stigler, George J., "Public Regulation of the Securities Markets," *The Journal of Business*, April 1964, pp. 112–133.

Tinker, T., *Paper Prophets: A Social Critique of Accounting* (New York: Praeger, 1985).

Tinker, A. M., B. Merino, and M. D. Neimark, "The Normative Origins of Positive Theories: Ideology and Accounting Thought," *Accounting, Organizations and Society*, vol. 7, no. 2, 1982, pp. 167–200.

U. S. Congress, Federal Regulation and Regulatory Reform, Subcommittee on Oversight and Investigations of the Committee on Interstate and Foreign Commerce of the U. S. House of Representatives (The Moss Report), Washington, D.C., 1976a.

———, The Accounting Establishment, Subcommittee Reports, Accounting and Management of the Committee on Government Affairs, (The Metcalf Report), U. S. Senate, Washington, D.C., 1976b.

Watts, Ross L. and Jerold L. Zimmerman, "The Demand for and the Supply of Accounting Theories: The Market for Excuses," *Accounting Review*, April 1979, vol. LIV, No. 2, pp. 273–306.

——— and ———, *Positive Accounting Theory* (Englewood Cliffs, New Jersey: Prentice Hall, Inc., 1986).

——— and ———, "Positive Accounting Theory: A Ten Year Perspective," *Accounting Review*, vol. 65, No. 1, January 1990, pp. 131–156.

THE DEMAND FOR AND SUPPLY OF ACCOUNTING THEORIES: THE MARKET FOR EXCUSES

Editors' Introduction: The following paper, Watts and Zimmerman's "The Demand and Supply of Accounting Theories: The Market for Excuses", marks the end of one era and the beginning of another. It declares the "normative" project of academics like Abraham Briloff, and other social critics of corporate accounting practice to be invalid; that there are no objective grounds in accounting theory for judging accounting practice as "good" or "bad"; all such judgments are mere excuses or apologies for advancing the interests of particular social constituencies, couched in a language of academic impartiality and objectivity. This thesis brings to fruition a tradition in economics and finance that was pioneered at the University of Chicago and Watts and Zimmerman's own University of Rochester. Not only did this overthrow the earlier "activist" (normative) forms of accounting— a residual from the remnants of the guild-professional phase of accounting— but it inaugurates a deregulatory movement in accounting for the Reagan-Bush era. The economic prize—in terms of distributional effects—was substantial: Watts and Zimmerman, and their Rochester and Chicago colleagues, were attempting to reverse a whole tradition of corporate regulation through accounting disclosure that stretched back to the 1933–34 Securities Acts.

THE DEMAND FOR AND SUPPLY OF ACCOUNTING THEORIES: THE MARKET FOR EXCUSES

ROSS L. WATTS, Associate Professor
JEROLD L. ZIMMERMAN, Assistant Professor
Graduate School of Management The University of Rochester.

ABSTRACT

This paper addresses the questions of why accounting theories are predominantly normative and why no single theory is generally accepted. Accounting theories are analyzed as economic goods, produced in response to the demand for theories. The nature of the demand is examined, first in an unregulated, then in a regulated economy.

Government regulation creates incentives for individuals to lobby on proposed accounting procedures, and accounting theories are useful justifications in the political lobbying. Further, government intervention produces a demand for a variety of theories, because each group affected by an accounting change demands a theory that supports its position. The diversity of positions prevents general agreement on a theory of accounting, and accounting theories are normative because they are used as excuses for political action (i.e., the political process creates a demand for theories which prescribe, rather than describe, the world).

The implications of our theory for the changes in the accounting literature as a result of major changes in the institutional environment are compared with observed phenomena.

This research was supported by the Center for Research in Government Policy and Business, Graduate School of Management, University of Rochester. The authors wish to acknowledge the suggestions of Ray Ball, George Benston, Richard Brief, Nicholas Dopuch, Nicholas Gonedes, David Henderson, Robert Holthausen, Michael Jensen, Melvin Krasney, Richard Leftwich, Janice Maguire, William Meckling, Philip Meyers, Katherine Schipper, William Schwert, Clifford Smith, and Jerold Warner. We also acknowledge the suggestions received on an earlier version of this paper presented at the Stanford Summer Research Colloquium, August 2, 1977 and the comments of the anonymous referees.

I. Introduction

The literature we commonly call financial accounting theory is predominantly prescriptive.[1] Most writers are concerned with what the contents of published financial statements should be; that is, how firms should account. Yet, it is generally concluded that financial accounting theory has had little substantive, direct impact on accounting practice or policy formulation despite half a century of research. Often the lack of impact is attributed to basic methodological weaknesses in the research. Or, the prescriptions offered are based on explicit or implicit objectives which frequently differ among writers.[2] Not only are the researchers unable to agree on the objectives of financial statements, but they also disagree over the methods of deriving the prescriptions from the objectives.[3]

One characteristic common to the prescriptions and proposed accounting methodologies however, is their failure to satisfy all practicing accountants and to be generally accepted by accounting standard-setting bodies. A committee of the American Accounting Association recently concluded that "a single universally accepted basic accounting theory does not exist at this time."[4]

The preceding observations lead us to pose the following question: What is the role of accounting theory in determining accounting practice? Our objective in this paper is to begin building a theory of the determinants of accounting theory. This theory is intended to be a positive theory, that is, a theory capable of explaining the factors determining the extant accounting literature, predicting how research will change as the underlying factors change, and explaining the role of theories in the determination of accounting standards.[5] It is *not* normative or prescriptive.[6]

Other writers have examined the relationship between accounting theory and practice. For example, Zeff (1974, p. 177) examines the historical relationship and concludes:

> a study of the U.S. experience clearly shows that the academic literature has had remarkably little impact on the writings of practitioners and upon the accounting policies of the American Institute and the SEC. *Too often, accounting theory is invoked more as a tactic to buttress one's preconceived notions, rather than as a genuine arbiter of contending views.* (emphasis added)

Horngren [1973, p. 61] goes further and suggests an explanation for accounting theory's limited impact on the setting of accounting standards:[7]

> My hypothesis is that the setting of accounting standards is as much a product of political action as of flawless logic or empirical findings.

Our tentative theory is consistent with both Zeff's and Horngren's obser-vations. It predicts that accounting theory will be used to "buttress precon-ceived notions" and further, it explains why. Our contribution to Zeff's and Horngren's ideas is to give them more structure so that we can make addi-tional predictions about accounting theory. The source of that structure is economics. We view accounting theory as an economic good and examine the nature of the demand for and the supply of that good.

Understanding why accounting theories are as they are requires a theory of the political process. We model that process as competition among indi-viduals for the use of the coercive power of government to achieve wealth transfers. Because accounting procedures[8] are one means of effecting such transfers, individuals competing in the political process demand theories which prescribe the accounting procedures conducive to their desired wealth transfers. Further, because individual interests differ, a variety of accounting prescriptions, hence a variety of accounting theories, is de-manded on any one issue. We argue that it is this diversity of interests which prevents general agreement on accounting theory.

While individuals want a theory which prescribes procedures conducive to their own interest, they do *not* want a normative theory which has their self-interest as its stated objective. The reason is that information is costly to obtain. Some voters will not obtain information on political issues person-ally. Those voters are not likely to support political actions which have as their stated objective the self-interest of others. The most useful theories for persuading uninformed voters are theories with stated objectives appeal-ing to those voters, e.g., the "public interest." As a result, individuals de-mand normative accounting theories which make prescriptions based on the "public interest". In other words, the demand is for rationales or excuses. Because it arises from the political process,the demand for normative, "pub-lic interest"-oriented accounting theories depends on the extent of the gov-ernment's role in the economy.

Section II analyzes the demand for financial accounting and accounting theory first in an unregulated economy, in which the only role of government is to enforce contracts, and then in a regulated economy. In Section III, we examine the nature of the supply of accounting theories. Because of the diverse demands for prescriptions, we expect to observe a variety of norma-tive theories. Further, we expect theories to change over time as government intervention changes. In Section IV we examine the effect of government intervention on extant accounting theory during the last century. Section V summarizes the issues and presents our conclusions.

II. The Demand for Accounting Theories

This section analyzes the demand for accounting theories in an unregulated economy (Part A) and the additional demands generated by government intervention (Part B).

A. THE DEMAND FOR ACCOUNTING THEORIES IN AN UNREGULATED ECONOMY

1. Accounting in an Unregulated Economy

Audited corporate financial statements were voluntarily produced prior to government mandate.[9] Watts [1977] concludes that the original promoters of corporations or, subsequently, corporate managers have incentives to contract to supply audited financial statements. Agreements to supply financial statements were included in articles of incorporation (or bylaws) and in private lending contracts between corporations and creditors.[10] These contracts increase the welfare of the promoter or manager (who is raising the new capital) because they reduce the *agency costs*[11] which he bears.

Agency costs arise because the manager's (the agent's) interests do not necessarily coincide with the interests of shareholders or bondholders (the principals). For example, the manager (if he owns shares) has incentives to convert assets of the corporation into dividends, thus leaving the bondholders with the "shell" of the corporation. Similarly, the manager has incentives to transfer wealth to himself at the expense of both the shareholders and bondholders (e.g. via perquisites).

Bondholders and shareholders anticipate the manager's behavior and appropriately discount the price of the bonds or shares at the time of issue. Hence, the promoter (or manager) of a new corporation receives less for the shares and bonds he sells than he would if he could guarantee that he would continue to act as he did when he owned the firm (i.e., when there were no outside shareholders or bondholders). This difference in the market values of the securities is part of the cost of an agency relationship, it is part of agency costs, and is borne by the promoter (or manager).[12] Jensen and Meckling [1976, p. 308] call it the "residual loss".

Because he bears the residual loss, the manager has incentives to make expenditures to guarantee that he will not take certain actions which harm the principal's interest or that he will compensate the principal if he does. These are "bonding" and "monitoring" expenditures and are additional elements of agency costs. Examples of such expenditures include contracting to restrict dividend payments and expenditures to monitor such dividend covenants.

The final element of agency costs is the utility of the increase in perquisites, wealth transfers, etc., the manager receives because of his actions as an agent. An equilibrium occurs when the net costs of an agency relationship, the agency costs, are minimized by trading-off the decreases in the promoter's (or manager's) utility due to the residual loss, the monitory and bonding expenditures, and the increased utility due to increased perquisites. The promoter or manager will write contracts for monitoring and bonding as long as the marginal benefits of these contracts (e.g., reduction of the residual loss) are greater than the marginal costs (e.g. the costs of contracting and the utility of any perquisites foregone). Moreover, since he bears the agency costs, the manager or promoter will try to write the contracts and perform the bonding or monitoring at minimum cost. In fact, the Jensen and Meckling analysis suggests that the equilibrium set of contractual devices is the one which minimizes the agency costs associated with the separation of management and control and with the conflict of interests associated with the different classes of investors.

Promoters and managers voluntarily included bonding covenants in corporate articles and bylaws in the nineteenth century. Dividend covenants were voluntarily included in company charters as early as 1620.[13]

Watts [1977] analysis of agency relationships suggests that the function of audited financial statements in an unregulated economy is to reduce agency costs. This theory predicts that accounting practices (i.e., the form, content, frequency, etc., of external reporting) will vary across corporations in an unregulated economy depending on the nature and magnitude of the agency costs. Agency costs, in turn, are, among other things, a function of the amount of corporate debt outstanding and of the relative share of equity owned by the manager.[14] These variables affect the manager's incentive to take actions which conflict with the interests of shareholders and bondholders. Agency costs also vary with the costs of monitoring managers, that, in turn depend on the physical size, dispersion, and complexity of the firm. Further, the practices underlying financial statements will vary across firms because an accounting practice which minimizes agency costs in one industry may not minimize those costs in another.

As an example of the association between agency costs and accounting procedures, consider management compensation schemes in the nineteenth century. Some management compensation schemes in the nineteenth century were included in corporate articles. Those schemes tied management compensation to the firms' "profits" [Matheson, 1893, pp. vii–viii] to reduce the divergence between the interests of the managers and shareholders.[15] At that time "profits" were effectively operating cash flows, since accrual accounting was not used. [Litherland, 1968, pp. 171–172] However, a cash flow "profit" index is susceptible to shortrun manager manipulation. The manager can reduce repairs and maintenance expenditures and increase cash flows and "profits,"[16] which would increase the manager's compensation.[17] In addition, reduced maintenance increases the ability of the corporation to pay current dividends. Such dividends could reduce the value of the creditors' claims and increase the shareholders' wealth.[18]

To reduce these agency costs of equity and debt, several contractual devices were used to decrease the likelihood that managers and shareholders would run down the value of the capital stock.

    i)   Dividends were restricted to a fixed proportion of profits, thereby creating a buffer.[19]

    ii) Reserve funds of fixed amounts had to be maintained if dividends were to be paid.[20]

    iii) Fixed assets were treated as merchandise accounts with changes in value (usually not called depreciation) closed to profits prior to dividend distributions.[21]

In the latter procedure, depreciation was treated as a valuation technique which had to be estimated only in profitable years, since dividends were paid only in these years. A typical company charter requiring depreciation is:

> The directors shall, before recommending any dividend, set aside out of the profits of the company, but subject to the sanction of the company in general meeting, such sum as they think proper as a reserve fund for maintenance, repairs, depreciation and renewals.[22]

The court interpreted this article and the term "proper reserve" as a mechanism to account for declines in the capital stock.[23] Thus, the existence of a depreciation covenant (and hence the presence of depreciation in the financial statement) or other restrictions on dividends was a function of the amount of fixed assets and the nature and magnitude of the agency cost of debt.

Capital market participants contract to supply capital. Managers and owners seeking capital have incentives to enter into contracts which limit the agency costs they incur. But these contracts must then be monitored and enforced since managers have incentives to circumvent the contracts. For example, the promoter or manager of a corporation may contract to restrict dividends to, or base management compensation on, profits after a deduction for depreciation because such a covenant enables him to sell bonds and shares at a higher price. However, *after* the contract is written the manager has incentives to minimize that depreciation charge, thereby leading to increased profits (and potentially increased management compensation) and dividends which transfer wealth from bondholders to shareholders (including management). Thus, contracts will reduce agency costs only if they include provisions for monitoring. Since audited financial statements are useful devices to monitor these voluntary agreements between owners and managers, these statements serve a useful role in the capital markets and owner and managers will agree to provide them in advance.

2. The Function of Accounting Theories

The preceding analysis suggests that accounting theories will serve three overlapping functions in an unregulated economy:

i) *Pedagogic Demand.* Accounting procedures are devised in order to reduce agency costs of contracts. Since these costs vary across firms, accounting procedures will vary, giving rise to diversity of techniques, formats, etc.[24] However, diversity in accounting procedures increases the difficulty of teaching the practice of accounting. Consequently, accounting teachers develop pedagogic devices (rules-of-thumb) to assist learning and to structure the variation found in practice. Theorists examine existing systems of accounts and summarize differences and similarities. These descriptions of practice highlight the tendencies of firms with particular attributes to follow certain accounting procedures.

Nineteenth century accounting texts and articles indicate that accounting theorists recognized the diversity of practice and attempted to distill general tendencies from the diversity. For example:

No fixed rules, or rates of depreciation can be established for general use, because not only do trades and processes of manufacture differ, but numerous secondary circumstances have to be considered in determining the proper course. It may, however, be possible to lay down some general principles which will always apply, or which, at any rate, may with advantage be held in view in deciding particular cases. [Matheson, 1893, p. 1]

Similarly, Dicksee and Tillyard's [1906] treatise describes current accounting practice for goodwill and the relevant court cases. Based on this description, the authors "enunciate general business principles and explain their practical application" [Dicksee and Tillyard, 1906, p. vii].

ii) *Information Demand.* In an unregulated economy there is a demand for writers to do more than just describe variations in accounting practice. There is a demand for predictions of the effects of accounting procedures on both the manager's and auditor's welfare via exposure to law suits. The auditor contracts with the shareholders (and creditors) to monitor management, and he is legally liable if he fails to report breaches of covenants in the corporation's articles or bylaws.[25] Furthermore, the demand for a given auditor's services is a function of the auditor's efficiency in monitoring management.[26] Hence, the auditor again has an incentive to understand how management's choice of accounting procedures affects agency costs.

Auditors would value information in the form of theories predicting how agency costs vary with accounting procedures. In particular, auditors would like to know how managers' actions and hence agency costs would be affected by alternative accounting procedures.

iii) *Justification Demand.* Early accounting textbooks warned that managers would use accounting to serve their own interests at the expense of shareholders. The second edition of Matheson [1893] contains examples of such warnings. Matheson provides illustrations of how managers can take advantage of deficiencies in the definition of depreciation, repairs, and maintenance charges to increase "profits" and their own compensation at the expense of shareholders and/or bondholders. For example, on page 5 he writes:

> The temptation to treat as Profit the Surplus of Income over Expenditure, without sufficient allowance for Deterioration, appears to be often irresistible. Thus, in the case of a Tramway undertaking in its first years of working, a dividend may be possible only by writing off little or nothing from the capital value of the cars, the harness, and the horses. This, of course, cannot last without the introduction of new capital, but in undertakings long established there yet may be epochs of fictitious profits due to various causes. For instance there may be neglect of repairs, which, when the necessity for them becomes evident, will involve a heavy outlay for renewals; or it may arise from actual fraud in postponing expenditure, so as to show large profits, which will raise the value of shares for stock-jobbing purposes. There are railways where the dividend income and the corresponding value of the shares have fluctuated considerably, not according to alterations in the real earnings, but according to alternate neglect and attention in regard to plant.

Accounting texts (and theories) which detail how managers seek to manipulate profits and the consequent effects of those manipulations on shareholders and bondholders not only improve the auditor's ability to monitor such behavior, but also provide the auditor with ready-made arguments to use against such practices in discussions with management. It is clear that Matheson's work fulfilled this role. William Jackson, a member of the Council of the Institute of Chartered Accountants in England and Wales, stated that he used Matheson's book in that fashion:

> To those who honestly and from conviction treat the subject on the only sound basis, it may seem superfluous to urge due consid-

eration of the arguments to convincingly set out in these pages; but Auditors, and especially those who have to deal with joint-stock or other concerns where the remuneration of the management is made wholly or partly dependent upon declared Profits, know in what varied forms resistance to an adequate Charge against profits for Depreciation is presented.

The fallacies underlying these objections present themselves again and again with the modifications caused by the lack of apprehension in some, or the ingenuity of others. *Mr. Matheson's work provides the Auditor with true antidotes to these fallacies, and it has been in past times used by the writer with satisfactory effect, where his own less-reasoned arguments have failed to convince.*

He therefore recommends it afresh to the notice and for the support, where necessary, of members of his own profession, and of those who, untrained in the practice of Auditing, are confronted with unfamiliar and specious pretexts for avoiding the unwelcome charge against Profits. [Matheson, 1893, pp. vii–viii](emphasis added)

B. THE DEMAND FOR ACCOUNTING THEORIES IN A REGULATED ECONOMY

This section extends the previous analysis of the demand for theories to include the effects of government. We assume that private citizens, bureaucrats, and politicians have incentives to employ the powers of the state to make themselves better off and to coalesce for that purpose. One way by which coalitions of individuals are made better off is by legislation that redistributes (i.e., confiscates) wealth.

1. Accounting and the Political Process

Farm subsidies, tariffs, welfare, social security, even regulatory commissions[27] are examples of special interest legislation which transfer wealth. The business sector is both the source (via taxes, antitrust, affirmative action, etc) and the recipient of many of these wealth transfers (via tax credits, tariffs, subsidies, etc.).

Financial accounting statements perform a central role in these wealth transfers and are affected both directly and indirectly by the political process The Securities and Exchange Commission (SEC) regulates the contents of financial statements directly (upward asset revaluations are not allowed, statements of changes in financial position must be prepared, etc.). The Federal Revenue Acts also affect the contents of financial statements directly (e.g., LIFO) In addition, regulatory commissions (e.g., state public utility boards, various banking and insurance commissions, the Interstate

Commerce Commission, the Federal Trade Commission) often affect the contents of financial statements.

Besides these more direct effects, there are indirect effects. Government commissions often use the contents of financial statements in the regulatory process (rate setting, antitrust, etc). Further, Congress often bases legislative action[28] on these statements. This, in turn, provides management with incentives to select accounting procedures which either reduce the costs they bear or increase the benefits they receive as a result of the actions of government regulators and legislators.[29]

Since public utilities have incentives to propose accounting procedures for rate-making purposes which increase the market value of the firm, their arguments are assisted if accounting standard-setting bodies such as the Financial Accounting Standards Board (FASB) mandate the same accounting procedures for financial reporting.[30]

Consequently, managers of utilities and other regulated industries (e.g., insurance, bank and transportation) lobby on accounting standards not only with their regulatory commissions but also with the Accounting Principles Board (APB) and the FASB.

Moonitz (1974 a and b) and Horngren (1973 and 1977) document instances of regulated firms seeking or opposing accounting procedures which affect the value of the firm via direct and indirect wealth transfers. Examples of other firms lobbying on accounting standards exist. Most of the major U.S. oil companies made submissions regarding the FASB's Discussion Memorandum on General Price Level Adjustments [Watts and Zimmerman, 1978].

2. The Effect of Government Intervention on the Demand for Accounting Theories

The rules and regulations which result from government regulation of business increase the pedagogic and information demands for accounting theories. Even beginning accounting textbooks report the income tax requirements of LIFO, depreciation, etc. Practitioners demand detailed texts explaining SEC requirements (e.g., Rappaport [1972]), tax codes, and other government regulations.

The justification demand for theories also expands with regulation. The political process in the U.S. is characterized as an advocacy proceeding. Proponents and opponents of special interest legislation (or petitions before regulatory and administrative committees) must give arguments for the positions they advocate. If these positions include changes in accounting procedures, accounting theories which serve as justifications (i.e., excuses) are useful. These advocacy positions (including theories) will tend to be based on contentions that the political action is in the public interest,[31] that everyone is made better off, that most are made better off and no one is harmed, or that the action is "fair," since those contentions are likely to generate less opposition than arguments based on self-interest. Often, those public interest arguments rely upon the notion that the unregulated market solution is inefficient. The typical argument is that there is a market failure which can only be remedied by government intervention.

Politicians and bureaucrats charged with the responsibility for promoting the general welfare demand public interest testimony not only to inform them of the trade-offs but also for use in justifying their actions to the press and their constituencies. Consequently, when politicians support (or oppose) legislation, they tend to adopt the public interest arguments advanced by the special interests who promote (oppose) the legislation.

i) *Examples of Public Interest or Market Failure Justifications*

The reported objective of the Securities Exchange Act of 1934 and of required disclosure is stated by Mundheim [1964, p. 647]:

> The theory of the Securities Act is that if investors are provided with sufficient information to permit them to make a reasoned decision concerning the investment merits of securities offered to them, investor interests can be adequately protected without unduly restricting the ability of business ventures to raise capital.

This objective stresses economic efficiency. The statement suggests that required disclosure can increase investors' welfare at virtually zero cost (i.e., that there is a market failure).

Examples of "public interest" justifications of accounting procedures are observed in rate-setting hearings for public utilities. For example, Public Systems, an organization that represents municipalities and rural electrification agencies, applied for a hearing on the Federal Power Commission's (FPC) Order 530 which allowed the use of income tax allocation in setting rates.[32] Order 530 increases the cash flow of electric utilities "at the expense of customers using electricity" and hence harms the interests of Public Systems. But, Public Systems did not argue that it is in its self-interest to oppose Order 530. Instead it argued that "normalization (income tax allocation) represents an *inefficient* means of subsidizing the public utility industry" [U.S. Congress, Senate, 1976, p. 683] (emphasis added). Bureaucrats also use public interest arguments to justify their actions.[33] For example, the former SEC Chief Accountant, John Burton, a bureaucrat, justified the disclosure regulations imposed during his term in office by arguing:

> In a broad sense we hope [that disclosure regulations] will contribute to a more efficient capital market . . . The way

in which we hope that will be achieved is first by giving investors more confidence that they are getting the whole story and second by encouraging the development of better tools of analysis and more responsibility on the part of the professional analyst to understand what's going on. We think that by giving them better data we can encourage them in the direction of doing a better job, thus leading, we hope, to more effective [sic] capital markets. [Burton (1975), p. 21.]

Government regulation creates a demand for normative accounting theories employing public interest arguments—that is, for theories purporting to demonstrate that certain accounting procedures *should* be used because they lead to better decisions by investors, more efficient capital markets, etc. Further, the demand is not for *one* theory, but rather for diverse prescriptions. On any political issue such as utility rate determination, there will be at least two sides. In the FPC Order 530 example, Coopers & Lybrand, who opposed Public Systems, wanted a theory which prescribed income tax allocation, while Public Systems wanted a theory which did not. When we consider that accounting methods are relevant to taxes, antitrust cases, union negotiations, disclosure regulations, etc., as well as utility rate-setting, we expect a demand for a multitude of prescriptions.

With increased government intervention in business, the demand for theories which justify particular accounting procedures (proposed in the self-interest of various parties) has come to eclipse the demand for theories which fulfill the pedagogic and information roles. We present evidence to support this proposition in Section V.

ii) *Rationality or "Theory Illusion"*

Until recently, it had been popular in the economics literature to assume that politicians, elected officials, bureaucrats, etc., acted in the "public interest" (the public interest assumption).[34] In order to determine which actions are in the public interest, politicians require theories which predict the consequences of alternative actions. "Rational," "public interest"-oriented politicians/bureaucrats would tend to use the theories which best predict (i.e., the "best" theories)[35] and hence those theories would predominate. Leading articles in the accounting literature are implicitly based on the public interest premise [AAA, 1966, p.5; AICPA, 1973, p. 17; Gonedes and Dopuch, 1974, pp. 48–49 and pp. 114–118; Beaver and Demski, 1974, p. 185], that the "best" theories prevail.

In recent years, however, economists have questioned whether the public interest assumption is consistent with observed phenomena.[36] They have proposed an alternative assumption—that individuals involved in the political process act in their own interest (the self-interest assumption). This assumption yields implications which are more consistent with observed phenomena than those based on the public interest assumption.[37]

The costs and benefits to voters of becoming informed, of lobbying, of forming coalitions, and of monitoring their representatives' actions are of central importance in a self-interest model of the political process. Downs (1957) suggests that the expected effect of one individual's vote on the outcome of an election is trivial and hence the individual voter has very little incentive to incur the costs of becoming informed on political issues. On the other hand, individual voters do have incentives to act as groups in the political process.

Economies of scale in political action encourage group participation. When several voters have similar interests on particular issues (e.g., members of a trade union), those voters can share the "fixed" costs of becoming informed and moreover can increase the likelihood of affecting the outcome of an election by voting as a bloc.[38]

The costs of political action also depend on the existing political institutions (e.g., whether political decisions are made by referendum or a vote of elected representatives) [Leffler and Zimmerman, 1977]. If we call the sum of the costs of political action the "transactions costs" of political decisions, the crucial question is "What is the magnitude of these transactions costs?" If the transactions costs of political decisions are high, self-interest motivated government servants will not always act in the public interest; if they are zero, they will.[39] Hence, if the transactions costs of the political process are high, government officials will not use the "best" theory available; if they are zero, they will.

As an example of the importance of positive political transactions costs, consider the manager of a utility advocating deferred tax accounting because of its effects on utility rates. The manager will argue that recognizing deferred taxes as current operating costs is in the public interest. The official responsible for allowing or not allowing this practice has a greater incentive to resist the lobbying efforts of the utility manager if other individuals (e.g., consumer advocates) lobby against the procedure. Whether those individuals lobby or not depends on the costs of consumers being informed about the effects of the accounting procedures on their welfare (which requires human capital), the costs of forming groups to oppose the procedure, etc. The manager's public interest theory (which is an "excuse" to cover a self-interest motive and need not be valid) increases the costs of others being informed and will tend to be accepted by the public official *if* the transactions costs are large enough.

We assume that political transactions costs are large enough to cause the acceptance of "invalid" theories, that the competition among excuses does not always lead to acceptance of the "best" theory. The usefulness of that assumption depends on the empirical consistency of its implications. It is an empirical question. The work by Posner [1974], Stigler [1971] and Peltzman [1976] supports the assumption.

The assumption that the transactions costs of the political process are non-zero is analogous to the assumption of non-zero transactions costs in capital markets.[40] In capital market theory it is typically assumed that transactions costs are zero despite the fact they obviously are not, because that assumption yields empirically confirmed hypotheses. Why, then, should political transactions costs be sufficiently more important than capital market transactions costs to warrant their inclusion in a political theory?

We suggest that there is an important difference between capital markets and the political process which makes transactions costs important in the latter case. There is, in the capital markets, a direct market for control. If the manager of a corporation is not maximizing the market value of the corporation's shares, then an individual can, by buying its shares, acquire control of the corporation in the capital markets and, therefore, obtain the right to make the decisions. That individual can change the corporation's decisions and reap for himself the capital gain from the increase in the value of the corporation's stock. If the Chairman of the Securities and Exchange Commission were not making decisions in the public interest, an individual could not directly buy the right to make those decisions and capture the benefits of the changed decision. Because direct payments to elected officials are illegal and payments in kind are generally more expensive, it is costlier to bribe congressmen, senators, etc., than to purchase a controlling interest in a corporation. It is also costly to establish indirect ways of achieving the same result.[41]

Notice that in our model of the political process everyone is rational. No one is being "fooled" by accounting theories; they are not "fooled" by "theory illusion."[42] If people do not investigate the validity of theories, it is because they do not expect such investigation to be worthwhile. If the expected benefits of investigation to an individual are small, he will make only a limited investigation.

Our assumption of high political costs is crucial to our theory. As we shall see in the next section, the assumption enables us to discriminate between the empirical implications of our theory and the implications of an alternative theory. This allows empirical testing. Ultimately, the test of the political cost assumption is whether the implications of the theory based on the assumption are confirmed or not by empirical tests. Thus, the merit of an assumption is judged by the predictions it generates. Those accounting researchers who build theories on the assumption that information is a pure public good (e.g., Gonedes and Dopuch [1974] and Beaver [1976]) often assert that information is a pure public good. Yet no tests of these theories have been provided. In Section IV we argue that implications of our theory are consistent with the evidence.

III. The Supply of Accounting Theories

Accounting theorists often view themselves as expert critics or defenders of accounting prescriptions (e.g., replacement cost, historical cost, etc.). They argue that accounting theory should be used to determine accounting practice and standards.[43] The ideal state of affairs to them is one in which theorists logically and objectively determine the merits of alternative procedures.[44] For example, Hendriksen [1977, p. 1] writes: ". . . the most important goal of accounting theory should be to provide a coherent set of logical principles that form the general frame of reference for the evaluation and development of sound accounting practices." Theorists tend to bemoan the fact that this ideal state does not exist and that corporate managers, auditors, and politicians do not allow them to determine accounting standards.[45]

Most theorists probably believe that an objective of their research and the reason they supply theories is to provide knowledge which will ultimately improve accounting practice. They would not regard themselves as supplying "excuses." But we suggest that the predominant contemporary demand for accounting theories (the demand for accounting in a regulated economy) is the demand for justifications—"excuses." If that empirical proposition is correct, the question is: How responsive is the supply side (accounting research) to changes in the nature and quantity of the economic good being demanded?

As long as there exists a large number of individuals who are able to supply a wide diversity of theories (i.e., as long as numerous close substitutes exist) at relatively low cost, then supply will be very responsive to demand. Stigler's observation succinctly summarizes this point:

. . . consumers generally determine what will be produced, and producers make profits by discovering more precisely what consumers want and producing it more cheaply. Some may entertain a tinge of doubt about this proposition, thanks to the energy and skill of Professor Galbraith, but even his large talents hardly raise a faint thought that I live in a house rather than a tent because of the comparative advertising out lays of the two industries. This Cambridge eccentricity aside, then, *it is useful to say that consumers direct production—and therefore, do they not direct the production of the words and ideas of intellectuals, rather than, as in the first view, vice-versa?* [Stigler, 1976, p. 347] (emphasis added)

The consumers ("vested interests") determine the production of accounting research through the incentives they provide for accounting theorists. The greater the prestige and articulation skills of an accounting researcher, the more likely practitioners, regulators and other academics will know his work and the greater the flow of both students and funds to his university. Researchers have non-pecuniary incentives to be well-known, and this reputation is rewarded by a higher salary and a plenitude of research funds.[46] Practitioners, regulators, and those teaching future practitioners are more likely to read or hear of the output of an accounting researcher if it bears on topics of current interest. As a result, the researcher who is motivated by pecuniary and non-pecuniary factors (e.g., "free" trips to conferences) will tend to write on the current controversies in accounting. Therein lies the connection to the demands of vested interests. Controversies arise in accounting when vested interests disagree over accounting standards. For example, the LIFO controversy arose when the Supreme Court outlawed the base stock method of valuing inventory for tax purposes and the American Petroleum Institute recommended LIFO to replace it, thereby reducing the present value of its members' taxes. The Internal Revenue Service resisted because of the effect on revenues. The parties demanded pro and con LIFO theories which were eventually produced. [Moonitz, 1974, pp. 33–34]

Accounting researchers often include a set of policy recommendations as part of their research project.[47] Those recommendations, made on the basis of some objective assumed by the researcher, may never have been intended to serve as an "excuse" for the corporate manager, practitioner or politician who prefers the recommended procedure for self-interest reasons. Nevertheless, the research findings will be favorably quoted by those with vested interests.[48] The more readable the research, the more frequently it is quoted, the more the researcher's fame increases. Similarly, criticisms of alternative accounting practices will be quoted by vested interests and will also increase the researcher's reputation.

The link between suppliers of accounting theory and consumers goes further than mere quotation. Partners in accounting firms, bureaucrats in government agencies and corporate managers will seek out accounting researchers who have eloquently and consistently advocated a particular practice which happens to be in the practitioner's, bureaucrat's, or manager's self-interest and will appoint the researcher as a consultant, or expert witness, or commission him to conduct a study of that accounting problem. Consistency in the researcher's work allows the party commissioning the work to predict more accurately the ultimate conclusions. Thus, research and consulting funds will tend to flow to the most eloquent and consistent advocates of accounting practices where there are vested interests who benefit by the adoption or rejection of these accounting practices.

The tendency of vested interests to seek out researchers who support their position produces a survival bias.[49] The bias is introduced by the vested interests. We do not mean to impugn the motives of accounting researchers who advocate particular practices. In fact, the more consistent the positions of the researcher and the greater his integrity, the more support he lends to the vested interest's position.

Given the rewards for supplying theories on controversial issues, we expect to observe competition in the supply of accounting theories related to those issues. The prescriptions for an issue are likely to be as diverse as the positions of vested interests. But despite this diversity, we do not necessarily expect accounting researchers to be inconsistent from issue to issue. Academic evaluation and criticism create incentives for each researcher to be consistent. However, the rationales given for observed accounting standards may well be inconsistent across issues and different sections of the same accounting standard.

Rationales differ (and are inconsistent) across accounting standards because a standard is the result of political action. The outcome depends on the relative costs which the various involved parties are willing to incur to achieve their goals. And these costs will vary with the expected benefits. The rationale given for a standard will be the successful party's rationale; and if it is a compromise, such as APB Opinion 16 on business combinations, mixtures of rationales will be used.[50] The same party is not successful in every issue; indeed many are not even involved in every issue. Further, vested interests (e.g., an insurance company) are not constrained to give consistent rationales across issues. Hence, we observe a party supporting historical cost valuation in some cases and market valuation in others.[51]

If political transactions costs are high so that there is a demand for excuses which are useful weapons in the political arena, if the demand for accounting theory is dominated by that demand for excuses, and if demand determines production, accounting theories will be generated by, not generate, political debates. We will observe the nature of accounting theory changing as political issues change. Accounting theory will change *contem-*

poraneously with or *lag* political issues. We will *not* observe accounting theory generally *leading* political action.

Contrast the preceding predictions to what we would expect under alternative theories of accounting theory. The only alternative theory which we can even partially specify is that theories in the accounting literature are used to further the "public interest" (i.e., they assist politicians or bureaucrats in producing regulations to further the "public interest"). In order for politicians or bureaucrats to use that literature we would have to observe the theories appearing in the literature before or, at best, at the same time as the relevant regulation. The appearance of the theories in the literature could not *lag* the regulation. Thus, we can discriminate between our theory and the alternative public interest theory if the appearance of theories in the literature tends to lead or lag regulation. If it tends to lead, the public interest hypothesis is supported. If it lags, our theory is supported. On the other hand, if the literature and regulation are contemporaneous we cannot discriminate between the two hypotheses.

It is important to remember that we are attempting to explain accounting theory as it is represented in the accounting literature (see footnote 1). It is conceivable that an accounting theory could be produced and used in the political process to institute a regulation, but not appear until later in the accounting literature. In other words, the "public interest" could, in fact, motivate the theory and the regulation but the publication of the theory could nonetheless lag legislation. In that case neither the public interest theory nor our theory could explain the accounting literature. In essence, we would be left without a theory of the literature. However, those who would argue such a scenario must then produce another explanation for, or theory of, the accounting literature.

In Section IV we compare the timing of general movements in the accounting literature to the timing of regulation to see if a priori the evidence supports our theory or the public interest theory. We do not present any formal tests which discriminate between the two theories, although we believe such tests could be performed (e.g., by using citation tests). However, the serious problem in doing a formal test is that the public interest theory, like other alternative theories, is poorly specified. Hopefully, this paper will cause others to better specify the public interest theory or specify alternative theories of the accounting literature so that testing is facilitated.

One or two papers discussing a topic prior to the time the topic becomes politically active is not sufficient to reject our theory, just as one or two "heads" is not sufficient to reject the hypothesis that a given coin is "fair." It is important to remember that as in all empirical theories we are concerned with *general* trends. Our predictions are for the accounting literature in general. We are not purporting to have a theory that explains the behavior of all accounting researchers or the acceptance, or lack of acceptance, of every published paper. There are many interesting phenomena that this theory, at this state of development, cannot yet explain. But this does not ipso facto destroy the value of the theory.

Our analysis suggests that the accounting literature is not the simple accumulation of knowledge and consequent development of techniques. It is not a literature in which, as Littleton suggests,[52] concepts become better understood and consequently leads to "better" accounting practices. Instead it is a literature in which the concepts are altered to permit accounting practices to adapt to changes in political issues and institutions.

In this section, the existence of close substitute suppliers of theories was shown to make the supply of accounting "excuses" very responsive to the demand. In the next section we argue that the evidence we have gathered is consistent with the proposition that the market for accounting research is the market for "excuses" and suggests that the theory will be confirmed in formal testing.

IV. The Empirical Relationship Between Government Intervention and Accounting Theory

If the demand for "excuses" is important in determining the output of accounting theorists, we expect to observe changes in accounting theory when a new law is passed which impinges on accounting practice. This section examines how accounting practice and theories were affected by several major types of legislation. We have selected three types of legislation which we believe have had a pronounced impact on accounting theory: the laws regulating railroads, the income tax laws, and the securities acts.

In this section we do not purport to present an exhaustive list of legislation which has created a demand for accounting "excuses" or to present a complete analysis of each type of legislation. Our objective is merely to present prima facie support for the hypothesis that accounting theory has changed *after* the introduction of government regulation.

When dealing with historical events such as government regulation, the "evidence" presented is always subject to interpretation and the ex post selection bias of the researchers. Critics can always charge that "strategic sampling" of references produced the results. In fact, much of the economic theory of regulation suffers from this ex post rationalization. However, at this early stage in the development of the theory, an ex post case study approach has yielded insights [Posner, 1974] and appears to be the logical and necessary precursor to a general theory of regulation. We are aware of these methodological problems. Even though the evidence we present is somewhat "casual," and not as "rigorous" as we would like, it is nonetheless evidence.[53] Furthermore, we have endeavored to choose the references from the standard, classical accounting literature. Undoubtedly, conflicting citations and references exist. Critics can, will, and should raise these conflicting citations, keeping in mind the statistical fallacies of drawing inferences based on sample sizes of one. We do not contend that all issues are settled, but rather encourage others to pursue, correct, and extend our analysis.

A. RAILROAD LEGISLATION

The growth of railroads is considered by many accountants to have been very important in the development of accounting theory. Hendriksen [1977, p. 40] lists it as one of the main influences on accounting theory in the period from 1800 to 1930. Littleton [1933, pp. 239–241] is more specific; he ascribes the development of depreciation accounting and the concern with depreciation in the literature in the nineteenth century to the growth of railroads.

There is no doubt that the development of railroads both in the U.S. and the U.K. affected the accounting literature on the nature of depreciation, including the question of charging depreciation as an expense [Pollins, 1956; and Boockholdt, 1977]. Holmes [1975, p. 18] writes:

> Depreciation was a knotty problem for these early railroad accountants. They argued over it, scorned it, denied it, anatomized it, and misused their own concepts. But in the end it was from the very ashes of their disagreements that our modern concepts of depreciation rose Phoenix-like fifty years later.

This literature existed at least by 1841 in the U.K. [*The Railway Times*, October 30, 1841, quoted in Pollins, 1956] and by 1850 in the U.S. [Dionysius Lardner's book quoted in Pollins, 1956] Although the debate did not result in depreciation being treated as an expense in either the U.S. or U.K.,[54] theories of depreciation were enunciated. Consequently, given our theory, we have to answer two questions:

1) why did this depreciation debate arise with the railroads (i.e., was there some government regulation or political action present in the case of the railroads that was not present for earlier corporations); and if so,
2) did that government regulation or political action precede the literature?

1) *The reason for the debate* was investigated by Littleton [1933]. He asserts that two conditions were necessary to the development of depreciation accounting—corporations with limited liability and long-lived assets. He suggests that limited liability was a necessary condition, because it led to covenants restricting dividends to profits and thereby created the demand

for financial statements which report profits (see Section II). Long-lived assets were important because, if they had not existed, there would have been no necessity to calculate depreciation to determine profits.

We think that Littleton's analysis is incomplete. *First,* agency costs of debt and equity exist whether or not a corporation has legally limited liability. Limited liability merely shifts some of the risk [Jensen and Meckling, 1976, pp. 331–332]. Given that the function of dividend covenants is to reduce the agency costs of debt, it is not surprising to observe them existing as early as 1620 for U.K. companies, long before limited liability was generally recognized for companies. We can easily amend Littleton's argument for this defect; for the first condition of limited liability we substitute the existence of dividend covenants.

Second, dividend covenants and long-lived assets would not necessarily lead to depreciation being treated as an *expense.* The dividend covenants place a lower bound on the equity participation of shareholders. As long as sufficient earnings have been retained in the past to cover the depreciation of fixed assets to the current time, there would be no necessity to deduct depreciation systematically each year. We do not observe depreciation being treated as an expense prior to this century. Instead it was treated as an allocation of profits.

This suggests that Littleton's analysis has not been supported empirically. Observation of his two conditions would not necessarily be accompanied by depreciation being treated as an expense. Littleton's two conditions existed in the seventeenth and eighteenth centuries (dividend covenants can be observed as early as 1620 and were included in company charters as a general practice in the eighteenth century). Limited liability for U.K. companies existed de facto at least by the 1730's and was explicitly recognized by 1784.[55] The U.K. trading companies of the seventeenth and eighteenth centuries certainly had long-lived assets—forts and ships. Yet, we do not observe any real concern with depreciation expense until the nineteenth century.

Littleton recognized that his analysis was inconsistent with observed phenomena and that some other variable was necessary to explain the absence of concern about depreciation expense in both accounting theory and practice. He eloquently expresses the inconsistency [Littleton, 1933, p. 240]:

> The simultaneous appearance of these two elements—active, long-lived assets and a special need for the careful calculation of net profit—seems to be essential to the recognition of the importance of depreciation. Before these two are joined depreciation is incidental to the profit calculation; afterward it becomes indispensable. First in the trading companies, later in the railroads, these two elements were united and the foundations for deprecia-

tion accounting were laid. But, so far as could be learned, the depreciation of ships and forts did not receive consideration in the trading companies' bookkeeping, while the railroads, as has been seen, did give considerable attention to the problem of wear and tear of roadway and equipment. *Apparently some third element was also needed, which was present in the case of the railroads* but not earlier. (emphasis added)

Littleton [1933, p. 240] suggests that the missing variable is knowledge, that it took 200 years for the nature of the corporation to become known. We suggest that a more plausible explanation is that, in the case of railroads, fares and rates were regulated by government on the basis of "profits."

Both in the U.S. and the U.K., some transportation prices were related before the existence of railroads. For example, the rates of the Fort Point Ferry (U.S.), incorporated in 1807, were, according to its charter, to be fixed by the court. [Dodd, 1954, p. 258] However, railroad rates came to be tied to profits. The early U.S. railroad charters often had provisions for the adjustment of their rates based on profits. For example, the charter of the Franklin Railroad Company, incorporated in Massachusetts in 1830, included the following provision:

> if at any time after the expiration of four years from the completion of the Road, the net income shall have amounted to more than ten percent per annum, from the date of the completion aforesaid, upon the actual cost of said Road, the Legislature may take measures to alter and reduce the rates of toll and income, in such manner as to take off the overplus for the next four years, calculating the amount of transportation and income to be the same as the four preceding years; and, at the expiration of every four years thereafter the same proceeding may be had. [Dodd, 1954, p. 260]

The charters of three other railroads incorporated in Massachusetts in the same year included a similar provision. [Dodd, 1954, p. 261]

The private acts of Parliament incorporating the early U.K. railroads typically fixed the maximum rates explicitly; but, in one notable exception, the Liverpool and Manchester Railway Act in 1826 limited the company's dividends to ten percent of the capital and required that its rates be reduced by five percent for each one percent of dividend above ten percent. [Pollins, 1956, pp. 337–338] Parliament soon began regulating railroad profits. In 1836, James Morrison sought to have Parliament restrict the profits of all railways. Clauses in Gladstone's 1844 Bill,

> authorized the Board of Trade to consider the position and profits of any railway which had a charter for fifteen years and to decide

whether to buy it up on prescribed terms or, alternatively, to revise all its charges if it had made a profit of more than ten percent on its capital for three consecutive years. [Cooke, 1950, p. 135]

Though these clauses were weakened in the actual Railways Regulation Act of 1844, a principle was established. Cooke [1950, p. 136] explains,

The Act therefore fell short of the designs of Gladstone's committee and it is notable not for any reform it accomplished but rather for the principle embodied in it, that railway companies were one example of a class of company which was formed under special Parliamentary sanction to carry on an undertaking of a special public nature. Since for this purpose it had special powers, it should therefore be subject to special scrutiny and (if necessary) control by the State on behalf of the public.

The question of railroad profits and the public interest was raised in the political process in both the U.S. and the U.K. in the nineteenth century. Hence, it is not surprising that questions of calculating profits and whether or not depreciation should or should not be charged as an expense were raised. The accounting methods of treating capital additions, depreciation, repairs and renewals, etc., could affect reported profits and hence the rates and market values of railroads. Thus, there was a demand for rationalizations of alternative procedures.

The political issue of railroad profits led several U.S. states (Virginia (1837), New Hampshire and Rhode Island (1841), New York (1855), Massachusetts (1869) and Illinois (1869)) to pass legislation which in some way regulated railroads, usually by "controlling extortionate rates". [Boockholdt, 1977, p. 13; Johnson, 1965, p. 218; and Nash, 1947, p. 2] According to Nash [1947, p. 3], "Several of the early state laws called for statements of provision for depreciation in annual reports but without definition as to what such provisions should be." Arguments for depreciation are expected to follow such regulations. Finally, in 1887 federal legislation established the Interstate Commerce Commission to prohibit unreasonable rates and price discrimination, control mergers, and prescribe a uniform system of accounts. The Interstate Commerce Commission adopted an accounting policy of charging "repairs or renewals of ties, rails, roadway, locomotives, and cars under the classification 'operating expenses' [which typically results in higher reported expenses than depreciation] but did not mention depreciation". [Littleton, 1933, p. 236]

Although railroads were the prime target of regulation, the rates of other public utilities were also regulated in the nineteenth century. A Gas Commission was established in Massachusetts in 1885 and two years later was expanded to regulate electric companies. Later, it was given control over capitalization and rates. [Nash, 1947, p. 3] Municipalities regulated water company rates [*Spring Valley Water Works v. Schottler* (1883) in Clay, 1932, p. 33] and such regulation led to legal disputes over whether depreciation should be considered in determining rates. [*San Diego Water Co. v. San Diego* in Riggs, 1922, pp. 155–157] In addition, states regulated the charges for grain elevators. [*Munn v. Illinois* (1877) in Clay, 1932, p. 30].

It is our hypothesis that rate regulation (primarily of the railroads) created a demand for theories rationalizing depreciation as an expense. Furthermore, we expect that the more popular of these theories would stress that it is in the "public interest" for depreciation to be treated as an expense. Without regulation there was no necessity for depreciation to be a charge, systematically deducted each year in determining net income. However, because rate regulation was justified in terms of restricting the economic profits of monopolists (or eliminating "ruinous" competition), regulation created a demand for justifications arguing for depreciation to be treated as an annual charge to profits. Furthermore, because regulatory legislation was often based on economic arguments, theories of depreciation came to be couched in terms of economic costs.

2) *The timing of the debate* appears to confirm our hypothesis that political action generated accounting theory, not vice-versa. As we have seen, the early U.S. railroad charters in the 1830's included provisions for regulation of profits. Those charters *precede* the debates observed in the accounting literature. The move by Morrison to have Parliament regulate the profits of U.K. railroads also *precedes* the debates.

B. INCOME TAX ACTS

The influence of the income tax laws on financial reporting *practice* is well known and much lamented by academics.[56] That influence is very obvious in the practice of charging depreciation to net income, rather than treating it as an allocation of profit. Saliers [1939, pp. 1718] describes the effect of the 1909 Excise Tax Law, the forerunner of the 1913 Income Tax Law:

> 'Financial looseness' describes the accounting practices of industries in general at that time. The company bookkeepers, when closing their books, based the amount of the depreciation charge on the amount of profit earned in that year. A lean year caused the property to receive little or no charge for depreciation, while a prosperous year caused a liberal allowance to be made. The authorities had reason for either action at their fingertips, shifting one side to the other as conditions warranted. But after the year 1909 the shift was to the side of larger depreciation charges, for

in that year the Corporation Excise Tax Law was enacted. This law levied a 1% tax on net income of corporations in excess of $5,000. This net income was said to be the figure resulting after deducting ordinary and necessary expenses and all losses, including an allowance for depreciation, from gross profit. Depreciation expense was made an allowable deduction and was universally deducted by those corporations affected by the act. The effect of this act on the growth of the use of the depreciation charge cannot be overemphasized. *It was the first instance in which the writing off of depreciation as expense was definitely advantageous. That fact alone insured its general application.* (emphasis added)

The influence of tax laws on accounting theory appears to be as dramatic as Saliers' description of the U.S. tax laws' effect on accounting practice, particularly with respect to depreciation. Concern with depreciation as an expense existed only in the railroad accounting literature until the 1880's. In that decade we observe a spate of U.K. journal articles and textbooks on the question of depreciation for corporations in *general*. We do not observe the same concern in the U.S. at that time. This raises the question of why the sudden concern with depreciation in the U.K., not just for public utilities, but for all corporations. Further, why did such a concern with depreciation for all corporations not manifest itself in the U.S.? Brief [1976, p. 737] suggests that the U.K. literature was motivated by a concern with "paying dividends out of capital." "Accountants sought first of all to clarify theory, and second, to understand their responsibility in these matters. However, they were offered little assistance from judicial and statutory authority which failed to specify rules of accounting behavior." Although the accounting authors of the time may have suggested that was the problem, we think it is a very unsatisfactory answer to the question of what really motivated the literature for two reasons. First, we have already noted that the "profits available for dividends" questions had existed for 260 years. Second, there was no uncertainty in the law as to when depreciation should or should not be deducted before determining "profits available for dividends." The legal decisions were consistent: if the corporate articles required a provision for depreciation, it had to be taken; if not it did not. As Litherland [1968, p. 171] states, "the question of depreciation was a matter of internal management with which the law had nothing to do. The Articles of the given company were to govern."

We suggest that the reason a general concern with depreciation for all corporations (and not just railroads) appeared in the U.K. literature in the 1880's and not before is that, prior to 1878, the U.K. tax laws made no allowance for depreciation. "In 1878 the law was modified to permit the deduction of a reasonable amount for the diminished value of machinery and plant resulting from wear and tear. Depreciation was not mentioned in the law and no amount was permitted for obsolescence." [Saliers, 1939, p. 255] Now there was an additional reason for arguing over the concept of annual depreciation and its level—taxes. [Leake, 1912, p. 180]

The income tax explanation for the late nineteenth century depreciation debate also explains the absence of that debate in the U.S. Brief's hypothesis does not. The first effective U.S. corporate income tax law was the Excise Tax Act of 1909 (which went into effect before it was declared unconstitutional).[57] Thus, in 1880 there was no federal tax motivation driving a debate over depreciation. There was in the U.S. in 1880 the problem of determining "profits available for dividend."

The tax laws affected not only the timing of depreciation discussions, but also the resulting concepts of depreciation and of accounting income. In the legal cases on "dividends out of profits," depreciation was regarded as a valuation procedure (see p. 9). Whether the amount of depreciation taken was sufficient or not would be decided in the event of a dispute. Administering the tax laws is less costly if the periodic valuation is replaced by an arbitrary proportion of historical cost. This saving was recognized in the early literature [Matheson, 1893, p. 15] and was the likely reason that both U.S. and U.K. income tax allowances for depreciation were based on historical cost. The demand for a rationalization of this procedure and other accruals under the tax law eventually resulted in the concept of income based on matching and the realization concept. Storey [1959, p. 232] reports this effect of the tax law as follows:

> [The realization concept] probably did not exist at all before the First World War, and at least one writer states that the first official statement of the concept was made in 1932 in the correspondence between the Special Committee on Cooperation with Stock Exchanges of the American Institute of Accountants and the Stock List Committee of the New York Stock Exchange. The letter referred to rejects the method of determining income by the inventorying of assets at the beginning and end of each period in favor of the recognition of profit at the time of sale. This concept of profit was gradually taking form during the period after the First World War and had become dominant in the field of accounting determination of net income by the later 1930's. *That it was influenced by the concept of income laid down by the Supreme Court in early income tax litigation is obvious.* (emphasis added)

The timing of the depreciation debates in the U.K. also appears to confirm our hypothesis that political action caused the observed change in accounting theory. The tax allowance of the depreciation deduction (1878) *precedes* the 1880's debates.

It might appear that the development of the profession could explain the difference in the timing of the concern with depreciation in the U.K. and U.S. The professional bodies did not really develop until the 1870's in the U.K. and until the 1890's in the U.S. [Edwards, 1968a, pp. 197–199] Hence, we could not observe depreciation debates in either country until those times. However, this alternative hypothesis is unsatisfactory on several counts. *First,* while the first professional society was not formed in the U.K. until 1854, Littleton [1933, p. 265] reports evidence of individuals (primarily lawyers) practicing accounting in the U.K. in the eighteenth century and suggests it is highly likely that accounting was practiced by lawyers in earlier times also. Similarly, there were public accountants in the U.S. at least as early as 1866. [Edwards, 1968a, p. 198] *Second,* the lack of a *formal* accounting profession did not prevent the appearance of the railroad depreciation literature in both the U.S. and U.K. in the 1840's and 1850's. *Third,* the formation of professional societies, itself, is likely to be due, at least partly, to political action. Accountants have incentives to lobby on government prescription of accounting practices: Given some economies of scale in lobbying, government intervention in accounting would be expected to produce professional bodies.

C. SECURITIES ACTS

There appear to be at least two major effects of the U.S. Securities Acts of 1933–34 on the accounting literature: they caused the objective of accounting to shift to what we call the "information objective"; and they stimulated a search for accounting principles. Both *follow* the Securities Acts.

1) *The Information Objective.* Prior to the Securities Acts accounting theorists tended to describe and base their prescriptions on the multiple objectives of accounting, and they listed the numerous users. Consistent with our analysis of accounting in an unregulated economy, the control, or stewardship role, was frequently stressed. For example, Leake [1912, pp. 1–2] includes the reasons for calculating profit and loss:

1. the stewardship role of management to "uphold the value of the capital investment and to ascertain and distribute the annual profits with due regard to the differential rights" of the various classes of capital;

2. profit sharing schemes between capital and labor;

3. income taxes; and

4. public utility regulation.

Daines [1929, p. 94] describes the "orthodox" or dominant objective of accounting as being "to reflect that income which is legally available for dividends." Sweeney [1936, p. 248] states that "the fundamental purpose of accounting should consist of an attempt to distinguish between capital and income."

In his book based on his doctoral dissertation, Sweeney adds other functions to the stewardship role:

> Business management guides the affairs of business. For its own guidance it depends heavily on reports submitted to it by its employees. Periodically it renders reports of its stewardship to the owners of the business. From time to time it also renders reports to bankers who have lent money to the business, to federal and state governments that tax or regulate business, and to the general financial public.
>
> The whole system of business, therefore, depends upon reports. Reports are made up largely of accounting statements. [Sweeney, 1936, p. xi]

Managers were frequently cited as important users of accounting. Paton [1924, p. 1] defines accounting as a

> mechanism and body of principles by means of which the financial data of the particular concern are recorded, classified, and periodically presented and interpreted, with a view, thereby, to the *rational administration of the enterprise.* (emphasis added)

After, the Securities Acts the providing of information to investors and creditors in order to aid them in making rational investment choices became the dominant objective in the literature. We call this the information objective. One of the earliest documents which illustrates this new emphasis on the investors decision is the AAA's 1936 "Tentative Statement on Accounting Principles." A number of "unsatisfactory" accounting procedures are discussed including upward asset revaluations.

> Occasional uncoordinated 'appraisals' produce in the average financial statement a hodgepodge of unrelated values of no explicable significance to *the ordinary investor,* if indeed they have any to the managements of the enterprises affected. [American Accounting Association, 1936, p. 189] (emphasis added)

Notice the emphasis given to investors. Hendriksen [1977, p. 54] also supports our contention that the objective changed "from presenting financial information to management and creditors to that of providing financial information to investors and stockholders." In a more recent example, *A*

Statement of Basic Accounting Theory [American Accounting Association, 1966, p. 4], the information objective is listed first among four objectives of accounting. The objectives are:

1. to provide information for decisions concerning limited resources by "individuals acting in their own behalf, such as the stockholders or creditors of a firm, by agents serving in fiduciary capacities, or by individuals or groups in business firms, in government, in not-for-profit organizations and elsewhere." [p. 4]

2. to effectively direct and control an organization's human and material resources,

3. to maintain and report on the custodianship of resources,

4. "to facilitate the operations of an organized society for the welfare of all." [p. 5]

Recent writers no longer even list management as a principal user of financial statements. The dichotomy of internal and external accounting has become complete.

The recent statement on accounting objectives, the FASB's Conceptual Framework Study [1976], also excludes management:

Financial statements of business enterprises should provide information, within the limits of financial accounting, that is useful to present and potential investors and creditors in making rational investment and credit decisions. [FASB, 1976, p. 10]

The dominance of the information objective arose, we suspect, as a public interest justification consistent with and in support of the raison d'être of the Securities Acts. The SEC was justified in terms of, and charged with, maintaining the orderly functioning of the capital markets. In particular the SEC was to protect the public from another stock market crash. That crash was alleged to have been caused in part by inadequate corporate disclosure, although very little evidence exists to support this claim.[58]

Although the SEC delegated the power to determine accounting standards for corporate disclosure to the accounting profession, there is evidence that it still exercised control over that determination. According to Horngren [1973] and Zeff [1972, pp. 150–160] the SEC managed by exception, threatening to intervene, or actually intervening in the standard-setting process whenever the Committee on Accounting Procedure (CAP) or the APB proposed a standard of which it did not approve. Consequently, proponents advocating particular accounting procedures would justify those procedures in terms of the SEC's stated objective—the public interest (which "requires" the information objective).

The hypothesis that the dominance of the information objective was caused by the Securities Acts is supported not only by the tendency of modern writers to cite the public interest as an objective along with the information objective (e.g., the fourth objective of *A Statement of Basic Accounting Theory* listed above), but by the tendency to argue that fulfillment of the information objective is necessary to the "public interest". An example of that latter tendency is provided by the FASB [1976, p. 3]

> Financial accounting and reporting is an important source of information on which investment, lending, and related decisions are based. Confidence in financial information is vital not only to ensure that individual decisions result in an equitable allocation of capital but to ensure continuing public support of the free enterprise system as a whole.

The close relationship between the information objective and the "public interest" is exemplified by the argument recently raised in the literature that information provided in accounting reports is a public good and that as a consequence, there may be an underproduction of information from society's viewpoint (i.e., there may be a market failure). If there is a market failure, the argument proceeds, the "public interest" may require disclosure laws requiring the provision of information to investors [Beaver, 1976, p. 66].

2) *The Search for Accounting Principles.* Before the Securities Acts most "of the accounting literature did not stray far from practice, prescriptions were usually based on rationalizations of practice (e.g., the matching concept). Even Sweeney's price-level accounting proposals of the 20's were based on practice. According to the author [Sweeney, 1936, p. xii] the work "has its roots in methods that were developed in Germany and France during the late inflation periods in those countries." There was, with the notable exceptions of Paton [1922] and Canning [1929], little effort devoted to establishing a theory of accounting.[59] Indeed, Chambers [1955a, p. 18] claims that except for Paton [1922] the word theory was not attached to any work in the accounting literature until after World War II.

Taggart describes the general situation in 1922 as follows:

> Some of the writers on theory, notably Sprague and Hatfield, not satisfied merely to describe practice, had earnestly addressed themselves to exposition of pure theory; but the textbook writers, for the most part, had quite naturally concerned themselves primarily with practice and with not much more than an occasional nod toward theory, where it seemed to bolster practice. Paton's *Accounting Theory* is concerned only with theory; it

touches on practice only for illustration or contrast; and it is quite the opposite of an apologia for practice. [foreword in the 1962 re-issue of Paton, 1922, p. v]

Canning [1929, p. 160] himself wrote, "accountants have no complete philosophical system of thought about income; *nor is there evidence that they have ever greatly felt the need for one.*[60] (emphasis added)

A potential explanation for the two famous departures from the orthodox accounting thought of the 20's [Canning, 1929; and Paton, 1922,] is that both were based on doctoral dissertations written in economics departments [Zeff, 1978, p. 16]. Undoubtedly, both authors were heavily influenced by economists as well as accountants. Canning himself writes, "I need not declare my obligation to Professor [Irving] Fisher for the influence of his writings upon my thought—that obligation appears throughout the whole book" [Canning, 1929, p. iv].

If Paton and Canning were harbingers of a change in accounting thought, we would expect to observe a shift in the orthodox accounting view during the 20's, following publication of their books. Alternatively, if Canning's and Paton's views were outliers or aberrations due to their economics training, we would expect to observe them modifying their views towards the orthodox position to ensure their survival as accounting academics.

Zeff [1978] presents evidence that Paton's views, at least, moved more towards the orthodox view during the 1920's and 1930's, than the orthodox view moved towards Paton's. Thus, it is difficult to argue that Paton and Canning were representative of a change in the accounting literature which influenced the passage of the Securities Acts. Instead, we suspect that much of the attention which Paton's and Caning's views received after the Securities Acts was a result of the Acts themselves.

The literature's concern with practice before the Securities Acts is not surprising (given our theory). Prescriptions based on rationalizations of practice are to be expected in an economy in which corporate reporting is not regulated. Theorists would base their prescriptions for individual firms on the current institutional arrangements determining practice (i.e., in terms of the agency or stewardship relationships, utility regulation, taxes, etc.). Hence, theory would be very concerned with practice. Further, because the advantages are to the individual firms, the theorist would not *require* all firms to follow his prescriptions, but expect his prescriptions to be adopted because of self-interest. The theorist would not try to specify accounting principles which all firms *should* adopt.

As we have noted, the Securities Acts were based on the argument that required disclosure is necessary to the "public interest". The idea was that without required disclosure capital markets would be less efficient. We do not observe this theory being generally advanced in the accounting literature prior to the Securities Acts.[61]

The justification for required disclosure is that the private incentives to adopt accounting prescriptions are insufficient. Hence, current accounting practice cannot serve as a basis for prescriptions. This justification sets accounting theory free from practice. It makes it possible to "build up a theory of accounting without reference to the practice of accounting" [Chambers, 1955a, p. 19]. Further, the justification caused the SEC to demand such theories.

Because they were to reform existing accounting practice, the SEC commissioners could not base regulations on practice; they required a theory or a set of accounting principles to justify their rulings.

Zeff [1972, pp. 133–173] documents the AICPA's initial search for accounting principles and the SEC's passing the responsibility for the determination of principles to the profession in SEC Accounting Series Release No. 4 (ASR 4).[62] Zeff also documents the search for accounting principles (or standards) by the succession of standard-setting bodies established by the profession. As noted, the SEC exercised control over the standard-setting bodies' search for accounting principles. Thus, we expect these bodies (like the SEC) to search for or demand accounting principles which do *not* describe existing practice.

We expect accounting theorists, who are accustomed to developing rules based on practice, to be perplexed by a demand for accounting principles not based on practice. *After* the SEC's call (in ASR 4) for accounting principles for which there is substantial authoritative support (1938), the accounting literature begins to discuss the nature of principles [Scott, 1941; Wilcox and Hassler, 1941; and Kester, 1942].[63] Further, as theorists come to observe less emphasis being placed on the practicality of their approach, we observe philosophical works becoming far removed from practice such as Chambers [1955a, 1955b, 1966], Mattessich [1957] and Edwards and Bell [1961].

It is instructive to compare the search for accounting principles in the U.S. to that in the U.K. where there has not been a government regulatory body with the statutory power to prescribe accounting procedures [Benston, 19, 6, pp. 14–30; Zeff, 1972, pp. 1–69].[64] Until recently there has been considerably less "progress" in the U.K. in the search for accounting principles [Zeff, 1972, p. 310 and Shackleton, 1977, pp. 17–21] and further, the "English began late" [Zeff, 1972, p. 310]. The evidence suggests that the U.K. search for principles is also a response to government pressure which arose out of various financial crises. [Zeff, 1972, pp. 39–40; Benston, 1976, pp. 15–17; and Shackleton, 1977, pp. 17–21].

The difference in the timing of the search for principles in the two countries is reminiscent of the 30 year difference in the tiring of the general depreciation debates in the U.K. and the U.S. That 30 year difference also coincides with a difference in the timing of government regulation (i.e., corporate income tax lags allowing depreciation as a deduction). The difference in timing cannot be explained per se by the fact that we are comparing two different countries. In the depreciation debates, the U.K. led, while the U.S. led in the search for principles.

The discussion in this section has suggested that much of accounting theory (e.g., the concepts of depreciation, accrual accounting, the application of the concept of economic income, and the idea that the objective of financial statements is generally to provide information to investors rather than to control agency costs), *follows* government intervention. Thus, the evidence is consistent with our hypothesis that much of accounting theory is the product of government intervention and that accounting theory satisfies the demand for excuses. The evidence appears to be inconsistent with what we have called the "public interest" hypothesis. Undoubtedly there are alternative theories which can also explain the timing of the accounting literature. The challenge is to those who would support those alternative theories to specify them and show that they are more consistent with the evidence than ours.

V. Conclusions

In our view, accounting theories have had an important role in determining the content of financial statements—although it might not be the role envisioned by the theorists. Instead of providing "an underlying framework" for the promulgation of "sound" financial reporting practices by standard-setting boards, accounting theory has proven a useful "tactic to buttress one's preconceived nations" [Zeff, 1974, p. 177]. While accounting theories have always served a justification role in addition to information and pedagogic roles, government intervention has expanded the justification role. The predominant function of accounting theories is not to supply excuses which satisfy the demand created by the political process; consequently, accounting theories have become increasingly normative.

We are not offering any judgments on the desirability of accounting theories fulfilling an excuse role. What we are arguing, however, is that *given* the existing economic and political institutions and the incentives of voters, politicians, managers, investors, etc. to become involved in the process by which accounting standards are determined, the only accounting theory that will provide a set of predictions that are consistent with observed phenomena is one based on self-interest No other theory, *no normative theory currently in the accounting literature (e.g., current value theories) can explain or will be used to justify all accounting standards, because:*

1. accounting standards are justified using the theory (excuse) of the vested interest group which is benefited by the standard;

2. vested interest groups use different theories (excuses) for difference issues; and

3. different vested interest groups prevail on different issues.

While a self-interest theory can explain accounting standards, such a theory will not be used to justify accounting standards because self-interest theories are politically unpalatable. As a consequence, *not only is there no generally accepted accounting theory to justify accounting standards, there will never be one.*

Notes

1. For example, see Canning (1929), Paton (1922), Edwards and Bell (1962), Sprouse and Moonitz (1962), Gordon (1964), Chambers (1966), and American Accounting Association (1966). We would prefer to reserve the term "theory" for principles advanced to explain a set of phenomena, in particular for sets of hypotheses which have been confirmed. However, such a definition of theory would exclude much of the prescriptive literature and generate a semantic debate. To avoid that consequence, in this paper (unless qualified) we use the word "theory" as a generic term for the existing accounting literature.

2. For example, Chambers (1966, Chapters 9–11) apparently adopts economic efficiency as an objective while the American Institute of Certified Public Accountants (AICPA) Study Group on the Objectives of Financial Statements (1973, p. 17) decided that "financial statements should meet the needs of those with the least ability to obtain information . . ."

3. Some writers (e.g., Chambers, 1966) make assumptions about the world without regard to *formal* empirical evidence and derive their prescriptions using those assumptions. Others (e.g., Gonedes and Dopuch, 1974) argue that prescriptions to achieve any given objective must be based on hypotheses which have been subjected to formal statistical tests and confirmed.

4. American Accounting Association, m (1977, p. 1). This report also reviews the major accounting theories.

5. The Committee on Concepts and Standards for External Reports, American Accounting Association (1977) examines many of these same questions, and the interested reader should refer to this committee report for an alternative explanation of these phenomena, specifically Chapter 4.

6. The terms "normative" and "prescriptive" are used interchangeably. See Mautz and Gray (1970) for an example of prescriptions to "improve" accounting research and hence its impact on practice.

7. See Sterling (1974, pp. 180–181) for Horngren's response to Zeff's initial remark.

8. Accounting "procedures", "techniques", and "practices" are defined as any com-

putational algorithm used or suggested in the preparation of financial accounting statements. "Accounting standards" are those "procedures" sanctioned or recommended by an "authoritative" body such as the APB, FASB, SEC, ICC, etc.

9. Benston (1969a) reports that as of 1926 all firms listed on the New York Stock Exchange published a balance sheet, 5% disclosed sales, 45% disclosed cost of goods sold, 71% disclosed depreciation, 100% disclosed net income, and 82% were audited by a CPA.

10. In the period 1862–1900, many U.K. companies voluntarily adopted the optional articles included in Table A of the 1862 U.K. Companies Act. See Edey (1968), Edey and Panitpakdi (1956) and Watts (1977). Examples of private contracts can be found today in any note or bond indenture agreement.

11. Jensen and Meckling (1976, p. 308) define an agency relationship as "a contract under which one or more persons (the principal(s)) engage another person (the agent) to perform some service on their behalf which involves delegating some decision making authority to the agent." There are at least two agency relationships which cause corporate promoters and managers to bear agency costs. The first is the relationship between shareholders (the principals) and the manager (the agent) and the second is the relationship between the bondholders (the principals) and the manager (the agent).

12. See Jensen and Meckling (1976) for a formal proof that he bears this cost.

13. See Kehl (1941, p. 4).

14. Agency costs are also a function of the tastes of managers for non-pecuniary income, the extent of managerial competition, the degree to which the capital markets and the legal system are able to reduce agency costs, etc. See Jensen and Meckling (1976, pp. 328–330).

15. The terms "shareholders" and "stockholders" are used interchangeably.

16. See Matheson (1893, p. 5) for a report that managers did in fact adopt this tactic in the nineteenth century.

17. See Matheson (1893, p. viii) for a statement that managers did in fact resist depreciation charges because of the effect on their compensation.

18. See Smith (1976, p. 42). Also, we find labor-managed firms in socialist countries faced with the same agency problem. Labor has less incentive to maintain physical capital than an owner-manager. Jensen and Meckling (1977).

19. For example, the General Bank of India had a provision in its charter limiting dividends to not more than ⅔ of net (cash) profits. DuBois (1938, p. 365).

20. The Phoenix Insurance Company, 1781, required a reserve fund of £52,000 before any dividends could be paid. Ibid.

21. See Littleton (1933, pp. 223–227).

22. *Dent v. London Tramways Company,* 1880 in Brief (1976, p. 193).

23. "Take the case of a warehouse: supposing a warehouse keeper, having a new warehouse, should find at the end of the year that he had no occasion to expend money in repairs, but thought that, by reason of the usual wear and tear of the warehouse, it was $1,000_p$ worse than it was at the beginning of the year, he would set aside $1,000_p$ for a repair or renewal or depreciation fund, before he estimated any profits; because, although that sum is not required to be paid in that year,

it is still the sum of money which is lost, so to say, out of capital, and which must be replaced." Ibid.

24. Prior to the creation of the Securities and Exchange Commission (SEC) in 1934, much variation existed in accounting procedures. See Blough (1937, p. 7). In an unregulated economy, the market itself regulates the amount of diversity of accounting procedures. There are economies associated with using existing practices and terminology. If the firm adopts previously unknown accounting practices, then the users of the statements (i.e., creditors monitoring shareholders and shareholders monitoring management) will incur costs in learning the new accounting procedures. If creditors and shareholders have alternative uses of their capital (i.e, capital markets are competitive) the costs of the new procedures are ultimately borne by the shareholders and managers. Hence, new procedures (and increased diversity) will be implemented only if their added benefits offset the costs they impose.

25. See the Leeds Estate Building Company case in Edwards (1968b, p. 148).

26. Share prices are unbiased estimates of the extent to which the auditor monitors management and reduces agency costs (see Fama (1970) and Gonedes and Dopuch (1974) for a review of the evidence on market efficiency). The larger the reduction in agency costs effected by an auditor (net of the auditor's fees), the higher the value of the corporation's shares and bonds and, ceteris paribus, the greater the demand for that auditor's services. If the market observes the auditor failing to monitor management, it will adjust downwards the share price of all firms who engage this auditor (to the extent to which the auditor does not reduce agency costs), and this will reduce the demand for his services.

27. See Stigler (1971), Posner (1974), and Peltzman (1976).

28. The reported profits of U.S. oil companies during the Arab oil embargo were used to justify bills to break up these large firms.

29. See Watts and Zimmerman (1978) for a test of this proposition. Also, see Prakash and Rappaport (1977) for further discussion of these feedback effects. See a bill introduced into the Senate by Senator Bayh [U.S. Congress, Senate, Subcommittee on Anti-trust and Monopoly (1975, pp. 5–13) and (1976, p. 1893)]. Note that it is absolute size and profits which are used as a justification. On this point, see the "Curse of Bigness," Barron's, June 30, 1969, pp. 1 and 8. Also see Alchian and Kessel (1962, p. 162).

30. The Interstate Commerce Commission based its decision to allow tax deferral accounting on APB Opinion No. 11. See Interstate Commerce Commission, *Accounting for Federal Income Taxes,* 318 I.C.C. 803.

31. Other writers have also recognized the tendency for advocates to use public interest arguments. For example, Pichler (1974, pp. 64–65) concludes that the accounting profession has increased its economic power via control over entry "through legislation justified as protecting the public interest." (p. 64) "In most cases, *public rather than professional interest was cited as the primary reason for* [the legislation]." (p. 65) (emphasis added)

32. U.S. Congress, Senate (1976, p. 59), "Metcalf Report."

33. McCraw (1975, p. 162). Also, see U.S. Securities and Exchange Commission (1945, pp. 1–10).

34. For a summary of this literature see Posner (1974) and McCraw (1975).
35. By "best" theory, we mean the theory most consistent with observed phenomena. Such theories allow public officials to predict the outcomes of their actions, thereby helping them select actions which increase social welfare.
36. See Posner (1974).
37. For analyses of the political process based on this assumption see Downs (1957), Jensen (1976), Meckling (1976a and b), Mueller (1976), Niskanen (1971), Peltzman (1976), Stigler (1971), and Leffler and Zimmerman (1977).
38. Stigler (1971) attempts to explain the regulation of an industry on the basis of variation of coalition costs, free-rider costs, etc., with such variables as group size, homogeneity of interests, etc.
39. The social choice literature (see Mueller, 1976) discusses the conditions which guarantee Pareto-efficient decisions by regulators.
40. See Fama (1976) for a review of capital market theory.
41. See Zimmerman (1977) for further discussion of this issue. Essentially, the reason it is costlier to purchase "control" of the political system (via a system of bribes, payoffs, etc.) is that the legal system does not enforce those contracts to the same extent that the state enforces the property rights of residual claimants in corporations. Hence, more (costly) monitoring is required to enforce contracts between politicians/bureaucrats and other parties.
42. Buchanan and Wagner (1977, pp. 128–130) introduce the concept of "fiscal illusion" as a systematic bias in individuals' perceptions of the differential effects of alternative taxing procedures. They hypothesize "that complex and indirect payment structures create a fiscal illusion that will systematically produce higher levels of public outlay than those that would be observed under simple-payment structures." (p. 129) It could be argued that individuals also suffer from "theory illusion" (i.e., that more complex theories obscure political behavior). We do not subscribe to this phenomenon, but offer it as an alternative explanation.
43. Mautz (1966, p. 6) and Sterling (1973, p. 49).
44. Ijiri (1971, p. 26) states, "Accounting theorists are scientific observers of accounting practices and their surrounding environment. Their theories are required to have the highest degree of objectivity."
45. Moonitz (1974b) does not believe that accounting research should be the sole source for setting practice, but that it should have a role, "Almost everyone agrees that research is an essential component of the process of establishing accounting standards." (p. 58) He goes on to suggest that "accountants must curb the power of the management," (p. 68).
46. Even though we have argued the existence of close substitutes, all researchers will not be earning the same compensation. Higher compensation will accrue to the most prolific, articulate, and creative advocates—to those who are able to establish early property rights in a topic and thus must be cited by later theorists.
47. See Beaver (1973) for an example of policy prescriptions based on accounting research.
48. An interesting case in point is the work of Ijiri (1967 and 1975). Ijiri claims to be a postivist—the purpose [of this book] is a better understanding of the foundations of accounting as it is and not as someone thinks it ought to be." (1967, p.

x) He states that his work "is not intended to be pro-establishment or to promote the maintenance of the status quo. The purpose of such an exercise is to highlight where changes are most needed and where they are feasible." (1975, p. 28) But then in the same monograph (pp. 85–90) Ijiri presents a defense of historical costs, saying, "Our defense of historical cost should not, however, be interpreted to mean that historical cost is without any flaw." (p. 85) Ijiri concludes this defense with a statement—"We should in fact try to improve the accounting system based on historical cost not by abandoning it, but by modifying it (e.g., through price level adjustments) and supplementing it with data based on other valuation methods" (p. 90). Despite being a professed positivist, Ijiri is making a strong normative statement. No wonder the AAA (1977, p. 10) committee when summarizing Ijiri (1975) concludes—"[he] defends historical costs against the criticisms of current-cost and current value. . . ." At least part of the "market" views Ijiri as a defender of the status quo.

49. Just as in any market those who produce what is demanded have a better chance of survival than those who do not.

50. See Zeff (1972, pp. 212–216) for an account of this compromise.

51. Ernst & Ernst (1976) has proposed that replacement costs be used for depreciable assets while historical costs be continued for other assets.

52. "There is little evidence of fresh ideas regarding depreciation until the middle of the nineteenth century. The appearance of steam railroads at that time directed attention as never before to fixed assets and their associated problems of maintenance, renewal and improvement. Out of the discussion and experience which followed, new ideas about depreciation took form and the ground was prepared for a better comprehension of the real nature of depreciation itself." Littleton (1933, p. 227).

53. It is tempting to suggest citation tests of the theory (i.e., the frequency of articles on a subject increases with regulation). Besides the obvious costs of such a test, it suffers from the interpretation bias of the researchers. Also, how should changes in terminology be controlled? We would welcome anyone who can overcome these methodological difficulties to perform the tests.

54. The general practice in both countries came to be the writing-off of the value of fixed assets at the time of retirement of the asset.

55. See DuBois (1938, pp. 94–95) for a report on the incorporation proceedings of the Albion Flour Mill in 1784. In those proceedings, the Attorney General gave an opinion on limited liability which caused DuBois to conclude that, "for England at any rate, the fact of incorporation either by the Crown or by Parliament came to be the criterion for the extent of limited liability" (p. 96). Note, however, that it was theoretically possible for shareholders of insolvent companies to be made subject to calls. (See DuBois, pp. 98–103). DuBois (p. 95) recognized that de facto limited liability existed in the 1730's and 1740's: "it should be noted that through the financial tribulations of the Charitable Corporation, the York Buildings Company, and the Royal African Company, which in the thirties and forties were making life miserable for their creditors, there was no suggestion of any attempt to proceed against the personal estates of the members of the corporation."

56. Hendriksen [1977, p. 49] states: "The effect on accounting theory of taxation of business incomes in the United States and in other countries has been considerable, but it has been primarily indirect in nature . . . While the revenue acts did hasten the adoption of good accounting practices and thus brought about a more critical analysis of accepted accounting procedures and concepts, they have also been a deterrent to experimentation and the acceptance of good theory."

57. An increase in the effective corporate tax rate from less than 1% in 1909 to over 7% in 1918 further stimulated the concern for depreciation in the U.S. (Source: *Historical Survey of the Untied States,* U.S. Department of Commerce (1975), p. 1109).

58. See Benston (1969 a and b). The U.S. Securities and Exchange Commission (1945, pp. 1–3 and Part X) report makes this claim although Sanders (1946, pp. 9–10) disputes much of their arguments.

59. The Federal Reserve Board published a 1917 bulletin (*Uniform Accounting*) written by Price, Waterhouse & Co. in response to the Federal Trade Commission threatening to establish a federal accountant's register, but the bulletin "consisted of mainly audit procedures." (Carey, 1969, pp. 1:29–135).

60. Canning's principal intentions were not to reform existing practice or to construct a general theory but rather to make "the work of the professional accountant more fully intelligible to those in other branches of learning" (1929, p. iii).

61. The theory does appear in *The Journal of Accountancy* in October, 1930 (see Hoxsey, 1930), but the author is not an accounting theorist; instead he is an employee of the New York Stock Exchange. The theory also appears in the writings of Ripley in the popular financial literature in the 20's (e.g., Ripley, 1926). However, Ripley is also not representative of the financial literature.

62. ASR 4 stated that "financial statements filed with this Commission [which] are prepared in accordance with accounting principles for which there are *no substantial authoritative support,* . . . will be presumed to be misleading or inaccurate." (emphasis added) ASR 4 created a demand for some procedure or device to provide "substantial authoritative" support.

63. Storey (1964, p. 3) supports our contention that the Securities Acts were "landmark events" and directly related to the search for accounting principles.

64. See Sanders (1946) for an overview of the different prevailing attitudes in the U.S. and U.K. in the 1940's.

References

Accounting Principles Board, *Opinion 16, Business Combinations,* (New York: American Institute of Certified Public Accountants, 1970).

Alchian, Armen and Reuben Kessel, "Competition, Monopoly and the Pursuit of Money," in *Aspects of Labor Economics,* (Princeton University Press: N.B.E.R., 1962), pp. 157–175.

American Accounting Association, "A Tentative Statement of Accounting Principles Affecting Corporate Reports," *Accounting Review,* (June 1939), pp. 187–191.

American Accounting Association Committee on Basic Accounting Theory, *A State-*

ment of Basic Accounting Theory, (Chicago: American Accounting Association, 1966).

American Accounting Association, Committee on Concepts and Standards for External Reports, *Statement of Accounting Theory and Theory Acceptance* (Sarasota: American Accounting Association, 1977).

American Institute of Certified Public Accountants, *Objectives of Financial Statements,* (Trueblood) Report of the Study Group on the Objectives of Financial Statements (New York: American Institute of Certified Public Accountants, 1973).

Barron's, "Curse of Bigness," Dow Jones & Company (June 30,m 1969), pp. 1 and 8.

Beaver, William H., "What Should Be the FASB's Objectives?", *Journal of Accountancy,* (August, 1973), pp. 49–56.

Beaver, William H., "The Implications of Security Price Research for Disclosure Policy and the Analyst Community," in *Financial Information Requirements for Security Analysis,* ed. A. R. Abdel-khalik and T. F. Keller, Duke Second Accounting Symposium, Duke University (December 1976), pp. 65-BI.

Beaver, William H. and Joel S Demski, "The Nature of Financial Accounting Objectives: A Summary and Synthesis," *Studies on Financial Accounting Objectives,* supplement to the *Journal of Accounting Research* (1974), pp. 170–187.

Benston, George J., "The Value of the SEC's Accounting Disclosure Requirements," *Accounting Review,* (July 1969a), pp. 515–532.

———, "The Effectiveness and Effects of the SEC's Accounting Disclosure Requirements," in *Economic Policy and the Regulation of Corporate Securities,* ed. Henry G. Manne (Washington, D.C.: American Enterprise Institute, 1969b), pp. 23–79.

———, *Corporate Financial Disclosure in the UK and the USA,* (Westmead, U.K.: Saxon House, 1976).

Blough, Carman G., "Some Accounting Problems of the Securities and Exchange Commission," *The New York Certified Public Accountant,* (April 1937), pp. 3–14.

Boockholdt, James L., "Influence of Nineteenth and Early Twentieth Century Railroad Accounting on Development of Modern Accounting Theory," unpublished working paper

Brief, Richard P. (ed.), *The Late Nineteenth Century Debate over Depreciation, Capital and Income* (New York: Arno Press, 1976)

Buchanan, James M. and Richard E. Hagner, *Democracy in Deficit: The Political Legacy of Lord Keynes,* (New York: Academic Press, 1977).

Burton, John C., "An Interview with John C. Burton," *Management Accounting,* (May, 1975), pp. 19–23.

Canning, John B., *The Economics of Accountancy* (New York: Ronald Press, 1929).

Carey, John L., *The Rise of the Accounting Profession,* Vols I & 2 (New York: American Institute of Certified Public Accountants, 1969).

Chambers, Raymond J., "Blueprint for a Theory of Accounting," *Accounting Research,* (U.K.) (January 1955a), pp. 17–25.

———, "A Scientific Pattern for Accounting Theory," *Australian Accountant* (October 1955b), pp. 428–434.

———, *Accounting, Evaluation and Economic Behavior* (Englewood Cliffs, NJ: Prentice-Hall, 1966).

Clay, Cassius M., *Regulation of Public Utilities*, (New York: Henry Holt and Company, 1932)

Cooke, C.A., *Corporation, Trust and Company* (Manchester, U.K.: Manchester University Press, 1950)

Daines, N.C., "The Changing Objectives of Accounting," *The Accounting Review*, (June 1929), pp. 94–110.

Dicksee, Lawrence, *Depreciation, Reserves and Reserve Funds* (1905), reprinted by Arno Press (New York, 1976).

Dodd, Edwin M., *American Business Corporations Until 1860* (Cambridge, Mass.: Harvard University Press, 1954)

Downs, Anthony, *An Economic Theory of Democracy* (New York: Harper and Row, 1957).

DuBois, Armand B., *The English Business Company After the Bubble Act 1720–1800* (New York: The Commonwealth Fund, 1938).

Edey, Harold C., "Company Accounting in the Nineteenth and Twentieth Centuries," reprinted in *Contemporary Studies in the Evolution of Accounting Thought*, ed. Michael Chatfield (Belmont, California: Dickenson Publishing Co. Inc., 1966), pp. 135–143.

———, and Prot Panitpakdi, "British Company Accounting and the Law 1844–1900," in A. C. Littleton and B. S. Yamey (eds.) *Studies in the History of Accounting* (Homewood, Illinois: Richard D. Irwin, Inc., 1956), pp. 356–379.

Edwards, Edgar O. and Philip W. Bell, *The Theory and Measurement of Business Income* (Berkeley and Los Angeles: University of California Press, 1961).

Edwards, James D., "The Antecedents of American Public Accounting," *Accounting Research* (January 1956) reprinted in *Contemporary Studies in the Evolution of Accounting Thought*, ed. Michael Chatfield (Belmont, California: Dickenson Publishing Co., 1968b), pp. 144–166.

Ernst & Ernst, *Accounting Under Inflationary Conditions*, (Cleveland: Ernst & Ernst, 1976).

Fama, Eugene F., "Efficient Capital Markets A Review of Theory and Empirical Work," *Journal of Finance* (May 1970), pp. 381–417.

Fama, Eugene F., *Foundations of Finance* (New York: Basic Books Inc., 1976).

Financial Accounting Standards Board, *An Analysis of Issues Related to Conceptual Framework for Financial Accounting and Reporting: Elements of Financial Statements and Their Measurement* (Stamford, Conn.: FASB, 1976).

Gonedes, N. and N. Dopuch, "Capital Market Equilibrium, Information Production and Selecting Accounting Techniques: Theoretical Framework and Review of Empirical Work," *Studies on Financial Accounting Objectives*, supplement to the Journal of Accounting Research (1974), pp. 48–129.

Gordon, Myron J., "Postulates, Principles and Research in Accounting," *The Accounting Review* (April 1964), pp. 251–263.

Hendriksen, Eldon, *Accounting Theory*, 3rd ed. (Homewood, Illinois: Richard D. Irvin, Inc., 1977).

Holmes, William, "Accounting and Accountants in Massachusetts," *Massachusetts CPA Review* (May–June 1975), pp. 18–21.

Horngren, Charles T., "The Marketing of Accounting Standards," *Journal of Accountancy*, (October 1973), pp. 61–66.

————, "Setting Accounting Standards in the 1980's," in Norton Bedford, ed. *Accountancy in the 1980's—Some Isues*, ed. Norton Bedford (Reston, Va.: The Council of Arthur Young Professors, 1977).

Hoxsey, J.M.B., "Acounting for Investors,": *Journal of Accountancy*, (October 1930), pp. 251–284.

Ijiri, Yuji, *The Foundations of Accounting Measurement* (Englewood Cliffs, NJ: Prentice-Hall Inc., 1967).

————, "Logic and Functions in Accounting," in *Accounting in Perspective*, eds. Robert Sterling and William Bentz (Cincinnati: South-Western Publishing Co., 1971).

————, *Theory of Accounting Measurement* (Sarasota, Florida: American Accounting Association, 1975).

Edwards, James D., "Some Significant Developments of Public Accounting in the United States," *Business History Review* (June 1956), reprinted in *Contemporary Studies in the Evolution of Accounting Thought* ed. Michael Chatfield (Belmont, California: Dickenson Publishing Co., 1968a), pp. 196–209.

Interstate Commerce Commission, *Accounting for Federal Income Taxes*, 318 I.C.C. 803, U.S. Government Printing Office.

Jensen, Michael C., "Towards a Theory of the Press," published paper, Graduate School of Management, University of Rochester, June 1976.

————, and William H. Meckling, "Theory of the Firm: Managerial Behavior, Agency Costs and Ownership Structure," *Journal of Financial Economics*, (October 1976), pp. 305–360.

————, and William H. Heckling, "On 'The Labor Managed' Firm and the Codetermination Movement," Public Policy Working Paper Series GPB 77-2, Center for Research in Government Policy and Business, Graduate School of Management, University of Rochester, February 1977.

Johnson, Arthur M., *Government-Business Relations* (Columbus, Ohio: Charles E. Merrill Books, 1965).

Kehl, Donald, *Corporate Dividends* (New York: The Ronald Press Company, 1941).

Kester, Roy B., "Sources of Accounting Principles," *Journal of Accountancy*, (December 1942), pp. 531–535.

Leake, P. D., *Depreciation and Wasting Assets and Their Treatment in Assessing Annual Profit and Loss* (1912), reprinted by Arno Press (New York 1976).

Leffler, Keith and Jerold Zimmerman, "A Theory of Municipal Government: Agency Costs, Organizational Form, and Scale," working paper, Graduate School of Management, University of Rochester (July 1977).

Litherland, D. A., "Fixed Asset Replacement a Half Century Ago," reprinted in *Contemporary Studies in the Evolution of Accounting Thought*, ed. Michael Chatfield (Belmont, California: Dickenson Publishing Co. Inc., 1968), pp. 167–175.

Littleton, A. C., *Accounting Evolution to 1900* (1933), reprinted by Russell & Russell (New York 1966)

Matheson, Ewing, *The Depreciation of Factories, Mines and Industrial Undertaking and Their Valuation* (1893) reprinted by Arno Press (New York 1976).

Mattessich, Richard, "Towards a General and Axiomatic Foundation of Accountancy; with an Introduction to the Matrix Formulation of Accounting Systems." *Accounting Research,* (October 1957), pp. 328–355.

Mautz, Robert K., "The Role of the American Accounting Association in Accounting Research," *Research in Accounting Measurement,* eds. Robert Jaedicke, Yuji Ijiri and Oswald Nielsen (American Accounting Association, 1966).

———, and Jack Gray, "Some Thoughts on Research Needs in Accounting," *The Journal of Accountancy,* (September 1970), pp. 54–62.

McCraw, Thomas X., "Regulation in America: A Review Article," *Business History Review,* (Summer 1975), pp. 159–183.

Meckling, William H., "Towards a Theory of Representative Government," presented at the Third Annual Conference on Analysis and Ideology, Interlaken, Switzerland, June 4, 1976 (1976a)

———, "Values and the Choice of the Model of the Individual in the Social Sciences," *Revue Suisse d'Economiec Politique et de Statistique* (Dec 1976b), pp. 545–560.

Moonitz, Maurice, "Accounting Principles—How They are Developed," in Robert Sterling (ed.) *Institutional Issues in Public Accounting,* (Lawrence, Kansas: Scholars Book Company, 1974a), pp. 143–171.

Moonitz, Maurice, *Obtaining Agreement on Standards* (Sarasota, Florida: American Accounting Association, 1974b)

Mueller, Dennis C., "Public Choice: A Survey," *The Journal of Economic Literature* (June 1976), pp. 395–433.

Mundheim, Robert H., "Foreward, Symposium on Securities Regulation," *Law and Contemporary Problems,* (Summer 1964), pp. 647–652.

Hash, Luther R., *Anatomy of Depreciation* (Washington, D.C.: Public Utilities Reports, Inc., 1947).

Niskanen, William A., *Bureaucracy and Representative Government* (Chicago: Aldine-Atherton, 1971).

Paton, William A., *Accounting Theory—With Special Reference to the Corporate Enterprise* (New York: The Ronald Press Company, 1922). Re-issued in 1962 by A.S.P. Accounting Studies Press, Ltd. Reprinted by Scholars Book Co., Houston, 1973.

———, *Accounting* (New York: Macmillan Company, 1924).

———, and A. C. Littleton, *An Introduction to Corporate Accounting Standards* (American Accounting Association, 1940).

Peltzman, Sam, "Towards a More General Theory of Regulation," *Journal of Law and Economics,* (August 1976), pp. 211–240.

Pichler, Joseph A., "An Economic Analysis of Accounting Power," in *Institutional Issues in Public Accounting,* ed. Robert Sterling (Lawrence, Kansas: Scholars Book Co., 1974), pp. 45–73.

Pollins, Harold, "Aspects of Railway Accounting Before 1868," *Studies in the His-*

tory of Accounting, eds. A. Littleton and B. Yamey (Homewood, Illinois: Irvin, 1956), pp. 332–355.

Posner, Richard A., "Theories of Economic Regulation," *Bell Journal of Economics and Management Science,* (Autumn 1974), pp. 335–358.

Prakash, Prem and Alfred Rappaport, "Information Inductance and Its Significance for Accounting," *Accounting, Organizations and Society,* Vol. 2, ho. 1, (1977), pp. 29–36.

Rappaport, Louis H., *SEC Accounting Practice and Procedure,* 3rd ed. (New York: Ronald Press, 1972).

Riggs, Henry E., *Depreciation of Public Utility Properties* (New York: McGraw Hill Book Co., 1922)

Ripley, William Z., "Stop, Look, Listen!", *The Atlantic Monthly,* (September, 1926), pp. 380–399.

Saliers, Earl A., *Depreciation; Principles and Applications,* 3rd ed. (New York: Ronald Press Company, 1939).

Sanders, Thomas H., "A Review of Reviews of Accounting Progress," *Journal of Accountancy,* (January 1946), pp. 9–26.

———, Henry R. Hatfield and Underhill Moore, *A Statement of Accounting Principles* (New York: American Institute of Certified Public Accountants, 1936).

Scott, DR, "The Basis for Accounting Principles," *Accounting Review,* (December 1941), pp. 341–349.

Shackleton, Ken, "Government Involvement in Developing Accounting Standards: The Framework," *Management Accounting* (U.K.), (January 1977), pp. 17–21.

Smith, Clifford, "On the Theory of Lending," unpublished paper, Working Paper Series No. 7635, Graduate School of Management, University of Rochester, 1976.

Sprouse, Robert T. and Maurice Moonitz, "A Tentative Set of Broad Accounting Principles for Business Enterprises," *Accounting Research Study No. 3* (New York: American Institute of Certified Public Accountants, 1962).

Sterling, Robert R., "Accounting Research, Education and Practice," *Journal of Accountancy,* (September 1973), pp. 44–52.

Sterling, Robert R. (ed.), *Institutional Issues in Public Accounting* (Lawrence, Kansas: Scholars Book Co., 1974).

Stigler, George J., "The Theory of Economic Regulation," *Bell Journal of Economics,* (Spring 1971), pp. 3–21.

———, "Do Economists Matter?", *Southern Economic Journal,* (January 1976), pp. 347–363.

Storey, Reed K., "Revenue Realization, Going Concern and Measurement of Income," *Accounting Review,* (April 1959), pp. 232–238.

Storey, Reed K., *The Search for Accounting Principles* (New York: American Institute of Certified Public Accountants, 1964).

Sweeney, Henry W., *Stabilized Accounting* (New York: Harper & Bros. Publishers, 1936)

U.S. Congress, Senate, Subcommittee on Antitrust and Monopoly of the Committee of The Judiciary, Hearings, *The Petroleum Industry,* Part I, 94th Congress, 1st Session, 1975.

US Congress, Senate, Subcommitte on Reports, Accounting and Management of the Committee on Government Operations, *The Accounting Establishment: A Staff Study* (Metcalf Report), 94th Congress, 2nd Session, 1976.

U.S. Department of Commerce, Bureau of the Census, *Historical Statistics of the United States, Colonial Times to 1970* (Washington, U.S. Government Printing Office, 1973)

U.S. Securities and Exchange Commission, "Administrative Policy on Financial Statements," *Accounting Series Release No. 4*, (April 25, 1938).

——, *Tenth Annual Report of the Securities and Exchange Commission: Fiscal Year Ended June 30, 1944* (1943)

Watts, Ross L., "Accounting Objectives," working paper series no. 7408, Graduate School of Management, University of Rochester, April 1974.

——, Corporate Financial Statements, A Product of the Market and Political Processes", *Australian Journal of Management*, (April 1977), pp. 53–75.

—— and Jerold L. Zimmerman, "Towards a Positive Theory of the Determination of Accounting Standards," *Accounting Review*, (January 1978), pp. 112–134.

Wilcox, E. B. and R. H. Hassler, "A Foundation for Accounting Principles," *Journal of Accountancy*, (October 1941), pp. 308–314.

Zeff, Stephen A., *Forging Accounting Principles in Five Countries: A History and an Analysis of Trends*, Arthur Andersen Lecture Series (Champaign, Illinois: Stipes Publishing Co., 1972).

Zeff, Stephen A., "Comments on Accounting Principles—How They are Developed," in *Institutional Issues in Public Accounting*, ed. Robert R. Sterling (Lawrence, Kansas: Scholars Book Co., 1974), pp. 172–178.

Zeff, Stephen A., "Paton on the Effects of Changing Prices on Accounting 1916–1955," unpublished manuscript (March 1978).

Zimmerman, Jerold L., "The Municipal Accounting Maze: An Analysis of Political Incentives," *Studies on Measurement and Evaluation of the Economic Efficiency of Public and Private Nonprofit Institutions*, supplement to the *Journal of Accounting Research* (1977), pp. 107–144.

PREPUBLICATION DEBATE

Editors' Introduction: This prepublication debate highlights many of the historical and institutional schisms in the accounting profession and academia. George Foster's teaching notes from Stanford University reflect that school's strong affiliations with corporate management (corporate capital) that contrast with the links to the accounting profession and the finance sector (finance capital) of Chicago and Watts and Zimmerman's University of Rochester. Stanford's sobriquet of "the Harvard of the West" emphasizes these corporate management allegiances. The relationships between interests and positions are neither direct or simple, however, in very general terms, the deregulation movement—that the Excuses Paper broadly endorsed—was most favored by the finance sector, the Big Eight accounting firms, and their (captive) institutions of the American Institute of Certified Public Accountants, the American Accounting Association, and universities like Rochester and Chicago. Tepid opposition to deregulation, ranging from indifference to mild dissent, was to be found among the smaller, craft-oriented, less commercialized accounting firms, managerialist academics at schools like Stanford, and those academics who still revered the tradition of accounting as a public service. Steve Zeff, the then editor of *The Accounting Review,* reflected and interesting confluence of these pressures. As a historian by training, he was better versed than most in the public service tradition of "accountability"; as an accounting academic and journal editor, he displays a scrupulous adherence to an ideology of "impartiality" and "objectivity". These inclinations do not run together: the former was likely to breed a skepticism about the Excuses Theory paper, the latter would lean towards giving it a fair hearing.

PREPUBLICATION DEBATE

GEORGE FOSTER, ROSS WATTS, STEVE ZEFF, JEROLD ZIMMERMAN, AND ANONYMOUS REVIEWERS

DATE: APRIL 3, 1980

TO: B419C PARTICIPANTS

FROM: GEORGE FOSTER

SUBJECT: WATTS-ZIMMERMAN ON "THE MARKET FOR EXCUSES"

The attached correspondence is reproduced with the permission of Watts, Zimmerman, and Zeff. I am Reviewer #2. It gives insight into the "politics" of the review process. I recommended that an earlier version of the paper not be published in its (then) existing state. Reviewer's #3 and #4 recommended acceptance. Zeff sent the March 31st letter and then subsequently reversed his decision contingent upon some further revision of the manuscript. Ex poste, I still think my arguments are correct but I also fully agree with Zeff's decision to publish the "final" version of the paper.

[From Reviewer #2]

DATE: NOVEMBER 1977

TO: S ZEFF

ABOUT: "THE DEMAND FOR AND SUPPLY OF ACCOUNTING THEORIES: THE MARKET FOR EXCUSES"

1. This paper attempts a very ambitious task—to explain the development of the immense financial accounting theory literature. Unfortunately, too

much is attempted in one paper with the result that little more than casual supposition is presented. The paper states:

> "Even though the evidence we present is somewhat 'casual', and not as 'rigorous' as we would like, it is nonetheless evidence and is the only way to 'test' the propositions put forward" (p. 26).

This review will show that (a) the argument and evidence is more casual than the above comment admits, and (b) more rigorous testing is possible and should be done.

2. On p. 20 the authors note an assumption regarding transaction costs in (a) capital markets, and (b) political processes that is important in their argument:

> "We suggest that there is an important difference between capital markets and the political process which make transactions costs important in the latter case." (p. 20)

If this assumption is incorrect many of the distinctions as regards the demand for accounting theories between regulated and unregulated economies are much less important. The paper should attempt to quantify transactions costs in both capital markets and political processes. For instance, what is the cost of purchasing a controlling interest in General Motors? Is it less than the cost of bribing a congressman? The paper argues that such questions are important but backs off any attempt to address them. The casual hypothesizing on p.20 is totally inadequate support for such a key assumption in the argument. The Zimmerman (1977) paper is referred to for further discussion of this issue. This paper, unfortunately, also avoids any attempt to explicitly quantify transaction costs.

The problem with not quantifying these costs is that it is easy to ex poste explain any event with the "model—if "reality" approximates that of the market solution (political process) one waves one hand and concludes that transactions costs are small (large). In short, one never gets the chance to reject the "model" unless one estimates transaction costs *first* and *then* examines if the observed result is consistent with the "model's" prediction.

There is evidence that the paper underestimates capital market transactions costs. They state:

> In capital market theory it is typically assumed that transaction costs are zero despite the fact they obviously are not, because that assumption yields empirically confirmed hypotheses. (p.20)

The paper fails to mention even one such hypothesis that has been "empirically confirmed". Consider portfolio diversification. The zero transaction cost model predicts investors would hold fully diversified portfolios. This prediction has not been empirically confirmed. Lease, Lewellen and Schlarbaum (*Journal of Finance,* May 1974) report that in a survey of 990 customers of a brokerage firm three out of every four individuals hold less than 15 stocks.

3. A key argument in the paper is that there are incentives on the demand side for researchers to supply the theories that vested interests demand:

> If the demand for accounting theory is dominated by the demand for excuses which are useful weapons in the political arena, then accounting theory will vary over time as political issues vary. . . . Individual researchers may change their position but also different researchers become successful as their prescriptions come to fit the demands of the vested interests. (p.25)

No evidence is presented that any individual researcher has become successful this way. Either the argument should be dropped or supported with detailed evidence. I suggest the author(s) take five of the most successful researchers of the past decade—Beaver, Demski, Gonedes, Hakansson and Kaplan—and document in detail how their "prescriptions (have) come to fit the demands of the vested interests." The "vested interests" should be named. It is only by such detailed documentation that one can be confident there is substance and not just rhetoric in this paper.

Footnote 1 of p. 25 implies that Ernst and Ernst (1976) is inconsistent in its accounting submissions. The paper claims that this inconsistency as being predicted by their model. Unfortunately, the paper does not document the nature of the inconsistency. It should be explicitly stated so that Ernst & Ernst can respond.

A related point is that prescriptive theories have been used as excuses by different vested interests on different issues. In footnote 1 on p.1, eight so-called prescriptive theories are referenced. Nowhere in the paper is direct evidence presented that any one of these referenced theories have been used as excuses. For instance, what vested interests have used Chambers (1966) as an excuse and on what issues?

4. The section on "railroad legislation" and "the empirical relationship between government intervention and accounting theory" has substantive defects. The paper makes no attempt to go to the original literature (e.g., early accounting or engineering journals). Rather, it relies on secondary sources, whose filter for selecting examples can differ from this paper. They need to

go to the original literature, randomly sample the articles published before, during, and after the railroad legislation, and then present profiles of the percentage of articles and pages on depreciation accounting. The paper's model predicts the percentage after will exceed the percentage before. With this data, it is thus possible to test the model's predictions; of extreme importance, the possibility of the model being rejected is admitted.

At present the paper only presents instances consistent with its "model"—it is difficult to believe that these instances were randomly chosen. A model that predicts railroad legislation had nothing to do with the depreciation debate is given no chance of being accepted or rejected. An accounting historian suggested to me that the uniform accounting debate for trade associations was the most likely explanation for the depreciation literature.

The point is that alternative models do exist and refined testing to discriminate between them is necessary. Selecting (ex poste) isolated cases consistent with one model cannot in any sense provide this model discriminating evidence.

5. The section on "Securities Act" and "the empirical relationship between intervention and accounting theory" also has substantive defects. The paper argues that "the passage of the Securities Acts and ASR #4 were responsible for the search for an underlying framework" (p.38). The Sanders, Hatfield and Moore (1938) and Paton and Littleton (1940) studies are consistent with this point. But how does one justify the continuation of such theories in the 1945-1965 period, e.g., Vatter, Alexander, Staubus, Edwards and Bell etc. If the answer is to keep the Acts in existence, why has there been relatively little activity since 1970? The paper asserts "our theory can answer that question." (p.39). They do have an ex post explanation, but it does not explain why the problems in imposing an underlying framework were first recognized in the 1970's and not in, say, 1953. The paper needs to *quantify* the factors on the demand and supply side and show that the theory first predicted a drop in the supply of new theories in the late 1960's to early 1970's and not before. Without such quantification, one can always pull one of N factors out of the "hat" and assert it to be the dominant one when ex poste explaining developments in the accounting theory literature.

6. The "Securities Act" section argues that since 1933 theorists have been induced to concentrate on the "information objectives" of investors to supply the "public interest" justification of the Securities Acts. Three 1941-1977 authors are cited, each of whom supports the above argument. Unfortunately, the paper selectively ignores works inconsistent with the argument. For instance, Edwards and Bell justify much of their case for business income on its usefulness for management decisions. Chambers argues his

model is equally relevant to both internal and external decisions. The wheat trader decision model in Sterling (1970) is an internal management one. In short, due to the paper's selective citation one cannot accept the evidence in this section as supporting the above argument. The author(s) should examine all major works in this period if they want their results to be believable.

7. In several parts of the paper, I have marked up additional points requiring attention.

[From Reviewer #3]

Comments on "The Demand for and Supply of Accounting Theories: the Market for Excuses"

The author should renumber footnotes to conform to our house style.

Early on, the author should define *agency-cost,* as though to a bright first-year student. Otherwise, readers will get lost.

Page 6, 1st full paragraph. The author might explain that "loss" is here being used in the highly specialized sense of "potential equity contribution not received." As things stand, much of this page is at first obscure.

Page 10, note, line 5. Does the author mean *creditors?* If so, I'm confused.

Page 11, paragraph ii, line 5. I suggest *was* for *is.*

Pages 23-24. I'm uneasy here: perhaps the most prominent financial accounting theorists today are Sterling, Chambers, Beaver, Gonedes . . . people whose research does *not* support significant selfish interests (as far as I can see). The author should respond to this apparent contradiction.

Page 41, last complete sentence. Similarly, I'd like to know in detail how the four major general accounting theories that emerged in the 1960s (1. Sterling and Chambers' current-exit-value approach, 2. Edwards and Bell's current-entry-value approach, 3. Lawson's cash flow approach and 4. Henriksen's and Jones' work on general purchasing power adjustments) satisfied the demand for excuses. I can see this for (4), somewhat for (2), but not at all for (1) and (3) -nor for such a less general theory as Thomas' arguments against allocation.

Pages 44-45 (top). Would the author care to comment on Sterling's recent appeals to/for scientific standards? This seems to return one to Cole's 1915 position (quoted on page 42).

This paper's basic idea is brilliantly provocative.

[From Reviewer #4]

1. I should point out that I know little of the methodology of historical research and it is not clear whether I would know a good piece if I saw one. I am aware of Hempel's criterion for "historical explanation"—complete specification of sufficiency conditions. This work does not appear to satisfy the Hempel criterion; however I sincerely doubt if there are many works that do.

2. My opinion is therefore a somewhat uninformed one. My opinion is that this manuscript should be published. I base this opinion on two grounds. First, the methodology appears (to a non-historian) reasonable. Second, I think publication will provoke public thinking and debate on an important issue. Indeed, is there any more important issue to an academic than "what academics is about"?

3. I would hope that the authors would at least think about, and provide commentary on, the generality of their work. Doesn't their theory apply to virtually all social science theory construction? Economic and sociological arguments are often invoked as a justification for a particular political action. Was not an externality argument advanced by Anita Bryant in her campaign against homosexuals? Indeed, it may even extend to physical sciences. Genetics was used as an argument favoring certain Nazi policies. (As an afterthought, what demand prompted the authors to undertake this theory construction effort? In other words, does their theory explain their own actions in writing this manuscript?)

REPLY TO REVIEWER #2

1. a) What does "more casual" mean? Does the Reviewer have some index of casualness? We recognize that the evidence presented does not come from a computer tape and is not subject to large-scale statistical testing. However, that does not mean it is unimportant. Formal tests of hypotheses using large samples are not a necessary condition of empirical research. Many of those tests address irrelevant issues.

    We address this problem in the paper. It appears to us that Reviewer #2 has *no perspective* when it becomes necessary to trade-off substance and testing by formal econometric techniques.

    b) Reviewer #2's suggestion for more "rigorous" testing (expanded on in his point 4) is *naive*. What he suggests would add an appearance of "rigor", but not any substance. We respond to this suggestion in footnote 50 in the revised manuscript (p. 27).

Citation tests would be at least as casual and at least as subject to ex-post selection bias as our procedures. Our theory predicts changes in the *nature* of the literature. For example, we suggest the nature of depreciation charges changed with railroads and tax laws. Counting pages on depreciation does not answer that problem. Besides that, we have the problem of controlling for expansion of the literature for other reasons. We suggest citation tests would merely impose costs.

2. We address this point in the revised version (p. 21). The Reviewer is questioning assumptions. He appears to forget that in standard empirical methodology, the test of an assumption is, its ability to generate confirmed hypotheses. If the Reviewer wants to question assumptions for which we don't have direct evidence, why stop with our assumption of high political transaction costs, why not attack other assumptions such as individual rationality, etc.

Despite Reviewer #2's comment, there is good reason to believe that the assumption of high political transaction costs will produce better predictions than the assumption of low political transaction costs. The observation that there is *no* formal market for political controls is *not* casual evidence. Whether he likes it or not, Reviewer #2 would have a hard time denying that observation's empirical validity. Given the lack of such a formal market and the legal costs to side-payments, you would have to be *extremely prejudiced* to argue that this would *not* impede the market for political control vis-a-vis the market for corporate control.

3. We consider the suggestion that the document how the output of the "most successful" individual researchers has come to serve vested interest impractical and impolitic. *First,* it is not entirely clear that those quoted are the "most successful" researchers. We would suggest that the Reviewers' selection of successful researchers reflects his own biases. *Second,* the objective of our theory is to predict general tendencies in the literature. In asking us to explain the actions of particular individuals, Reviewer #2 is asking us to do something efficient markets theorists have not been able to do, i.e., explain each individual investor's behavior or each security's price behavior (e.g., why did XYZ's share price fall when Briloff published an article analyzing its financial reporting?)

To prevent others falling into this trap along with Reviewer #2, in the last paragraph of p. 25 of the revised version we have pointed out explicitly the nature of Reviewer #2's request for evidence on *individual* researchers.

4. See our reply to 1 (b) above for our response to the suggestions for "testing" our theory.

We recognize that we did not make it clear how our theory could be refuted in the earlier draft. We have remedied that defect in the revised version (see p. 25 of the revised version).

5. This point has been answered above. Quantification, per se, is not a goal of theory. It is desirable, if possible, but if not possible we can still have theory. Further, we can always generate numbers and get associations—the question is can the numbers and associations measure what we want them to measure? We would hope otherwise, but we expect that any quantifications Reviewer #2 suggests will be useless.

6. See footnote 68 on p. 45 of the revised paper.

REPLY TO REVIEWER #3

1. The footnotes have been renumbered.

2. Page 6 has been rewritten to clarify the definition of agency costs.

3. The footnote on page 10 has been rewritten.

4. "Is" has been substituted for "was" on page 11.

5. Our answer to the Reviewer's concern with pages 23-24 is contained in the last paragraph of page 25 of the revised version.

6. Our answer to point 5 also answers the Reviewer's question about page 41 of the old version.

7. We prefer not to comment on Sterling's approach.

REPLY TO REVIEWER #4

We also think that arguments in the paper apply to areas outside accounting. However, we would prefer that this paper remain an accounting paper—it is already very long. The other academic areas will recognize the paper if they think it is relevant. In fact, Armen Alchian has already requested permission to publish the paper in the International Institute for Economics reprint series.

[From Reviewer #2]

DATE: FEBRUARY 1978

TO: S. ZEFF

ABOUT: REVISION OF "THE DEMAND AND SUPPLY OF ACCOUNTING THEORIES, THE MARKET FOR EXCUSES"

1. a) The authors' comment:

> "Reviewer #2 has *no perspective* when it becomes necessary to trade-off substance and testing by formal econometric techniques. . .

> Not once in my review did I mention econometric techniques. Not once in my review did I suggest one had to use such techniques to address issues of substance. I find their judgment about my perspective (or lack thereof) rather hastily formed.

   b) The authors' comment:

> "We recognize that the evidence presented does not come from a computer tape and is not subject to large-scale statistical testing. However that does mean that it is unimportant. . .

> Not once in my review did I suggest they use computer tape evidence. Not once in my review did I suggest they undertake "large-scale statistical testing". The purpose of this comment escapes me.

   c) What I did suggest was that they give serious consideration to reducing the ex post sample selection bias apparent in their paper. Consider the section on pp. 44-47 documenting the "emergence of the public interest objective". In my review I noted that only three 1941-1977 authors are cited in the paper, each of whom supported their argument. I suggested "the authors should examine all major works in this period if they want their results to be believable". I will expand upon this suggestion as the evidence on pp. 44-47 is totally inadequate to test or support any hypothesis. Take all accounting theory books and monographs reviewed in *The*

Accounting Review since its inception. Then draw up a table as follows:

OBJECTIVES MENTIONED

	(1) Management	(2) Investors	(3) Creditors	(4) Public Interest	(5) Others
Hatfield	✔	✔			
Sweeney					
Paton & Littleton					
etc.					

The author's hypothesis predicts that (a) the number of ticks in the public interest box should increase significantly after the 1933 Act and (b) the number of ticks in the management box should drop ("recent writers no longer even list management as a principal user of financial statements" p.46). By using an independent criteria such as the work must have been reviewed in *The Accounting Review,* one can place more confidence in conclusions drawn from such a table than is possible from the evidence presented on pp. 44-47. Of extreme importance, the possibility of the authors hypothesis being rejected by the data is admitted.

2. I suggested the authors use citation tests to reduce the ex post bias. Their response was:

> Reviewer #2's suggestion . . . is *naive.* What he suggests would add an appearance of "rigor", but not any substance.

I'm not sure the authors understand the purpose of using citation tests. They are an attempt to reduce ex post selection bias by conducting an experiment that someone who has a different frame of reference can replicate. The authors state "our theory predicts changes in the *nature* of the literature." They predict more debate in relationship to depreciation as an expense. One could count (a) the number of pages on depreciation and (b) the number of pages on depreciation as an expense and see if the ratio of (b)/(a) changed at the time railroad legislation was introduced. This test would capture any change in the *nature* of the literature; using the ratio of (b)/(a) would control for any expansion of the literature. In short, citation tests do offer the chance for the authors to expose their hypotheses to more rigorous testing. I find my suggestion far from "naive."

The authors' other response was that it "would merely impose costs." I do not deny it would impose costs. But there is no free lunch in research, especially historical research. The authors could well examine Yamey's critique of Sombart's hypothesis that double-entry was important in the development of capitalism (JAR, Autumn 1964, 117-136). Yamey takes 20 journal pages to examine evidence on one specific issue and makes extensive use of source documents. This paper attempts to cover the depreciation literature in six quarto double spaced pages and avoids any detailed attempt to use source documents. This is illustrative of my initial comment that "too much is attempted in one paper with the result that little more than casual supposition is presented."

3. The authors make the following response to my suggestion for documentation that *any* individual researcher has become successful by providing "excuses":

> We consider the suggestion . . . impractical and impolitic . . . To prevent others falling into this trap along with Reviewer #2, in the last paragraph of p.25 of the revised version we have pointed out explicitly the nature of Reviewer #2's request for evidence on *individual* researchers.

It is not clear to me that I have fallen into any trap. The paragraph on p.25 argues they, like the information content studies, are addressing issues at the aggregate market level whereas my comment was made at the individual level. This argument is fallacious. There is not one market based piece of evidence in this paper (which is most strange given the subtitle of "The Market for Excuses"). Perhaps if their evidence was based on academics who provide the most cogent or most timely "excuses" (theories) having the highest salaries this point would be valid. But no such evidence is presented. Rather, their evidence is also at the individual level, e.g., pp. 44-47 quotes Hatfield, Leake, Paton, Paton & Littleton, etc. In short, the authors base their arguments for market level phenomena on individual authors and then describe my call for more specific individual author evidence as "impractical and impolitic". The authors should at least recognize that nowhere do they have aggregate market evidence to test their hypotheses. Why not admit they are dealing with general trends in the writings of individuals?

Their reply to my comment is thus more an evasive tactic than a considered response. Could it be that they will not provide the evidence I called for because no such evidence exists? Could their refusal to name the "vested interests" who use the "excuses" be because no such "vested interest" operates in the way they argue? I don't know the answers to these questions but their evasive attempts to sidestep them are disturbing.

4. The authors argue that prior to the 1933 Securities Act, there was "little effort devoted to establishing a general theory of accounting . . . an integrated set of accounting prescriptions for all firms" (p.38). My reading of the literature is very different. Indeed, every major proposal of "accounting prescriptions for all firms" had been proposed (or motivated) by 1930. GPLA was proposed by Middleditch (1918) and Sweeney (see his articles in 1920's-his book was finished in 1927, despite its 1936 publication). Replacement cost was proposed by Paton (1922) and Sweeney (1927). The NPV approach was outlined in Canning (1929). Although MacNeal's resale price proposals were published in 1939, he notes that they were motivated by an 1930 audit dispute with P.W. (see his book). In short, it is not clear that the 1920-1930 period was any more or less active a period for the accounting theory literature than the 1931-1940, the 1941-50 etc., periods. How do the authors reconcile the original proposals for "sets of accounting prescriptions for all firms" mostly being a pre 1933 phenomena with their hypothesis?

Professor Ross L. Watts and Jerold L. Zimmerman
Graduate School of Management
University of Rochester
Rochester, NY 14627

Dear Ross and Jerry:

The Demand for and Supply of Accounting Theories:
The Market for Excuses

During the last week, I have been studying the comments of Reviewers 2 and 3 in relation to the contents of the second version of your manuscript, and I have concluded that at least two of the points raised by the former (in which the latter joins to some degree) are deserving of further additional work. In citing the relatively few authors on pages 37-41 and 44-47, you open yourselves to the charge of *post hoc, ergo propter hoc.* Unless you rather thoroughly and, in an historical sense, rigorously examine the evolution of thought among major researchers in the literature, it is very difficult to rebut the criticism that the evidence is insufficient to warrant an inference of *causality.* The selection of relatively few instances could be convenient or coincidental; the marshalling of a substantial number of instances all tending in the same direction (with but relatively few exceptions) would be much harder to rebut. In this important respect, I am afraid that if you wish to use historical evidence to suggest one or more hypotheses, it will be necessary that you devote more of your effort to historical research. I know from our private correspondence of last fall that you disinclined to do this, as you do not see your comparative advantage as falling in historical scholarship. I understand your argument, but the *need* for solid historical backing for your arguments demands that this dimension to your analysis be supplied. In my letter of last August, I suggested that you might be better advised to expand your paper into a monograph (you demurred), and I now believe that the case is even stronger than I then thought it to be. If you do not seize the opportunity now, you run the risk of being pilloried by all-too-enthusiastic critics once your paper is published, probably obliging you to defend yourselves with instances of that very kind of research. I would rather not see a very interesting and (in my opinion) plausible hypothesis shot down so easily. In this respect, I am in agreement with several of the substantive criticisms of Reviewer 2, and Reviewer 3 appears to agree.

   To be sure, Reviewer 2 made remarks largely to the same effect on the first version of your manuscript, but I confess that their validity and significance did not impress me as much on the first reviewing round as they do now. In part, the echoes from Reviewer 3 may have been a factor. I apologize for not appreciating the full force of these arguments earlier, but repetition is sometimes required before the weight of an argument becomes evident.

Setting aside the exchange of barbed remarks between you and Reviewer 2, some of his arguments are worthy of serious attention. I am not convinced, however, that his citation test would prove very much, but I do believe that if you would undertake to weave a theory of such enormous implications as you are doing, it is essential that your fortress be as solid as one can reasonably expect. If you would use a historical inquiry to support the reasonableness of your hypotheses, your sampling of the literature must be more solidly grounded and generalizable. I know you want your theory to be taken seriously, and it is imperative that readers not be allowed to conclude that you might have selectively sampled the literature in a manner that did not genuinely test your arguments.

Both of us—you and I—are in a dilemma. I would like to see your paper published in the Review, but I am persuaded by the reviewers that your historical defense falls well short of the assignment. You would like to see your paper published as an article (in the Review or elsewhere), but I would like to think that you are as aware as I that a really first-rate job veritably requires that you think in terms of a monograph. Even acknowledging your already great investment of time in this project, I think it would be a mistake to publish it in its present form.

On a formal level, Reviewer 2 recommends rejection, while Reviewer 3 counsels revision. It is not Reviewer 2's policy recommendation but the substance of several of his arguments (particularly 1(c), 3, and 4) which I find to possess convincing logic. I might add that Reviewer 2 also believes that the first 25 pages of your paper could be cut to five, owing to prior publication of much of the content. But, to use his words, the evidence adduced on pages 26-47 do not adequately control for ex post bias, and this, I believe, is at the heart of the matter. A much more complete analysis of the pertinent literature would vitiate this criticism as much as one could reasonably expect.

I hope you will not be put off by some of Reviewer 2's somewhat petulant remarks on your paper; many of his comments are quite worthy, while others probably were inspired by your rather strongly worded memorandum.

I leave the matter in your hands. I am willing to see another revision, but I frankly doubt that you can deal with the points mentioned above in an article-length manuscript. I do hope you will persevere with your interesting and highly provocative study and that you will not dilute the undoubted impact of your work by "hasty" publication.

I am enclosing the reports of Reviewers 2 and 3 as well as the manuscript marked by Reviewer 2. The marks in pencil in the manuscript are mine, and are confined to editorial details.

Sincerely,

Stephen A. Zeff

MARCH 10, 1978

Professor Stephen A. Zeff Editor,
The Accounting Review
Harvard Business School
Soldiers Field
Boston, MA 02163

Dear Steve:

We are grateful for the time and energy you have expended on our manuscript—"The Demand for and Study of Accounting Theories, the Market for Excuses." We could not ask more of an editor in that dimension. In this letter we wish to discuss several important issues which were raised in your March 1, 1978 correspondence. Some of these issues transcend the "Excuses" paper and are basic to the editorial policy of *The Accounting Review.*

As the "Excuses" paper took shape last year, we became concerned that its "unpopular"/controversial implications would preclude its acceptance by a journal whose readers include the core of the accounting research community where we hope to stimulate discussion. We were delighted at hearing you had become editor of *The Accounting Review,* for we believed then and we still believe that *The Review* is the proper forum for pursuing the ideas expressed in the "Excuses" paper.

The "Excuses" paper posits a new theory to explain accounting research. Every aspect of the theory is not complete, nor can it explain *all* observed phenomenon. If we knew where it was incomplete, we would correct those sections. But the theory is consistent with the evidence we have been able to gather. Furthermore, the paper has been read by several accounting historians (Brief, Previts, Zeff) and at least one business historian, Thomas McCraw (who is also at the Harvard Business School) and no one has informed us of a major factual error.

The criticisms raised in the March I referee reports revolve two around two issues. The model is not *completely developed* and we do not present thorough tests of the implications. On both counts we are in total agreement. However, the crucial question is—whether given these facts "Excuses" should be published in *The Accounting Review?* We believe the answer to this question is yes for two reasons.

First, it is unrealistic to expect new theories to arise fully matured, to be able to explain all observed phenomenon, and not to have defects. Second, most of the landmark, classical papers in accounting, finance, and economics either did not contain *any* evidence or contained evidence later shown to be wrong. Most of the original papers by Ijiri, Hakansson, Demski, Sterling, Chambers, Edwards and Bell, etc. were not *completely* developed nor did they contain any evidence. The original Gordon (*AR,* April 1964) article on income smoothing would not have been published if the criteria of rigorous tests were applied. The 1974 *JAR Supplement* paper of Gonedes and Dopuch provides no evidence to support the theory that corporate statements are a public good. Should that award-winning manuscript have been published?

Finance and economics also would be much poorer if editors had applied the completely developed and thorough evidence criteria. The original Modigliani and Miller article (*AER,* June 1958), which many consider a turning point in the revolution in financial theory, was deficient in its empirical evidence (see Weston, *SEJ,* October 1963). The landmark Miller and Modigliani paper on dividends (*JOB,* October 1961) contained *no* supporting empirical evidence. Sharpe's original exposition of the now famous capital-asset-pricing model (*JOF,* September 1964) was not complete and contained *no* evidence on the empirical validity of the model. Roberts' (*JOF,* March 1959) watershed article on stock price behavior that played such an important role in the development of the efficient markets hypothesis contained no *formal* evidence and no well-developed theory. In fact we cannot think of a single paper that introduces a new theory and at the same time is completely developed and thoroughly tested.

These landmark papers suggest that exposing new ideas generates discussion and subsequent analysis and testing by other researchers—activities which increase our stock of knowledge. Note the intellectual exchanges and subsequent empirical work which followed the landmark efficient markets, capital asset pricing, Miller-Modigliani capital structure, . . . papers and the result of these exchanges. If the objective of academic journals is to encourage new and innovate lines of research, requiring new theories to be completely exhaustive and extensively tested prior to publication is counter-productive.

We are not arguing for lowering the publication standards. Rather, we believe the *relevant* standard should be the extent to which the paper ultimately leads to an increase in our stock of knowledge. New ideas which stimulate further research are just as valuable (perhaps more so) as another rigorous, conclusive test of an existing theory. Further, we have no pretensions that the "Excuses" paper should/could be compared to the above "classics." But we do feel that a dangerous precedent will be set if *The Accounting Review* requires all new theories to be completely developed and conclusively tested.

Whether our analysis is right or wrong or whether the evidence we present is factually correct or complete, the "Excuses" paper forces people to think about the nature of accounting (and other social science) research in a fundamental way. And for this reason we believe that these ideas should be exposed to the widest possible audience. Referee 4 supports this conclusion—"publication will provoke public thinking and debate on an important issue. Indeed, is there any more important issue to an academic than 'what academics is about?'"

Your letter of March 1st re-emphasized the benefits of a monograph to reduce "the risk of being pilloried by all-to-enthusiastic critics." As academics we (Watts and Zimmerman) do not want to be protected from those who would "pillory" us. In fact we welcome such an intellectual exchange. And the place for that exchange is *The Accounting Review* since it has the widest circulation of the academic accounting journals. The "Excuses" paper could probably be published in a reputable economics journal (perhaps the *JLE*), but less discussion would be generated and what is generated will not be directed towards accounting.

Nor will a monograph have as much impact as a refereed journal article. Although it would allow more room to test the model formally, *conclusive* tests would require a tome and be equivalent to several Ph.D theses. Such length would be costly to read, reducing the exposure not to mention delaying the publication date by several years. Such a delay increases the likelihood that someone else would scoop many of the ideas in the "Excuses" paper. Moreover, if the paper were to appear in *The Accounting Review* many people, other than ourselves, would be working on the tests and extensions.

The enclosed attachment discusses specific points raised by the referees.

Finally, we have confidence that our analysis in the "Excuses" paper is, though incomplete (like all new theories), substantially correct. Furthermore, we expect it to stand the test of future critical appraisals. *But,* even if we are dead wrong, we bear the costs and the profession reaps the benefits of having a better understanding of the role of and the process generating accounting theories. We urge you to reconsider your recent decision to reject the "Excuses" paper and the implications this decision has for the editorial policy of *The Accounting Review.*

Yours sincerely,

Ross L. Watts   Jerold L. Zimmerman
Assistant Professor   Assistant Professor

MARCH 15, 1978

Professor Ross L. Watts and Jerold L. Zimmerman
The Graduate School of Management
The University of Rochester
Rochester, NY 14627

Dear Ross and Jerry:

The Demand for and Supply of Accounting Theories,
The Market for Excuses

I am impressed with the persuasiveness and eloquence of your letter of
March 10, and the thesis you advance about the completeness of new theories has much to recommend it. Moreover, I accept your point about an
editor becoming too paternal toward a manuscript, as if it were his responsibility to protect the authors from attack. As you may find when you begin
to edit the new journal which, it is rumored, you are about to receive from
North-Holland, the line between satisfying oneself of the standard of research competence and endeavoring to guard against frontal assaults can be
a thin one indeed, especially with ikon-breaking manuscripts such as yours.

Nonetheless, I have a responsibility to be satisfied that you have dealt
adequately with those matters which can be feasibly handled within the
confines of an article, and I still believe that you could benefit, especially
on pages 44-47, from (1) a more representative review of the large literature
and (2) a better integration of your ideas within that section and between it
and pages 41-43. In doing so, it would not be necessary to expand your
discussion (and thus lengthen the manuscript), but only to demonstrate to
the reader that you have examined a broader sweep of the literature (through
citations). You may well find that there may be better and more powerful
quotations for page 44 than the ones you show.

At a number of places, I have suggested specific items in the literature
that you should read. You will, I hope, observe that I am endeavoring to
help you with your paper, not argue against it. In some instances, however,
you have not adduced the best evidence in support of your case. I am enclosing a manuscript which I completed only last week, which, on pages 40ff,
vividly brings out further evidence in support of your thesis. Feel free to
quote it if you wish. Another citation to something I wrote and compiled is
shown on the cover sheet of your manuscript. These materials are cited
only for your information, and I do not mean to imply, or even to create the
inference, that I seek to have my writings cited. These happen to be convenient treatments of materials that would appear to relate to your work. On

page 43, you must guard against the inference by readers that you may be unaware of the logical fallacy, *post hoc ergo propter hoc*. If you cannot obviate the possible error, at least admit that, failing a more thorough examination of the literature (and even *with* it), the problem may exist. It is a pervasive problem in historical research, but the juxtaposition of "follows" and "product of" (in successive lines, indeed), cries out for some comment.

In your accompanying memorandum (page 4), you assert that Paton's was not a "formally structured general theory." I could agree that Canning's is more "formally structured" than Paton's, but I would quickly add that Paton perceived much more clearly than did the great majority of writers until the 1950s the linkages and linchpins between and among the various elements of a possible accounting theory. Canning preferred to deal at the general, conceptual level, while Paton suggested (albeit very imperfectly) the implications of this "theory" for practical measurement problems. In this sense, Paton's theory was more "complete" than even Canning's.

Regarding the comment by Reviewer 3 (referring to your reply No. 6 to Reviewer 2), you can argue, I think, that while Edwards and Bell, Sterling, and Chambers have been popular among academics, there are no telling signs that this popularity has spread beyond academe. In this regard, note the second paragraph on page 2 of Reviewer 3's comments on the second version. (I am aware of your assertion that Chambers' stature has diminished in Chicago, Stanford, and Berkeley, but I would not generalize with any confidence from the views held in the ten-or-so "high research" schools: including Rochester, Cornell, Northwestern, Texas and a few others. Remember that the term "academics" covers quite a lot of people whom you and I have never met!). To be sure, the SEC has required replacement cost disclosures, but these disclosures do not deal with the measurement of assets and income; they are disclosures. Nor have the writings of these authors been cited by the SEC. I am sure you are aware, however, that four New Zealand companies (Challenge, Haywrights, Skellerup, and Midland Coachlines) have, since 1974/75, included exit-value measures in supplementary statements, and I believe at least one of them cites Chambers by name. I am willing to agree that you cannot explain every bit of evidence with a single theory, even after "all" the research has been done. To be candid, on pages 25-26, you may need to confess that your theory may fail to explain some interesting phenomena—but that does not ipso facto destroy the value of a theory. I am not persuaded that your analogy with EMH on page 26 is valid. I mention a possible problem at the bottom of page 44. Did these changes in the literature result from (not only follow) the changing composition and size of the American market for corporate shares, or were they caused by the Federal legislation?

On page 46, I note that the Trueblood-like U.K document, *The Corporate Report*, also appeals predominantly to investors. What explains this development if not securities legislation, of which there is no direct counterpart to our securities acts? I would argue (and George Benston may agree) that the U.K. "legislation" has been occurring silently in the board rooms of Threadneedle Street and in the big houses on Pall Mall.

Something should be said about the superficial lack of parallel between these two countries, because you yourselves frequently invoke U.K. evidence in your paper.

On the top of page 43, your comment in relation to professional schools of accounting is, to me, not very strong. I think that the normative approach to instruction has been much stronger in the "elite" private and public universities than in the great majority. But it is point to ponder.

On page 38, it may be worthwhile (you can decide) to mention that both Paton's and Canning's treatises were doctoral in origin. What does this tell us about their representativeness? Both were doctorates in economics, a relative rarity (Hatfield was one) among early accounting writers.

The sentence on page 48 is my attempt at solving your completeness problem.

If I may presume to interpret my own words (on page 2), I was endeavoring to distinguish between those who find it convenient to cite that literature and those who are disposed actually to be influenced by the literature. I recall very vividly, in about 1964, writing to the Treasurer of E. I. du Pont de Nemours & Co. about that company's long practice of showing Reserve for Depreciation on the liability side. The Treasurer replied by citing "authority" from the literature—an article by Sidney Simon, with the title, "The Right Side for Accumulated Depreciation." It had appeared in the *Review* in 1959, was a distinctly minority position, was published well after du Pont began its practice, and, I am sure, had absolutely no influence on the setting of their policy. But it was "authority" in our literature. At the end of your manuscript it may be well to attempt to distinguish between the du Pont kind of reliance on authority and the willingness to expose one's views to contradiction by actually immersing oneself in the currents of the literature.

On page 23, I mention Sandy Burton's quickly prepared *Accounting for Business Combinations,* which FEI sought to use during the intense debates over pooling-purchase in 1970.

I have made a number of suggestions of a nonsubstantive nature. On page 29, you refer to U.K. corporations. In that country, they are called "companies." Your citation style is not precisely that of the *Review.* See "Instructions to Authors" in the front of the January, 1978 issue. For example: "The point was made many years ago [Canning, 1929, p. 251]." Not "The point was made many years ago [Canning (1929), p.251]." I might suggest also that square brackets, not parentheses, are our style.

In conclusion, I would like to see a revision which addresses the foregoing points as well as those I have scribbled in the attached copy of your manuscript. Send me three copies, together with your statement replying to this letter and my substantive comments in the manuscript.

I may decide to review the next revision myself, without assistance from others. I may seek the advice of Reviewer 3. It is pointless to go back to Reviewer 2, although I think he has raised some very interesting and worthwhile points.

In effect, I am willing to apply the thesis argued in your letter of March 10 to the instance of your paper. If, upon revision and with whatever advice I have obtained, I believe it should be published, I will not feel bound by the argument contained in my letter of March 1.

I hope and trust that this letter provides you with a solid basis for improving your manuscript.

Sincerely,

Stephen A. Zeff

P.S. Please return the attached copy of your manuscript with the three copies of the second revision, when the latter is submitted.

EPISTEMIC CRITIQUE 1

Editors' Introduction: Boer and Mosely's paper is the first of three critiques from within the academy—with reviewer comments and replies from Watts and Zimmerman included where available. These debates are important because they expose the stresses and strains within the mainstream intellectual community. They show that even the institution of the American Accounting Association is not monolithic, but is unstable, factionalized, and vulnerable to political change. What all three critiques have in common is that they undertake rather traditional "philosophical" attacks on Watts and Zimmerman's Excuses Theory (thus a typical component of Boer and Moseley's critique of Watts and Zimmerman's paper is their "Sampling of Imprecise Terms."

In the history of accounting thought (which is intimately bound up with the history of economic thought) philosophy, sociology, history, and politics began to part company with economics soon after Adam Smith. Some philosophical concerns have survived in contemporary accounting literature; they were never entirely erased and periodically return to haunt mainstream thinkers in times of theoretical (and social) crisis. In this tradition, Harvard-based Charles Christensen published one of the most authoritative critiques of the Excuses Theory in a 1983 issue of *The Accounting Review*. Rumor has it that Christensen's paper was the leading contender for the 1983 AAA Most Notable Manuscript Award in committee, and only strenuous arm-twisting by AAA insiders prevented Christensen from securing it. We will further examine the character of these insider critiques in the subsequent introductions; suffice it to say at this stage that they all tend to stem from analytic (traditional) philosophy, and are relatively weak in terms of their historical, sociological, and political content. In this sense they all fall within a conservative tradition and because they neglect the kind of sociological analysis that traces theoretical ruptures (like the Excuses Theory) to crises in the broader social system, they only reflect intermediate and provisional symptoms of "things to come."

EPISTEMIC CRITIQUE 1

GERMAINE BOER, OWEN MOSELEY, ROSS WATTS, JEROLD ZIMMERMAN AND STEVE ZEFF

OCTOBER 31, 1980

Dr. Jerold L. Zimmerman
The Graduate School of Management
University of Rochester
Rochester, NY 14627

Dear Dr. Zimmerman

According to the policy set forth by Steve Zeff in *The Accounting Review* we are supposed to send our comments on published papers to the authors before submitting them for publication. Professor Moseley and I are enclosing our Comments on your paper "The Demand for and Supply of Accounting Theories: The Market For Excuses." We would appreciate your response to these comments so we can submit them to Steve for publication.

Sincerely,

Germain Boer
Professor of Management

Some Comments on Logical Reasoning and "The Market for Excuses"

The paper on "The Demand for and Supply of Accounting Theories: The Market for Excuses" by Ross L. Watts and Jerold L. Zimmerman (hereafter referred to as WZ) contains some interesting concepts that are intuitively appealing to accounting researchers.* Their theory of how accounting theories develop includes many issues of importance to accounting scholars. Unfortunately, the impact of their theory is somewhat clouded by a number of serious methodological imperfections which we discuss in the following pages. However, the purpose of our paper is not merely to criticize the WZ work; we hope that our comments will reaffirm the need for logical reasoning and careful hypothesis formulation in all accounting research.

We have organized our comments into two sections: logical fallacies and general comments.

I. LOGICAL FALLACIES

Logic provides a set of rules that allow scholars to ask questions, gather evidence, and arrive at conclusions in a rigorous, rational manner. It prescribes a way of intellectually scrutinizing arguments to make sure that the conclusions are supported by the appropriate evidence and that the evidence is free of subjective judgements, is objectively sound, and is relevant to the conclusion. Researchers who deviate from any one of the rigorous demands of intellectually sound reasoning in order to produce results unsupported by their evidence commit a fallacy. We discuss four major logical fallacies in the WZ paper.

A. Fallacy Number 1: Argument from Ignorance

Researchers commit this fallacy whenever they attempt to place the burden of disproof on the reader, and then argue that the reader's inability to disprove the assertion is itself proof of the assertion. WZ call upon this fallacy to buttress their arguments at least five times in their paper as the following quotations indicate:

---

*Ross L. Watts and Jerold L. Zimmerman "The Demand for and Supply of Accounting Theories: The Market for Excuses," *The Accounting Review* (April, 1979) pp 273-305.

Editors' note: In some cases to avoid confusion, page numbers in the text have been deleted where they do not cross reference to the page numbers in this volume.

Page   Statement

288   In that case, neither the public interest theory nor our theory could explain the accounting literature. In essence we would be left without a theory of the literature. However, those who would argue such a scenario must then produce another explanation for, or theory of, the Accounting literature.

291   We do not observe depreciation being treated as an expense prior to this century.

291   Yet, we do not observe any real concern with depreciation expense until the nineteenth century.

294   We do not observe the same concern in the U.S. at that time.

299   We do not observe this theory being generally advanced in the Accounting literature prior to the Securities Acts.

In the first quotation WZ assume that the inability of researchers to develop alternative theories is proof of their own. The fact that we cannot come up with an alternative theory adds no support whatsoever to their theory; it reflects our inability to develop an alternative theory—nothing more and nothing less. Their lack of observation of concern about depreciation until the nineteenth century, likewise, tells us nothing about accountants' concern with depreciation prior to the nineteenth century; rather, it may be due to a lack of diligence on their part in searching out references or it may merely reflect the fact that such concerns were not written about extensively to this time. The same criticism applies to the last two quotes. Lack of observation tells us something about the WZ ability to observe, but it reveals nothing about the existence of these unobserved events.

Not finding an issue discussed is quite different from finding that the issue was not discussed. The former never proves the latter.

B. Fallacy Number 2: Post Hoc Ergo Propter Hoc

This fallacy is based on the false assumption that because two events stand in temporal succession they are therefore related. For example, WZ argue (page 294) that passage of tax laws stimulated the depreciation discussions in both the U.K and the U.S. because in both instances passage of tax laws preceded the appearance of the debates. Their assertion may be correct, but merely pointing out that the passage of tax laws preceded extended discussions of depreciation in both countries in no way shows that these laws caused the accounting interest in depreciation. They make the same mistake again when they point out that "The tax allowance of the depreciation deduction (1878) precedes the 1880s debates"

Their discussion of events surrounding the formation of the Securities and Exchange Commission provides another example of the *post hoc* fallacy. The authors in this discussion divide accounting literature into that published before passage of the Securities Acts and that published after the Securities Acts. They then attribute changes in the accounting literature to passage of the act. However, it may be just as plausible to argue that the social and economic events that gave rise to the Securities Acts also gave rise to the accounting literature, causing changes in this literature that lasted some time. If this were the case (and we are not arguing for this position) a casual review of the sequence of events could give one the impression that the Securities Acts caused the change in the literature.

In both the instances cited here WZ could have easily strengthened their arguments if they had looked at the comments of accountants contemporaneous with the passage of the laws. These comments might have supported the WZ position. Or, WZ could have looked at alternative explanations present in the social and economic forces of the time when the tax laws or securities laws were passed. For example, the securities laws were passed in the depths of the Great Depression, a period marked by thousands of company bankruptcies numerous embezzlements of company funds, and severely depressed stock prices. Surely these events must have had some impact on the accounting literature. The recent impact of the Equity Funding scandal on the accounting profession would seem to indicate that numerous episodes of such behavior, as there were at the time the securities acts were passed, would also impact the accounting literature. For instance, the embezzlement at the Union Industrial Bank of Flint, Michigan, in 1929 has many parallels with the modem Equity Funding case [Galbraith, 1961, p. 139], and it probably influenced the thinking of accountants at the time of its discovery. The WZ omission of the fact that the Great Depression might have influenced the accounting literature is a serious one since this event alone, which happened to coincide with passage of the securities laws, may completely account for the changes in the accounting literature that WZ attribute to the passage of the securities laws. Unfortunately the WZ selection of an isolated event which precedes the literature changes of interest to them causes them to fall into the *post hoc* trap.

C. Fallacy Number 3: Confusion of Condition and Cause
Scholars define "cause" as some specific event which brings about another event called the effect. Conditions, on the other hand, are the set of related circumstances under which the cause-effect relation takes place. The cause produces the effect, whereas the condition provides the opportunity for the operation of the cause. The fallacy arises when a researcher confuses condition and cause or regards them as identical. For example, an economist who

argues that economic prosperity in the United States is due to its democratic form of government may be overlooking the fact that the form of government merely provides the conditions for prosperity. As a further example consider the case of the shopkeeper who on his way home down a dark street is shot by a robber and dies, before his condition is discovered. The dark street provided the conditions that allowed his death to occur, but the bullet from the robber's gun caused his death.

Researchers who seek out the causes of past events face a particularly tough job of separating causes and conditions for they have to deal with a variety of causes: greater causes, lesser causes, more important causes, most important cause, the immediate cause, underlying causes, necessary conditions and sufficient conditions. Distinguishing between greater and lesser causes is relatively easy in some cases, but trying to identify a factor as the most important or key cause is a troublesome problem.

The simple presence of a cause does not mean it was causally operative. To say a particular accounting theory was caused by the Securities Acts may be an unwarranted conclusion because something else may have caused the theory. The researcher who reviews past events must also keep in mind that he can never examine all variables, and the nature of his research is such that he can never conclude he has found *the* cause of an event. The researcher can only assess the relative importance of various factors on the event in question. Such a judgement on the importance of an event can lead to a conclusion in the sense that an opinion is formed but not in the sense that a final answer is determined.

These brief comments about cause and effect and the conclusions about them show that researchers who study past events should be cautious about isolating a single factor as the causal element. However, WZ exhibit little caution on this matter. Consider this statement: "The timing of the depreciation debates in the U.K also appears to confirm our hypothesis that political action caused the observed change in accounting Theory." Maybe the political action was a condition instead of a cause, or maybe it plus some other factors influenced the event. Again, they say "The hypothesis that the dominance of the information objective was caused by the Securities Acts . . ." This statement indicates little doubt in the authors' minds about what event caused what effect. An even stronger statement appears later where WZ says "Further, the justification caused the SEC to demand such theories." This statement would be hard to support even if the authors had presented evidence, but they cite no documents, speeches, memos, phone calls, or personal conversations to indicate SEC commissioners were motivated by the justification (justification in this case refers to the notion that private incentives to adopt accounting prescriptions are insufficient) nor do they present any evidence that the SEC requested anybody to produce accounting theories (see the third section of this paper for our discussion of accounting theories).

WZ restrict their consideration of past events so severely that no elements such as economic conditions, social factors, or political forces can play a role in their theory even if these were the predominant causes influencing the effects they are studying. WZ exclude all possible causal factors except those that fit the narrow scope of their theory. They assume that all causation moves from government legislation to accounting theory developments, and they mention no other possible causes.

Perhaps the cause-effect relationships postulated by WZ are valid. However, their lack of attention to the cause-condition distinction, to the possibility of multiple causal factors, and their lack of solid evidence to support their cause-effect assertions provide little justification for the strong statements they make about the causes of events.

D. Fallacy Number 4: Fallacy of the Declarative Question

This fallacy consists of the use of a declarative statement about what will be found in past events. It violates a fundamental rule that says questions should have an open end that allows the researcher a choice of alternative explanations for what he finds. A researcher who approaches the study of historical events with a simple affirmative proposition that "X was the case" is predisposed to prove it. He will usually find evidence to illustrate his expectations if not to actually sustain them. If instead the researcher asks,

> "Was X or Y the case?" then he has an empirical advantage. And if he asks "Was X or not-X, Y or not Y, Z or not-Z . . . the case?" and if he designs X, and Y, and Z in such a way that his own preferences are neutralized, and if he leaves the way open to refinements in the form of X_1, Y_1, Z_1, and if he allows for still other unexpected possibilities, then the probability of empirical accuracy is still further enhanced. [Fischer, 1970, p. 24].

By stating what they expected to find in past events and then finding events that support these expectations WZ do not present evidence to support their theory. They merely show examples of events that are consistent with their expectations. However WZ did not covertly commit this fallacy; they did it openly. They admit their awareness of this problem, but they seem to lose their awareness when they write later pages. For example, after their confession of guilt, they make comments such as:

> The timing of the depreciation debates in the U.K. also appears to confirm our hypotheses . . .

The hypothesis that the dominance of the information objective was caused by the Securities Acts is supported not only by . . .

. . . the only accounting theory that will provide a set of predictions consistent with observed phenomena is one based on self interest.

The first two statements are consistent with an open ended question that looks at all possible events but this is not what WZ did. They stated what they wanted to find, and they found it. The finding and presenting of these cases causes no problems; it is the WZ assumption that these events provide sufficient evidence for them to make the kinds of statements mentioned above that is the problem. Furthermore, admitting that one has used a fallacious approach to looking at a problem does not make the approach correct. It may win the researchers praise for their frankness, but it will not make valid their invalid results. Finally, the third statement is completely unwarranted. Earlier in the paper WZ say "Our objective is merely to present prima facie support for the hypothesis that accounting theory has changed *after* the introduction of government regulation." Choosing phenomena consistent with a theory does not allow a researcher to later prove his theory by saying it is consistent with the observed phenomena.

II. GENERAL COMMENTS

A. Posner's Methods Versus the WZ Method
In justifying their ex post case study approach to looking at evidence to support their theory WZ cite a work by Posner [Posner, 1974] as an example of how this approach has been successfully used. It will be worthwhile to look at Posner's approach in some detail since WZ cite it as support for their methodology.

Posner looked at two theories of government regulation of the economy: the public interest theory and the interest group theory. His approach to looking at these theories differs significantly from the WZ method of looking at facts to support their theory. At the outset Posner states clearly that he favors the economists version of the interest group theory: "I shall argue that the economists version is the most promising, but shall also point out the significant weaknesses in both the theory and the empirical research that is alleged to support the theory." [Posner, 1974, p. 36]. Compare this statement with the WZ description of what they plan to do in their empirical work: "Our objective is merely to present prima facie support for the hypothesis that accounting theory has changed *after* the introduction of government regulation." Notice how Posner considers evidence for and against the theory he prefers, but WZ include only supporting evidence.

In reviewing the public interest theory of government regulation, Posner studied case studies and other empirical work that contradict the original assumptions of this theory. He then gives a reformulation of the public interest theory that has been offered in response to the criticisms of this empirical work, and goes on to show that this reformulation still does not adequately account for the empirical research findings. Posner's approach in attacking the public interest theory consisted of a literature review which identified cases that contradicted the theory (actually, he went far beyond a simple review of the literature and analytical arguments as well as the empirical data). Compare this approach to WZ. They did not gather evidence to contradict a theory, they gathered instances to support a theory. Gathering evidence to disprove what is generally accepted requires only a few clear cases contrary to the generally accepted idea, but to build a new theory requires more than a few cases confirming the theory. Posner's use of case studies in attacking the public interest theory seems to provide no support for the WZ approach.

Nor does the way he uses case studies in looking at the economic version of the interest group theory. Since Posner states at the outset that he favors this theory, we would expect him to cite case studies that support the theory, which he does. He cites numerous cases of regulation that are explained by the economic theory in areas such as public utilities, common carriers, and airlines. However, Posner devotes four pages to a discussion of the shortcomings of this evidence.

Clearly, then, Posner looked at cases that supported the theory he preferred, but he did not uncritically accept them. He analyzes weaknesses in the evidence, points out difficulties in using the evidence to support the theory, and admits that serious questions remain. WZ offer little criticism of their evidence. In fact, at one point they appear to purge the October, 1930, issue of the *Journal of Accountancy* from the accounting literature because it contained an article on a theory they said was not generally observed until after the Securities Acts of 1933-34. They justify this position by pointing out that the author of the offending article ". . . is not an accounting theorist; instead he is an employee of the New York Stock Exchange."

If this Posner paper is supposed to provide support for the WZ method of choosing events to support their proposed theory, it does so in a strange way. Posner used case studies, WZ used case studies, and there the resemblance ends Posner cites and discusses at length cases that do not support the theory he prefers; WZ include cases that support their preferred theory or that support theories they reject. Any evidence contrary to their theory gets little, if any, space. We are puzzled by this reference to Posner; his paper gives no support to the WZ method, his statements and conclusions are far more cautious than WZ, and he offers alternative explanations of events that do not match his preferred theory.

B. The Drifting Theory Definition

Because the WZ paper deals with the demand for and the supply of accounting theories it would seem logical for them to provide a carefully structured definition of accounting theory so readers could see what WZ mean by this term. Instead, the reader gets a footnote on the first page in which WZ define theory ". . . as a generic term for the existing accounting literature."(page 273) Presumably "existing accounting literature" is meant to include all periodicals and books dealing with the subject of accounting. Yet two pages later (page 275) they note that a diversity of interests prevents general agreement on accounting theory. Why would we want general agreement on the "existing accounting literature"? Surely WZ must be using some other definition. The one they may have had in mind is one used by Hendriksen in his book on *Accounting Theory:*

> . . . accounting theory may be defined as logical reasoning in the form of a set of broad principles that (1) provide a general frame of reference by which accounting practices can be evaluated and (2) guide the development of new practices and procedures. [Hendriksen, 1977, page I)

We don't know that this is the definition intended by WZ, but it does seem to fit the context in which the term was used on page 275 of their paper.

Still another possible definition appears later in a statement about auditors: "Auditors would value information in the form of theories predicting how agency costs vary with accounting procedures"(page 279) The apparent definition of theory here hinges upon its predictive ability, a characteristic not evident in earlier uses of the term. WZ add a fourth dimension to the term "accounting theory" when they seem to expand it to include the notion of justification or excuse.(page 280) Because of the apparently changing definition of "accounting theory," we found it difficult to follow their ideas. As a means of highlighting this definitional problem we prepared the following frequency distribution of the apparent definitions intended by WZ. We imputed the definition to the term from the context in which the term was used. Obviously our frequency distribution is not perfect, but it does seem to indicate that the definition of accounting theory varied from point to point throughout the paper.

Theory	Frequency
A	23
B	3
C	2
D	24
E	29

Key to theories

A. Definition similar to that of Hendriksen

B. Definition based on quantity of literature

C. Definition based on predictive power

D. Definition of theory as excuse or justification

E. Does not fit any of the above categories

Such variations in definition not only confuse the reader, they also seem to confuse the writers. Consider the paragraph beginning in the middle of the left column on page 283. The authors begin the paragraph using a definition of theory based on its predictive power. They argue that bureaucrats will use the theories that predict best "(i.e., the 'best' theories)" and that these theories will tend to predominate. In the last sentence of the same paragraph WZ cite several references which they claim are based on the premise that the best theories prevail. However, the term theory used in this last sentence appears to be one similar to that offered by Hendriksen. Arguing that the theories that best predict are the ones that predominate is different from saying that the theories that best provide a general frame of reference by which accounting practice can be evaluated [Hendriksen, 1977, page 1] will predominate. These are two different kinds of theories, yet WZ act as if they are identical.

Any thoughtful researcher can prove, disprove or remain neutral on the WZ theory just by choosing the appropriate accounting theory definition. If the quantity of literature definition is used, we can cite a clear contrary example to their theory by showing that approximately 23 accounting publications appeared in the two years prior to the formation of the Cost Accounting Standards Board, and approximately 28 appeared in the five years following its formation. This strongly refutes their theory. However, if we use any of the other definitions of theory, we can say nothing about their hypothesis. In the case of Medicare legislation we can show different results. In this case no accounting publications were listed in the *Accountants Index* prior to the enactment of Medicare legislation, but the *Accountants Index* shows 112 references alone in the 1967-68 edition approximately two years after the legislation became effective. Using the B theory definition we support the WZ theory, but any other theory definition leads to the opposite conclusion that Medicare legislation had no impact on accounting theory. Such flexibility of definition prevents researchers from making any test of the WZ theory.

It is easy to excuse an occasional ambiguous term or one that is vague. After all, the spoken and written language is used for many purposes. However, when the major thrust of a paper focuses on a specific term, the least the authors could do is give the reader some referents, some guidelines to use in defining the term, especially a term like "accounting theory."

C. The Soundness of the WZ Theory

Because WZ are offering a new theory, it might be worthwhile to look at the qualities such a theory should possess. Theories usually evolve from hypotheses which are tested by many researchers over time until enough evidence accumulates to allow researchers to say a theory has evolved. Because theories evolve from hypotheses one could possibly argue that the WZ proposition is more on the order of an hypothesis instead of a theory, a theory being a stronger statement than an hypothesis. Nevertheless, we will not quibble over such a distinction, but since hypothesis formulation is the first step on the road to a theory we will look at some criteria of a sound hypothesis and see how well the WZ theory measures up to them. An introductory book on logic by Searles provides a list of four elements that he says make up some of the criteria of a good hypothesis. [Searles, 1956, pages 237-238] For additional discussion of these issues see Cohen, [1934, pps. 207-215] and Nagel [1961].

1. The hypothesis should be capable of explaining, bringing into order, and summarizing a body of facts in the form of a possible law.

2. The hypothesis should be so formulated that it is susceptible to deductive and mathematical development of its consequences, i.e., the hypothesis should have predictive power.

3. The hypothesis should be consistent with the presuppositions, postulates, principles and already verified facts in the field of Investigation.

4. The hypothesis should adhere to the principle of parsimony.

The first principle requires the hypothesis to be so stated that researchers can prove or disprove it by a comparison with observed facts. It is not always easy to state the hypothesis in exactly this form, but at the least the hypothesis should raise questions which are subject to operational testing. Let's examine how well the WZ theory measures up to this criterion.

They name three sources of demand in an unregulated economy: pedagogic demand, information demand, and justification demand. Pedagogic demand means that accounting teachers develop" pedagogic devices (rules of thumb) to assist learning and to structure the variation found in practice." Empirical testing of the level of this demand faces a number of problems: What is diversity in practice? What qualifies as a pedagogic device? How do we observe the relationship between changes in the level of diversity and the number of rules of thumb? The pedagogic demand part of their theory seems to be so imprecise that comparison of this part of the theory to observed facts may be impossible.

The information demand for accounting theories is even more obtuse. This is the "demand for predictions of the effects of accounting procedures on both the managers and auditor's welfare via exposure to lawsuits." The authors offer no explanation of how this demand reveals itself. In fact, the whole notion is obscure. What kinds of accounting theory does this demand produce? The authors do not even help the reader by giving an example of the kind of accounting theory this demand would elicit. Such murkiness in the idea obviously dictates against any empirical testing of this form of demand for accounting theories.

The theories elicited by the justification demand for accounting theories are more clearly described. This demand relates to theories that show how managers manipulate profits and the effects of those manipulations on shareholders and bondholders. At least, in this case, we have some idea of the types of theories such demand calls forth, and we could crudely measure the quantity of such theories by counting publications in the accounting literature. However, the demand for these theories operates in the same mysterious manner as the other two demands. It is so poorly defined that operational measures for empirical testing could probably never be devised. The authors postulate that government intervention increases the pedagogic and information demands for accounting theories. Given the obscure definition of these demands any researcher would have a difficult time empirically testing this portion of the theory. However, government intervention is not defined by the authors either. Presumably such intervention could vary from a phone call to a corporate executive by a clerk in a regulatory agency to the passage of legislation such as the Securities Acts. The authors do not even restrict government intervention to matters related to accounting, but seem to include any governmental actions that affect business. Presumably their theory would predict that environmental protection legislation and legislation protecting employees in the workplace also bring about changes in accounting theory. Operational testing of changes in governmental regulation (which in the form presented in the WZ paper defies measurement) in relation to demand changes (which are unmeasurable given the WZ lack of precise definitions for these terms) would evade even the most diligent and imaginative researcher.

The WZ theory pertaining to the supply of accounting theories is another exercise in obfuscation and ambiguity. For example, one possible testable postulate offered in the WZ discussion of the supply of theories is this one: "The greater the prestige and articulation skills of an accounting researcher, the more likely practitioners, regulators, and other academics will know his work and the greater the flow of both students and funds to his university." At last something we can measure: students and money. However, measures of prestige are not well developed, and articulation skill measurement may pose somewhat of a problem too. Later in the same paragraph, the authors note that researchers will tend to write on current controversies in accounting. Here is something else we can measure: the number of researchers writing on a particular topic. We will still have difficulty determining which topics are controversial. Other statements similar to these appear in the supply of accounting theories section of the paper, and they pose the same problems as the ones mentioned here.

The imprecision of the WZ theory makes comparison of observed facts to their theory an inconclusive exercise. Clear definitions of key elements of the theory are nonexistent, and without such clear definitions researchers would merely be comparing concrete facts to a poorly specified theory. Furthermore, as our earlier analysis shows, the WZ constantly changing definition of accounting theory would make empirical tests of their theory most difficult even if they had provided clear definitions of the terms used in various components of the theory. In a comparison to the first criterion of a good hypothesis, the WZ theory fails.

The second criterion says the theory should have predictive power. The lack of precise definitions makes any clear predictions impossible with the WZ theory.

The third criterion states the hypothesis should relate to already established facts. However, since WZ attempt to explain phenomena in a manner different from previous efforts, this criterion does not seem to apply to their theory. Finally, the fourth criterion says the theory should adhere to the principle of parsimony, and this their theory does seem to do. It focuses on a small number of factors; they just neglect to define them for us.

This analysis indicates that the WZ theory fails to meet some of the criteria for a good hypothesis in such a serious way that any rational, logical researcher would have a difficult time supporting the statement that WZ have presented a good theory.

D. The General Lack of Precision

We have already pointed out the omission of definitions for key terms used in the theory and the lack of a clear definition of accounting theory. There are numerous other instances of imprecise language in the paper. Rather than burden the reader with a lengthy position of these cases we have prepared a table of the more disturbing examples.

A Sampling of Imprecise Terms

WZ STATEMENT	COMMENT
"Congress often bases legislative actions on these statements."	How frequently is often?
"Often, those public interest.	Ditto
"Consequently, when politicians support (or oppose) legislation, they tend to adopt the public interest arguments advanced by the special interest."	What does tend mean? No examples or references are provided by WZ to support this statement.
"Leading articles in the accounting literature.	What makes an article a leading one? Is it the frequency with which it is referenced by other authors?
"Accounting researchers often include a set of policy recommendations."	How frequently is often?
"Our predictions are for the accounting literature in general"	WZ give no list of typical journals or books to indicate what they mean by "accounting literature in general."
"Furthermore, we have endeavored to choose references from the standard, classical accounting literature."	What is the standard, classical accounting literature? Footnote 61 seems to say the October, 1930, issue of the Journal of Accountancy Is not part of the standard, classical accounting literature.
"Yet we do not observe any real concern with depreciation expense."	What is real concern? How does it differ from other types of concern?

"In that decade we observe a spate of U.K. journal articles and textbooks on the question of depreciation for corporations in general."	How many articles and books total a spate? Surely the authors could give a simple count, especially since they can tell us the precise period the "profits available for dividends" question has existed: 260 years.
"Recent writers no longer even list management as a principal user of financial statements."	How recent is recent? Do WZ mean writers who began publishing after 1960, 1970, or do they mean publications appearing after some other date?
"Before the Securities Acts most of the accounting literature did not stray far from practice."	What fraction of accounting literature is most? What is the accounting literature?
"We expect accounting theorists, who are acustomed to developing rules based on practice, to be perplexed by a demand for accounting principles not based on practice."	What is an accounting theorist? Footnote 61 seems to exclude authors who provide cases contrary to the WZ theory.

These examples of inadequately defined and fuzzy terms are important not just for pointing out a general inattention to precise terminology by WZ, but they are also important because many of these terms are critical to the WZ theory. For example, the empirical evidence gathered by WZ presumes some precise definition of "standard, classical accounting literature." The authors offer none. The definition of accounting theorist is also crucial to their empirical work; again we get no precise definition of this term. Their use of the term "often" allows them to judge for the reader whether an event occurs frequently enough to impact other events. Readers should be allowed to make these decisions for themselves. These examples of imprecise language, the omission of a definition of accounting theory, and the equivocal description of key elements of the theory make the paper somewhat difficult to interpret.

E. Depreciation: Unobserved and Observed
As we noted in the beginning of our paper, the WZ inability to observe depreciation being treated as an expense prior to the nineteenth century could be due to their lack of a diligent search of the accounting literature. For example, Littleton states that:

Depreciation was an old idea even in the nineteenth century. In his text of 1588, John Mellis credits "Implements of householde" account for the amount judged to be "consumed and worn", and debits "profit and loss" account for the same amount, "lost by decay of householde stuff." [Littleton, p. 83]

Littleton adds: "The preferred theory and method of today are both very similar. As to theory, the consensus is that depreciation is a periodic expense. That was the idea in . . . examples from the sixteenth and seventeenth centuries." [Littleton, p. 83)

These comments by Littleton seem to indicate that the notion of depreciation as an expense has been in existence far longer than WZ suggest. Perry Mason in a 1933 article in *The Accounting Review* [Mason, 1933] gives three cases of depreciation recognition, one from the seventeenth and two from the eighteenth centuries. He also comments:

If the records were available for inspection, one would expect to find evidence of some understanding of the phenomena of depreciation as far back in history as the origin of written records of business affairs. [Mason, 1933, p. 209]

These two citations do indicate that the depreciation concept and the recording of depreciation in the accounting records existed far back in history. Depreciation entries existed prior to the nineteenth century even though WZ state ". . . we do not observe depreciation being treated as an expense prior to this century."

As we noted earlier, the WZ inability to observe depreciation being treated as an expense indicated only that they did not observe it. We have. The Littleton reference clearly suggests the idea existed earlier than WZ seem to indicate, and the Mason article also gives evidence to support the proposition that depreciation expense was recorded long before the nineteenth century.

We cite these references to show that the WZ statements about depreciation appear to be much stronger than the evidence justifies. Also, these two references point out again that not observing something is quite different from observing that something does not exist. It is possible that WZ are fully aware of the Littleton and Mason references; they could have excluded the citations because they honestly felt the references had no bearing on the theory. Such feelings are understandable given the nondefinition of accounting theory, the imprecise specification of their theory and the use of vague and ambiguous terms throughout the paper.

III. CONCLUDING REMARKS

It might be argued that the first time a theory is presented we should expect some problems in interpreting the theory because it is new, and we can accept this position. However, much of the imprecision in this paper seems to stem from the authors' avoidance of the rigors of logical reasoning and hypothesis formulation. There is nothing about the newness of a theory that permits its author to avoid definitions of key elements of the theory, e.g., accounting theory, classical accounting literature. Nor does the newness of a theory allow its authors to selectively choose evidence to support their theory and then conclude that such evidence is sufficient to prove the theory. Newness provides no excuse for illogical and imprecise reasoning. It is regrettable that the WZ paper has so many flaws because the authors deal with interesting issues of potential value to accounting researchers.

References

Cohen, Morris R., and Ernest Nagel, *An Introduction to Logic and Scientific Method* (Harcourt, Brace and Company, 1934).

Fischer, David Hackett, *Historians' Fallacies: Toward a Logic of Historical Thought* (Harper & Row, Publishers, 1970).

Galbraith, John Kenneth, *The Great Crash,* 1929 (Houghton Mifflin Company, 1961).

Hendriksen, Eldon S., *Accounting Theory* (Richard D. Irwin, Inc., 1977).

Hexter, J. H., *The History Primer* (Basic Books, Inc., 1971).

Littleton, A. C., *Essays on Accountancy* (University of Illinois Press, 1961).

Mason, Perry, "Illustrations of the Early Treatment of Depreciation" *The Accounting Review* (September, 1933), pp. 209-218.

Nagel, Ernest *The Structure of Science: Problems in the Logic of Scientific Explanation* (Harcourt, Brace and World, 1961)

Posner, Richard A. "Theories of Economic Regulation," *Bell Journal of Economics and Management Science* (Autumn, 1974), pp. 335-358.

Searles, Herbert L., *Logic and Scientific Methods: An Introductory Course* Second edition (The Ronald Press Company, 1956)

Watts, Ross L., and Jerold L. Zimmerman, "The Demand for and the Supply of Accounting Theories: The Market for Excuses," *The Accounting Review* (April, 1970), pp. 273-305.

Professor Stephen A. Zeff
Jesse M. Jones Graduate School of Administration
Rice University
Houston, TX 77001

Dear Steve:

My coauthor and I sent the enclosed comment to Professors Ross L. Watts and Jerold L. Zimmerman on October 31, 1980, and have had no response from them. should we assume there are no misconceptions or misinterpretations in our paper? If so, would you please begin processing our comment on their paper. Otherwise, would you let us know how we should get Professors Watts and Zimmerman to reply.

Since we were unsure on how to proceed, we decided to send you a copy of our comment and the letters we sent to Professors Watts and Zimmerman. Let us know how you want to handle this matter, and we will do what we can to cooperate with you.

Sincerely,

Germain Boer
Professor of Management

DECEMBER 16, 1980

Owen Graduate School of Management
Vanderbilt University
Nashville Tennessee 37203

Professor Jerold L. Zimmerman
Graduate School of Management
University of Rochester
Rochester, NY 14627

Dear Professor Zimmerman:

Steve Zeff suggested I drop you a note to remind you to respond to the comment my coauthor and I mailed to you on October 31, 1980. In case you have mislaid the comment or if it did not arrive in the first place, I am enclosing another copy for your use.

We look forward to hearing your response.

Sincerely,

Germain Boer
Professor of Management

cc: Owen Moseley

The Graduate School of Management
University of Rochester
Rochester, New York 14627

Professor Germain Boer
Owen Graduate School of Management
Vanderbilt University
Nashville, TN 37203

Dear Professor Boer:

With reference to your letter to Jerry Zimmerman dated December 16, 1980, I advise that we have read your comment on our paper and will respond in detail. However, we have many other pressing commitments including running a journal and I cannot promise our formal reply before the end of January.

Yours sincerely,

Ross L. Watts
Associate Professor

cc: Steve Zeff

FEBRUARY 6, 1981

The Graduate School of Management
The University of Rochester
Rochester, New York 14627

Professor Germain Boer
Owen Graduate School of Management
Vanderbilt University
Nashville, TN 37203

Dear Professor Boer:

I enclose two copies of our reply to your comment on our "excuses" paper.

Yours sincerely,

Ross L. Watts
Associate Professor

Reply to Boer and Moseley

R. L. WATTS AND J. L. ZIMMERMAN

Boer and Moseley conclude that our article "The Market for Excuses" is subject to "serious methodological imperfections" (p. 1). Boer and Moseley's arguments are at variance with the methodological approach prevailing in empirical research in economics (and other social sciences) and, indeed, in the physical sciences. In essence many of the serious imperfections lie not in our article, but in Boer and Moseley's lack of knowledge of scientific methodology.

To demonstrate that many of Boer's and Moseley's criticisms reflect a lack of knowledge of methodology and in fact are inconsistent with the methodology of normal science, we first outline the nature of science and scientific methodology (Section I), we then analyze each of the criticisms in view of traditional scientific methodology. Section II addresses the criticisms Boer and Moseley classify as logical fallacies and Section III addresses the criticisms they classify as general comments.

I. THE NATURE OF SCIENTIFIC METHODOLOGY

In our article we explicitly stated what we consider a theory: a set of "principles advanced to explain a set of phenomena, in particular" . . . "sets of hypotheses which have been confirmed" (p. 273, fn. I). That is a definition which is conventional in economics (e.g., Friedman, 1953, Part I) and in the physical sciences (e.g., Popper, 1959, p. 59). The objective of a theory is "to explain phenomena"; to predict phenomena not yet observed (see Friedman, 1953, p. 7). Phenomena "not yet observed" does not mean future phenomena, it includes phenomena which occurred in the past, but on which you have not yet collected evidence. Explaining means predicting. The goal of science is to produce theories which predict (see Braithwaite, 1953, p. 1; Poincaré, 1952, Chapter I; and Popper, 1959, Chapter III).

Logic plays a role in developing theories. Theories are based on assumptions and logic is used to derive propositions. However, given the logic of the theory is correctly developed, logic does not determine whether a theory is supported by the scientific community or not. Acceptance depends on the extent to which the empirical propositions (predictions) of the theory are consistent with observed phenomena (see Toulmin, 1953, p. 12; Friedman, 1953, p. 8; Popper, 1959, p. 109).

By their very nature theories are caricatures of reality. Assumptions are made which it is expected will capture the essence of the phenomena which is to be explained. As a consequence, theories typically do not explain all of the phenomena of interest. This is true in the physical sciences as well as the social sciences. For example, current theories of physics cannot fully explain the existence of black holes. Further, the abstraction of theories also causes their predictions to not exactly fit the observed phenomena even in the physical sciences (see Toulmin, 1953, pp. 70-73).

In developing and testing theories scientists do not look at all the facts and come up with a general model. Such a procedure is logically impossible. In order to make a general statement, we have to ignore some of the facts particular to some observations. As indicated above it is this abstraction which leads to the inability of the theory to explain, to perfectly fit, all observations.

Instead of looking at all the facts (i.e., all the phenomena), scientists develop theories, make predictions and then look at the facts. The theories tell them which facts to look at. As Popper (1959, p. 59) puts it "Theories are nets cast to catch what we call 'the world': to rationalize, to explain, and to master it." Theories tell us what facts are relevant and what are not; where to fish. We have a classic example of this in the physics. In investigating the structure of matter physicists predicted the existence of quarks and then successfully looked for them.

A theory is tested by developing hypotheses and then comparing those hypotheses to the evidence. This usually involves many observations. If the observations are consistent with the hypothesis the hypothesis is confirmed. *Confirmation does not prove the hypothesis or the theory correct.* As Friedman (1953, p. 9) writes "If there is one hypothesis that is consistent with the available evidence, there are always an infinite number that are." A theory comes to be accepted after its hypotheses have with stood substantial empirical testing (see Popper, 1959, p. 109), i.e., have been confirmed in strong and numerous empirical tests.

In the fight for acceptance, a theory is almost always in competition with other theories. As Popper (1959, p. 108) writes, "We choose the theory which best holds its own in competition with other theories; the one which, by natural selection proves itself the fittest to survive." Competing theories are important in testing a hypothesis. If no competing theories have been advanced we have no way of deciding what variables to control other than those indicated by the theory being tested (as indicated above there are an infinite number of alternative possibilities). In that case no control other than that suggested by the theory being tested would be necessary. However, if competing theories exist, we use situations where the competing theories give us different predictions to test the theories.

It is important to note that scientists do *not* worry about the infinite number of estimated possible alternative explanations. They only concern themselves with theories which have been advanced and are sufficiently specified to be capable of explaining the phenomena of interest. The reason for this is apparent. Facts can only be organized and interpreted with the aid of a theory.

Because a theory's hypotheses are general propositions, those hypotheses are not rejected on the basis of isolated observations which contradict a given hypothesis. As Popper (1959, p. 86) writes, "a few stray basic statements (observations) contradicting a theory will hardly induce us to reject it as falsified." Indeed, once a theory is accepted even contradictory observations which are reproducible will not lead to the theory's rejection if an alternative theory which explains more phenomena is not available. Newtonian physics is a superb example of this. Numerous systematic anomalies to Newtonian physics were observed before Einstein advanced his theories, but Newtonian physics was not rejected. In effect you stay with the "best" explanation until a "better" one is advanced (see Kuhn, 1970 for a discussion of the way in which one theory replaces another).

From the above it should be apparent that the test of a theory is not a simple matter of logic. For example, it should be clear that a theory is not rejected because of one contradictory observation. Now, armed with this knowledge of scientific methodology, let us turn to Boer and Moseley's criticisms.

II. OUR "LOGICAL" FALLACIES

1. Fallacy Number 1: Arguments From Ignorance
According to Boer and Moseley this fallacy occurs when researchers "attempt to place the burden of disproof on the reader, and then argue that the

reader's inability to disprove the assertion is itself proof of the assertion." Boer and Moseley claim we commit this fallacy at least five times. It is apparent we do not commit this fallacy at all. Nowhere in our paper do we claim to prove anything. As we noted in Section I "proof" of a theory is not possible. The five instances Boer and Moseley cite do not amount to this claim and all are consistent with normal scientific methodology. Let's examine them:

i) Page 288. This statement is completely in accord with the normal competition among theories for acceptance. The point being made is that if the circumstances arises where neither our theory nor the public interest theory can explain a particular observation, we do not reject those theories (if they can explain other phenomena). Rejection only occurs in favor of another theory.

ii) Page 291 (2 quotes). These statements are made in the context of discriminating between Littleton's explanation for the practice of taking depreciation and our own. The conditions for depreciation to be charged as an expense and for individuals to be concerned with depreciation under Littleton's model are observed with the trading companies of the seventeenth century. Thus, Littleton expects those companies to have charged depreciation as an expense in the seventeenth century. Our model does not predict depreciation to appear until there was a regulatory incentive. Such an incentive appeared with the railroads, hence we predict depreciation expense would appear at that time (i.e., in the nineteenth century). We have the classic case of two alternative models with differential predictions. One predicts depreciation in the seventeenth century, the other predicts depreciation in the nineteenth century. The lack of observation of and concern with depreciation being generally taken as an expense until the nineteenth century does provide evidence on the two models: It confirms ours and contradicts Littleton's.

The statements about our lack of observation of depreciation being taken as an expense are specious. It is always possible that observations were overlooked. However, we doubt that we overlooked the *general* phenomena of depreciation being taken as an expense. For if we did we are in company with many others, *including Littleton.* On the same page we provide a quote from Littleton that indicates he agrees with our statement. In fact, he even tries to explain why depreciation was not observed prior to the nineteenth century

iii) Pages 294 and 299. Our comments on the criticisms of page 291 apply here as well. These observations do discriminate between the alternative hypotheses (they do not "prove") and we are not the only ones who have observed them.

2. Fallacy Number 2: Post Hoc Ergo Propter Hoc

We, like most empiricists, realize that you cannot infer a relationship (e.g., causality) from statistical association, time series or otherwise, and we are not making that mistake on the pages referenced under this criticism. The relationship or causality can only be inferred by use of a theory. For example, our theory indicates that the 1878 tax laws provide incentives for taking depreciation hence we expect depreciation to appear as a general phenomenon after those laws. The observation that such an event occurs *is* confirmation of our theory. Within that theory the tax laws *caused* the appearance of depreciation.

The charge that we have made this fallacy probably arises from Boer and Moseley's odd perception that we are trying to prove our theory (see above). We recognize, and we thought most accounting researchers also recognized, that "If there is one hypothesis that is consistent (sic) with the available evidence, there are always an infinite number that are" (Friedman, 1953, p. 8). We cannot prove a theory and hence causality. The causal statements we make are purely within the confines of our theory.

3. Fallacy Number 3: Confusion of Condition and Cause

Our reply to this charge is the same as our reply to the claimed fallacy number 2, whether an event is causal or not depends on the theory, it cannot be inferred from observation alone. We do not suggest otherwise.

i) "The timing of the depreciation debates in the U.K. also appears to confirm our hypothesis that political action caused the observed change in accounting theory".

This quote is clearly in accord with scientific methodology. Our theory has implications for the timing of the debates, i.e., provides a hypothesis. Those implications are apparently consistent with the evidence, so we write that they "confirm" *(not prove)* our hypothesis and by inference the theory. The causation is explicitly referred to as part of the hypothesis (i.e., that the causation is implied by the theory).

ii) "The hypothesis that the dominance of the information objective was caused by the Securities Acts . . ."

Contrary to Boer and Moseley's statement this sentence does not amount to a statement of our belief. The sentence continues ". . . is supported by" and then refers to two empirical tendencies which are consistent with ("confirm") our theory. There is no logical fallacy here.

iii) "Further, the justification caused the SEC to demand such theories"
(p. 299). This interpretation of causality comes from our theory. As we stated
above one cannot observe causality, it can only be inferred from a theory.
In the section from which the quote is taken we are contrasting the implications of our theory with the alternative theory. The particular paragraph is
outlining the effect of the publicly stated rationale for the Security Acts in
terms of our theory—it is not a statement of fact.

The last paragraph of Boer and Moseley's comments on this claimed
fallacy indicates another defect in their knowledge of empirical methodology, i.e., that you have to hold all other factors constant in testing a theory.
That is impossible and is not a requirement in testing a theory. As the
Friedman quote (above) indicates, there are an infinite number of alternative
hypotheses. We are only required to hold constant variables suggested by
competing theories. Since no other theory of the literature has been advanced, strictly we had nothing to control. However, we tried to control for
the "public interest" theory which is implicit in many writer's statements
because it is popular. Such control requires specification of that theory.
We specified that theory as we perceived it and came up with differential
predictions as to the timing of events. Ex post, based on our results Boer
and Moseley apparently want to specify that theory differently. They are
welcome to do that. However, to test their theory against ours they must
find some other predictions which discriminate.

4. Fallacy Number 4: Fallacy of the Declarative Question
This is a very interesting fallacy. It effectively refutes scientific methodology; One apparently is not to specify a theory and formulate hypotheses
before looking at the data and testing the hypotheses. Instead one is to look
at the data and then choose an explanation or hypothesis. This inductive
logic viewpoint is incredibly naive, even though it did prevail in the accounting literature in the 1950's and early 1960's, and is not the methodology of
science. Popper (1959, p. 106) puts the point well:

> Thus the real situation is quite different from the one visualized
> by the naive empiricist, or the believer in inductive logic. He
> thinks that we begin by collecting and arranging our experiences,
> and so ascend the ladder of science. Or, to use the more formal
> mode of speech, that if we wish to build up a science, we have
> first to collect protocol sentences. But if I am ordered 'Record
> what you are now experiencing' I shall hardly know how to obey
> this ambiguous order. Am I to report that I am writing; that I
> hear a bell ringing; a newsboy shouting; a loudspeaker droning;
> or am I to report, perhaps, that these noises irritate me? And
> even if the order could be obeyed: however rich a collection of

statements might be assembled in this way, it could never add up to a *science*. A science needs points of view, and theoretical problems.

As we indicated in Section II, theories tell the researcher where to look. We don't deny that our theory told us what to look for and where to look. As Boer and Moseley say, we do not try to hide that fact. There is nothing to hide, we are merely following normal scientific methodology. Our situation is analogous to the physicists who predicted quarks and then went and looked for them.

The first two quotes Boer and Moseley give in this section are completely consistent with science as we explained above. The third quote is our prediction which is contained in the conclusion. At that point we have concluded our case for our model and we are looking forward as is common in academic articles. The fact that the quote is our prediction and has nothing to do with the testing of the theory using the past should be obvious to most readers.

5. Conclusions on Logical Fallacies
The preceding discussion makes it painfully clear that the "logical fallacies" Boer and Moseley claim we commit are in fact not committed. The problem is that Boer and Moseley try to force our application of scientific methodology into a methodology whereby one observes masses of data and infers the nature of the world from the data. We do not use that latter methodology; we do not attempt to prove anything. We do not use that methodology because as has been recognized in the literature on the philosophy of science for a long time, that methodology is not only naive, it is impossible.

III. GENERAL COMMENTS

Many of Boer and Moseley's comments in this section are, like the supposed "logical fallacies", driven by their lack of familiarity with scientific methodology and their perception that inductive logic should be the basis of empirical work.

1. Posner's Methods Versus the WZ Method
In the "excuses" paper we reference an article by Posner (1974) in which he reviews theories which have been advanced to explain the observed pattern of government regulation of the economy. We reference that article in 2 basic ways: i) as providing examples of a theory of political action based on individual self-interest and ii) as an example of the use of empirical cases to provide evidence on alternative theories. We do not, as Boer and Moseley suggest, cite Posner's paper to provide support for our selection of evidence.

We do not need such support. As we indicated above, *our* theory tells us where to look for the evidence.

As Boer and Moseley point out, Posner provides cases which are inconsistent with each of the theories of regulation he assesses, including the economic theory of regulation. Further, Boer and Moseley criticize us for not seeking such evidence. However, the reason Posner provides such examples is that he is surveying an established literature on the theory of government regulation in which there are many competing theories. The competition among those theories has led to the emergence of the examples.

In our case, there is no literature on a theory of the accounting literature. We are not reviewing a set of theories which have been advanced and criticized in many articles (there is *no* such literature). The only alternative hypotheses we have for ours are those we infer from the public interest theory which appears to be implicit in the accounting literature. That literature does not specify that theory so we have no reference points for establishing a great number of discriminatory examples.

Another point (which we clearly make in our paper) is that we are (as Boer and Moseley quote us) presenting "prima facie support" for the hypothesis that accounting theory has changed *after* the introduction of government regulation. We are trying to make a case for serious consideration of a theory (the first expressly proposed), we are not reviewing an established literature, we hope to start a literature. Nor are we (contrary to Boer and Moseley's belief) trying to prove any hypothesis. As we indicate above such proof is impossible.

One final note on this section is that a few clear cases contrary to a generally accepted idea may disprove that idea but they do not necessarily lead to rejection of that theory, as the history of science shows (see the anomalies in Newtonian physics and other such anomalies reported in Kuhn (1970)).

2. The Drifting Theory Definition

In writing the "excuses" paper we were confronted by the problem of the use of the word theory. We, as researchers have a clear definition of theory (i.e., the definition given in Section II) and we made that clear in the "excuses" paper (see footnote 1). The problem is, as we indicated in footnote 1, that the word theory is used in the accounting literature to include not only the model that is meant to explain the world, but also the specification of a normative criterion to evaluate procedures and the actual derivation of prescriptions (e.g., see the Hendriksen definition quoted by Boer and Moseley on p. 11). Hence, we used the word to encompass what is referred to as accounting theory in the accounting literature. That is what we meant as using "the word 'theory' as a generic term for the existing accounting literature" in footnote 1. With hindsight it is clear that we did not make that definition as clear as we might have.

Given our definition, our paper provides an explanation as to why we want agreement on theory—see our Section IV.C. Further, it is clear that Hendriksen's definition falls within ours as does the predictive ability notion of theory, (which is basically the definition in Section II, above). Theories in the accounting literature are either explanations of phenomena (e.g., the capital asset pricing model used by empiricists) or explanations of phenomena combined with some normative superstructure (e.g., Chambers' assumptions about the capital market behavior combined with a goal provides his prescriptions—see Ball, 1972, for a discussion of Chambers' assumptions).

When we discuss the *use* of accounting theories we talk about their justification role. Contrary to Boer and Moseley's assertion that is *not* another definition. Theories which purportedly explain phenomena (i.e., theories which fit our definition) can be used as a justification or excuse. They do not have to be confirmed theories. Likewise normative models (such as Chambers') can also be used as excuses. Such use does not imply another definition.

Part of Boer and Moseley's problem is again their lack of understanding of empirical methodology (i.e., science). This is demonstrated in their discussion of our use of the word theory on our page 283 (see Boer and Moseley, p. 12). They claim we begin with predictive ability and end with a normative model (i.e., we use Hendriksen's definition). However, the issue is one of predictive ability. A normative model which guides the development of procedures necessarily relies, explicitly or implicitly, on a theory of the world (i.e., a theory that is supposed to predict or explain). For example, Chambers' papers implicitly incorporate hypotheses about stock price reactions to accounting numbers. We didn't spell this out because we assumed that with the enormous growth in the empirical literature in accounting in the last 15 years that most readers understood empirical methodology. Perhaps we should have devoted some more space to these methodological issues.

We do not know which references Boer and Moseley classified in category E, but it is clear that their categories A and C fit within the definition of theory we chose in the "excuses" paper (though only C fits the definition in science). It is also clear that category D is not a definition but a *use* of one of the definitions in A or C. Boer and Moseley's suggestion that we define theory based on the quantity of literature is absurd (category B). We mentioned citation tests as a way of *testing* our theory, not as a definition. For example, consider the notion of auditor independence. Assume for the purposes of the example that our theory predicted that theories on independence would follow a particular regulation. We could test that prediction using the relative frequency of articles prescribing independence or assessing the empirical effect of independence before and after the regulation. Those tests are tests of the timing implied by our theory, they are not a new definition of theory.

3. The Soundness of the WZ Theory

The comments in this section also reveal an unfamiliarity with science. No theory ever emerged complete and we are sure there is no such thing as a complete theory in social science. Our theory is not fully specified and is vague in many areas. We do not pursue all the possible testable propositions, because that would involve a lifetime. Consequently, we had to choose where to develop our propositions which would be sufficiently specified to be testable. We chose to pursue the effect of government intervention on the timing of changes in accounting theory. Those timing propositions are eminently testable. For example, either the practice of depreciation being deducted as an expense began before the 1878 U.K. tax laws or it did not. It is also apparent what we meant by government intervention. The example of three government bills affecting economic incentives should be sufficient.

The timing predictions are not the only testable predictions our theory presents (though they are the only ones we test). Boer and Moseley, themselves, point out others (p. 16).

It is also clear that other testable propositions (not presented in the paper) can be derived from our theory as presented in the "excuses" paper. In fact, even Boer and Moseley are ?? derive implications. As they suggest, our theory "would predict that environmental protection legislation and legislation protecting employees in the workplace also bring about changes in accounting theory."

The comments in this section about our changing definitions of accounting theory are answered in Section III.2 (above).

4. The General Lack of Precision

The comments in this section are similar to those in the preceding section. It is a request for a complete theory. It is an impossible request and reflects the inductive logic era of the accounting literature that occurred in the 1950's and 1960's.

5. Depreciation Observed and Unobserved

We have little doubt that our observations about depreciation not being generally charged as an expense until the nineteenth century railroads and the 1878 U.K. tax law are correct. We have observed samples of corporate financial statements from the eighteenth and nineteenth centuries in the U.S. Their treatment of depreciation is consistent with what we observe in descriptions of English accounts prior to the nineteenth century. Depreciation was not deducted systematically each year. Assets were valued and any gain or loss charged *directly* to profit and loss appropriation. Note that we recognize that method of accounting on p. 291 of the "excuses" paper. As we stated, what changed with the railroads and taxes was that depreciation became an expense calculated on the basis of historical cost.

The Littleton quotes provided by Boer and Moseley show how little care they put into reading our paper or their own source.

i) The description of one practice in the first quote is consistent with practice as we describe it prior to the railroads.

ii) Littleton proceeds in the Boer and Moseley reference (Littleton, 1961, p. 84) to indicate that depreciation did indeed change from an occasional inventory valuation to systematic depreciation much as the same as he does in the quote we provide in the "excuses" paper. In fact, if Boer and Moseley really believed their out of context quotations, weren't they worried that Littleton pondered over the lack of a systematic depreciation charge before the railroads?

The Mason quotation falls into the same category as Littleton's. First we suggest the example is the type of depreciation we described as existing prior to the railroads in the "excuses" paper. Second, by Littleton's own admission and our observation of actual statements there was not a general tendency for systematic depreciation charges. There may have been occasional exceptions, but we refer the reader back to our discussion of the nature of scientific methodology for the relevance of such observations.

The bottom line is Boer and Moseley do *not* observe what they claim to observe.

IV. CONCLUSIONS

It is apparent that Boer and Moseley's criticisms suffer from a lack of knowledge of the methodology of science. It is regrettable that we did not anticipate that this may be a problem among the readers of the *Accounting Review*. However, our oversight can readily be solved by publication of their paper and our reply.

Apart from the inclusion of a section on methodology and an additional sentence on our definition of theory, Boer and Moseley's criticisms would not cause us to revise our "excuses" paper.

References

Ball, R. (I 972), "Changes in Accounting Techniques and Stock Prices", in *Empirical Research in Accounting: Selected Studies 1972,* supplement to Vol. 10 of *Journal of Accounting Research.*

Braithwaite, R. B. (1953), *Scientific Explanation,* reprinted by Cambridge at the University Press, 1968.

Friedman, M. (1953), "The Methodology of Positive Economics", Part I of *Essays in Positive Economics,* reprinted by the University of Chicago Press, 1966.

Hendriksen, E. (1977), *Accounting Theory,* 3rd ed., ed. Richard D. Irwin.

Kuhn, T. S. (1970), *The Structure of Scientific Revolutions,* The University of Chicago Press, 2nd ed.

Poincaré, H. (1952), *Science and Method,* reprint of the first English translation by Dover Publications.

Popper, K. R. (1959), *The Logic of Scientific Discovery,* reprinted by Harper Torch Books 1965.

Posner, R. A. (1974), "Theories of Economic Regulation", *Bell Journal of Economics and Management Science* (Autumn).

Toulmin, S. (1953), *The Philosophy of Science,* reprinted by Harper Torch Books, 1960.

FEBRUARY 16, 1981

Professor Stephen A. Zeff
Jesse H. Jones Graduate School of Administration
Rice University
Houston,
TX 77001

Dear Steve:

Owen Moseley and I have reviewed the rebuttal of Professors Watts and Zimmerman to our comment on their article entitled "The Demand for and the Supply of Accounting Theories: The Market for Excuses", and we still feel that our comments are valid. Accordingly, we are sending you our original comment and the rebuttal for your consideration for publication in *The Accounting Review*. Regardless of whether our view or that of the authors ultimately prevails, publication of this discussion is worthwhile because this exchange addresses some important issues all accounting researchers should consider when conducting research.

I look forward to hearing your decision on publication of this paper.

Sincerely,

Germain Boer
Professor of Management

cc: R. L. Watts

Reviewer's Memo to authors of 'Some Comments on Logical Reasoning and "The Market for Excuses".

[Reviewer #1]

The reasoning and mode of exposition employed in the WZ paper certainly invite criticism. However, I found your critique seriously inadequate in a number of places.

I. LOGICAL FALLACIES

A

P. 288. I agree that there is something odd about WZ's reasoning here. Whether arguments or theories appear in the literature before or after a regulatory decision is not a matter which is capable of assuming the weight WZ give it in discriminating between the rival 'public interest' and 'excuses' metatheories. Rather, it is the *type* of arguments or theories appearing in the literature which provides evidence in support of the 'excuses' meta-theory. The 'public interest' metatheory requires the emergence of arguments and theories which explain or predict the impact of different practices on various components of the public, so as to enable regulators to prescribe those practices which coincide with a given concept of the 'public interest'. The 'excuses' metatheory requires the emergence of prescriptive arguments or theories which are tendentious rationalizations of existing or proposed practices, available to be used as "ammunition" by interest groups or as "defenses" by beleaguered regulators (another interest group). At least until recently, it is certainly arguable that the bulk of the prescriptive arguments and theories offered as the literature has belonged to the latter category. (For example, the concept of "service potential" provides a post-hoc ratio-nalization of certain kinds of interperiod cost allocation. As such, it is poten-tially helpful to regulators in framing and defending accounting standards on such matters as fixed asset depreciation, and to the accounting profession as a whole in defending arbitrary practices adopted for pragmatic reasons). This suggests a possible reformulation of the WZ theory, mentioned fur-ther below.

P.291, 294 and 299. By "we do not observe" WZ are (obviously, I would have thought) referring to observers of accounting phenomena in general, not merely to themselves. Your comments therefore miss the point. Have *you* observed the phenomena whose occurrence they are denying?

B and C

I consider that WZ are, in various places, imprecise and tendentious in their use of the word 'cause' and in their imputation of causality. (Nor do I consider their reply to your comments satisfactory on this point) But I find your discussion of the conceptual problems of causation unilluminating. Actually, I thought that ever since Hume (1730) 'aroused' Kant from his dogmatic slumbers', scholars had been rather wary of defining "cause". Does one not rather follow J. S. Mill (1843) and speak of necessary or sufficient conditions? Perhaps one could say that a conjunction of all those conditions which a given theory states to be necessary for the occurrence of a given event may add up to a sufficient condition which "causes" that event according to the theory. In that case, where all the necessary conditions obtain except one, then the occurrence of that one condition may be said to "trigger" the event. The word "cause" is often loosely used to mean "trigger" in this sense.

WZ are presumably arguing that the passage of the Securities Acts *triggered* the emergence of certain arguments or theories in the accounting literature. You are right in saying that they fail to mention other conditions which were contemporaneous and might have jointly provided a sufficient condition for the emergence of that literature *without* the Securities Acts. In other words, concern for the workings of the Stock Market and the protection and information of investors might have motivated *both* the Securities Acts *and* the shift in emphasis in the literature.

To argue this is not to refute WZ's theory but to call for a partial reformulation of it: Accounting is a pragmatic discipline in which "theories" have been used to tidy up and/or to justify particular practical responses to perceived problems and, of course, to help conceptualize those problems. As such, accounting "theories" may be used by regulators, regulatees or any other interested party. *There is a market for that kind of "theory"*, in spite of (or, perhaps, because of) its epistemologically dubious character. This partial reformulation concerns the 'demand' side of the market for accounting theories. I return to the 'supply side' below.

D
Your criticism of WZ's method has some validity but misses the essential point, viz. did WZ genuinely look for counterexamples to their theory so as to refine it (i.e. what Lakatos calls the "negative heuristic of a research program")? For it is hardly an achievement to find *some* events in the past which *agree* with their theory (i.e. that their theory 'retrodicts'). These issues also concern section A of your 'general comments'.

II. GENERAL COMMENTS

A
The counterexamples which WZ cite are the work of Ripley and Hoxsey. These are counterexamples to the 'supply' side aspect of their theory: sup-

ply of these bits of theory was clearly not *triggered* by the passage of the Securities Acts. How they deal with these counterexamples is, as you suggest, a crucial issue in appraising the robustness of their thinking. They defend their theory by arguing that, of the authors in question, Hoxsey is "not an accounting theorist but an employee of the New York Stock Exchange", while Ripley "is also not representative of the financial literature in the 1920's". That is, they try to deny these pieces of literature the status of 'bits of theory'. This is a pretty inept defense, especially given the loose definition of theory which, as you rightly point out, they are using. However, its ineptitude doesn't entail the invalidity of their theory, they have merely neglected an opportunity for refining it.

One possible refinement is the one already proposed above: it is the *type* of theories or arguments appearing in the literature, rather than the *timing* of their appearance with respect to some allegedly critical event, which supports the 'excuses' metatheory.

Of course, the 'excuses' metatheory requires that there be some practical response to a perceived problem—a response for which the argument or theory appearing in the literature provides a justification. But there is nothing necessarily wrong in the theory appearing *before* the response is translated into an actual regulatory decision, *provided* the theory exhibits the characteristic of being a tendentious rationalization. It would not be surprising to see a few examples of such theorizing appearing during the gestation period of the Securities Acts.

This reformulation may take care of the Hoxsey and Ripley counterexamples as well as those relating to the CASB. However, it doesn't deal with a further counter-example cited by yourselves, namely that depreciation of fixed assets had been thought of, and to a limited extent practised, long before the regulatory and taxation issues of the nineteenth and twentieth centuries forced accountants to seek to refine their ideas on "matching expenses and revenue."

Consideration of the depreciation counterexample mentioned in Section E of your "General Comments" indicates that WZ's account of the 'supply side' of the market for accounting theories requires further refinement. Accounting theories may either be produced for immediate application as rationalizations (demand-led production) or they may be produced autonomously, as the result of scholarly endeavor, in which case they will enter the inventory of available but currently undemanded rationalizations (supply-led production). However, the socioeconomic rewards for supply-led production are rather meager, hence the rarity of accounting theories from this source. Finally, it is possible that rationalizations originally produced in response to pedagogic demand may later serve as ammunition or as defenses in the regulatory arena.

The WZ metatheory would thus be reformulated, so as to provide explanations for the original production of accounting theories, as well as for the subsequent reemergence of certain of these theories after periods of neglect. It would also predict (and 'retrodict") that the emergence or reemergence of prescriptive theories in the accounting literature would be triggered by debates among accountants concerning major pragmatic issues of the kind which prescriptive theories attempt to address. These debates might in turn have been triggered by regulatory action or might be in anticipation of possible regulatory action.

B

For the reasons just given, your argument based on the literature preceding and following the formation of the CASB does not "strongly refute" WZ theory. Probably, the opposite is true, given the possible refinements of the theory mentioned above. That WZ have failed to make any such refinements is a fair criticism of their methodology. Moreover, they duck this issue in their reply.

C, D and E

How can one prove or disprove an empirical theory? Your comments under this section betray a failure to distinguish between theory structures consisting of analytical propositions, such as the theories of mathematics and formal logic, and empirical theory structures. See Lakatos (1970, 1971) for an illuminating account of what happens to empirical theories when counterexamples are encountered.

Again, the fact that depreciation was an old idea even in the nineteenth century does not refute WZ. Their theory (as reformulated) does not demand that 'excuses' be *new;* only that they be either "produced" or "taken out of inventory" when pragmatic considerations demand.

Finally, I don't think that the fact that WZ use the word "theory" to mean either "theory" or "argument" is particularly significant in the context.

Conclusion

I think you have both failed to grasp the Lakatosian "hard core" of the WZ theory and misunderstood the issues of methodology involved in empirical theory construction. Consequently I find much of the content of your comments ineffective as criticism of WZ and undeserving of publication. I would suggest that you rewrite your comments confining them to pointing out the counterexamples (perhaps you can find a few more) as well as WZ's failure, in their original paper, to do anything constructive with those of which they showed awareness.

Reviewer Report on 'Some Comments on Logical Reasoning and "The Market for Excuses"'

[Reviewer #as2]

GENERAL COMMENTS

As a reviewer, I am caught in a dilemma regarding this manuscript. I sympathize with the authors' sentiments and I feel that a rigorous Comment on the WZ paper is warranted. However, I also feel that this manuscript does not do a good job either in raising all the points that should be raised or in expressing those points which it does discuss. The manuscript considers two aspects of the WZ paper: the logic of its construction and the precision of its presentation. With respect to the latter, the authors' points should have been brought up and rectified in the original review process. Much of their editorial criticism is correct, but it really doesn't contribute to the state of accounting knowledge [see point 2 below]. With respect to the discussion of logic, the authors take a very convoluted route to discuss a straightforward issue, the testing of hypotheses. I have attempted to restate and compress their arguments in point I below. I think that the essence of their argument can be stated in two or three pages, not the ten which are consumed here. Finally, I think that the manuscript adopts an unnecessary and counterproductive manner of expression which attacks the original authors' intelligence and integrity.

SPECIFIC COMMENTS

1. Logical Fallacies
The authors (hereafter referred to as XY) describe four logical fallacies, each with a catchy title and each taking one or two typed pages to describe. I think that fallacies A, B, and D are really the same issue, and could be more clearly and precisely discussed by considering the formal logic of hypothesis testing. The argument hinges on how one "proves" a theory, and what it means for WZ to present evidence "consistent with" their theory. Logical conjectures are presented in the form:

$$\text{if A, then B.} \qquad (1)$$

The equivalent contrapositive statement is:

if not B, then not A.   (2)

Researchers usually state their conjectures in form (1), but test them in form (2). For example, consider an information content study of earnings announcements. The researcher conjectures that earnings releases cause changes in stock prices by changing investor beliefs. However, he constructs a *null hypothesis* of the form:

if earnings contain no information, then stock prices will not change.

if   A   , then B.

The researcher then examines stock prices, and if they *do* change at earnings announcements, he infers:

stock prices changed, therefore I reject "earnings contain no information"

if not B   , then not A.

The researcher refers to his findings as *consistent with* the hypothesis that earnings releases do cause stock price changes, because this is one (of perhaps many) alternative hypotheses to the rejected null.

Note that finding B itself is inconclusive; the theory says that A implies B, but says nothing about whether other conditions also may imply, even in A's absence. In reading the WZ paper and XY comment, it seems to me that the WZ hypothesis could be stated as:

if accounting theories are excuses, then accounting theories will appear after regulations.

if A   , then B.

XY argue that locating instances of B (accounting theories following regulations) does not prove that condition A holds. This argument is logically correct.

Note that there are other ways to pursue the question; consider these two:

if accounting theories are in the public interest, then accounting theories will precede regulation.

if C   , then D   (3)

if accounting theories are excuses, then accounting theories will not precede regulation.

if E   , then F   (4)

XY's quote of Littleton [p. 18], is cited as a case of D (which cannot prove C) and "not F" (which can disprove E). Without belaboring things further, these two examples illustrate the key dispute; WZ's detection of theories following regulations doesn't "prove" anything because *it doesn't disprove anything*. Research proceeds by lining up all the potential hypotheses, conducting experiments which can *disprove* each, and knocking down the losers until only one is left standing; it is the "not B" and "not F" outcomes which teach us something.

The authors' final sentence in the section [p. 8] hints at this understanding. "Choosing phenomena consistent with a theory does not allow a researcher to later prove his theory by saying that it is consistent with the observed phenomena." However, it shouldn't take eight pages to reach this statement. Since the authors want to discuss logic, they should discuss it rigorously and tersely. Pages 2 through 10 (8, 9 and the top of 10 really continue the "logic debate") hint at the fundamental issue, but fail to state it clearly. As an aside, fallacy 3 is exceedingly vague, and the authors offer no help in separating causes from conditions at the empirical level.

2. Drifting Theory Definition and Lack of Precision

XY criticize WZ for apparent shifts in the meaning of the term "theory', and WZ reply that their own definition is precisely stated in footnote 1. XY go to great lengths in this criticism (a tabulation of occurrences of the word "theory") and expand the criticism to include other terms, again with a table While I sympathize with XY's sentiments, these issues should have been cleared up in the review process for the original paper. There is a marked distinction between a Comment which contributes to the store of theoretical or empirical knowledge and editorial suggestions aimed at improving the exposition of a paper. The latter, while important in the running of a Journal, do not merit publication to the entire readership. Note that I am not saying that XY are incorrect, but only that the bulk of this section is not proper material for the Comment section of the Review. A brief two-paragraph discussion [like the first half of the first paragraph in this section and the closing paragraph would suffice.

3. General Tone of the Comment and the Reply

Writing published comments on the work of others is a touchy business. I will admit to occasionally skimming through the Comment section of the Review to see who is cutting up whom and how deftly they can turn the knife. However, clever phrases which impugn either an author's intelligence or his integrity only invite a reply in kind, to the mutual embarrassment of all involved. Allow me to pull some quotations out of context:

Argument From Ignorance
Lack of diligence on their part
WZ exhibit little caution
the narrow scope of their theory
their confession of guilt
they purge fan article] from the accounting literature
Such variations confuse the writers
Any thoughtful researcher can prove
The WZ theory is another exercise in obfuscation and ambiguity
they just neglect to define (factors) for us
authors' avoidance of the rigors of logical reasoning

It is apparent that XY are pretty worked up about the WZ paper, as are many other academic accountants. Nevertheless, a carefully reasoned Comment which makes its points concisely and in an emotionally neutral tone will accomplish the same intellectual goals. I fear that the current manuscript will generate much more heat than light.

APRIL 23, 1981

Professor Germain Boer
Owen Graduate School of Management
Vanderbilt University
Nashville. TN 37203
Dear Cermain:

Some Comments on Logical Reasoning, and "The Market for Excuses"

On the basis of comments received from the reviewers, I have decided not to accept your manuscript for publication in the *Review*. I am enclosing the reviewers' comments. The reviewers are labeled 1 and 2 so that you can link the marked manuscripts with the comments shown separately.

Reviewer 1 wavered between recommending revision or rejection, and Reviewer 2 recommended rejection. It is evident from both of the reviewers' reports that a very substantial revision would be necessary, and it is not contemplated that revisions of such pervasive character be undertaken while a manuscript is under active editorial review. As you will observe, the reviewers would have you go in different directions, and I hope you will use their extensive comments in order to decide whether you might like to entertain a substantial revision and eventually submit a manuscript afresh to this journal. The submission fee would apply, and I would retain the reviewer whose suggestion you were to adopt. A new reviewer would be added. But it is quite clear that there are too many problems with this proposed Comment to recommend a coherent revision at this stage.

If you do resubmit the Comment, it will be necessary, as before, to obtain the written reaction of Watts and Zimmerman.

I might add that Reviewer I informs me that, in his view, the logic parts could be done in a maximum of five pages. Reviewer 2, by contrast, would have you concentrate instead on counterexamples. Both of the reviewers are particularly competent on research method.

Thanks for sending your paper to the *Review,* and I regret that the outcome was not favorable.

Sincerely

S. A. Zeff

Owen Graduate School of Management
Vanderbilt University
Nashville
Tennessee 37203

Mr. Stephen A Zeff
Jesse H. Jones Graduate School of Administration
Rice University P.O. 1892
Houston,
Texas 77001

Dear Steve:

Owen Moseley and I have studied the reviewers' comments and have decided to ask you for a third review before we undertake any major revision.
We make this request because Reviewer 1 seems to have such a strong bias
in favor of the Watts and Zimmerman paper that we feel he was unable to
give an objective review of our paper. The Reviewer seems to feel that WZ
have developed a theory. If an individual believes this, he must reject most
of our criticisms because we say they have not developed a theory. Evidence
of Reviewer 1's belief in a WZ theory arises in the four occasions (see
circled numbers) that he says reformulation of the WZ "theory" could easily
accommodate our objections, and his final comment says we have failed to
grasp the "hard core" of the WZ theory.

Furthermore, his second paragraph illustrates one of our criticisms about
the imprecise language in the paper; the Reviewer explains what WZ meant
by the word "we". The reviewer then proceeds to commit the fallacy of
argument from ignorance by asking if we (Boer and Moseley) have observed
the phenomena WZ say they have not observed. Such a comment seems to
indicate that the Reviewer is so strongly committed to the WZ theory that
he is willing to commit one of the same fallacies they commit.

This reviewer provides additional examples where he defends the WZ
theory. For example, his comments in the paragraph labeled "D" on page 2
implies that because WZ did not genuinely look for counter examples to
their theory we cannot criticize them for not looking for such examples. At
the top of page 3 the reviewer says that ineptness on the part of WZ in
excluding literature that contradicts their theory does not invalidate their
theory but merely provides an opportunity for them to refine their theory.
On this same page the reviewer explains away our depreciation criticism as
simply an indication of the need for further refinement of the WZ theory.

The Reviewer's comments about depreciation on page four of his review seem confused. We say depreciation is mentioned before the nineteenth century and WZ says it is not. The Reviewer seems to think we are saying something quite different.

Reviewer 2 seemed more interested in the content of our comment than in defending or criticising WZ. However, his comments attribute more credit to our creativity than we deserve. He assumes we created the titles for the logical fallacies when in fact Argument from Ignorance comes from Searles, *Logic and Scientific Method: An Introductory Course,* and Fallacy of the Declarative Question was coined by Fischer in *Historians' Fallacies.* The other two are discussed in many introductory logic books. Also, this Reviewer seems to think that the "Argument from Ignorance" implies something about the intellectual ability of WZ, but this fallacy makes no such assertion.

This Reviewer wants the logical fallacy section condensed, and it could be done. Since any logical fallacy involves the violation of some rule of logic one could simply present the relevant logic rules and then say WZ did not follow them. However, we were using the approach Fischer used in his book (we enclose a few pages for you) which involves some discussion of the specific fallacy. Since most of *The Accounting Review* readers are not logicians, we felt they would appreciate some discussion of the logical fallacy instead of a technical discussion of logic rules.

We recognize that as an editor you must exercise judgement in deciding what to publish, and we respect your judgement. In our case we would ask you to consider getting another review before we undertake another major revision of this paper.

Sincerely,

Germain Boer
Professor of Management

OCTOBER 14, 1981

Mr. Stephen A. Zeff, Editor
The Accounting Review
Jesse H. Jones Graduate School of Admin.
Rice University
P.O. Box 189,
Houston, Texas 77001

Dear Steve:

Enclosed is a copy of our revised comment on the Watts-Zimmerman paper. As soon as we receive their response, we will formally resubmit the paper for publication. We have worked hard to change the tone of the paper, and I think the present version has far fewer barbs than the previous one.

Hopefully, we can submit this one to you soon.

Sincerely,

Germain Boer
Professor of Management

OCTOBER 14, 1981

Professor Jerold L. Zimmerman
The Graduate School of Management
University of Rochester
Rochester, New York 14627

Dear Professor Zimmerman:

Enclosed is a revised version of our comment on your paper. The reviewers of the original paper suggested substantial changes, and Steve Zeff wanted us to get your response to this revised version before sending the paper to his reviewers again.

We would appreciate receiving your response, so we can start the review process again.

Sincerely,

Germain Boer
Professor of Management

OCTOBER 20, 1981

Rochester, New York 14627

Professor Germain Boer
Owen Graduate School of Management
Vanderbilt University
Nashville, TN 37203

Dear Professor Boer:

Thank you for your letter of October 14, 1981 and a copy of the revised
Boer and Moseley paper. Since the revised version of your comments are
not substantially different from the first version, we do not want to delay
the *Review's* consideration of your manuscript by revising our comments.
Most of our initial reactions continue to apply and hence it does not seem
worthwhile now to make minor modifications to our initial reply. We will
make changes in our reply when we see the final version of your comments.
But, we suspect that most of our revisions will be to align our remarks with
your final comments (e.g., eliminate sections that you have eliminated, etc.).
    Thank you for giving us the opportunity to see the revisions.

Sincerely,

Ross L. Watts
Jerold L. Zimmerman
Associate Professors

Mr Stephen A Zeff, Editor
The Accounting Review
Jesse H. Jones Graduate School of Admin
Rice University
P O Box 1892
Houston, Texas 77001

Dear Steve

Enclosed is our revised comment on the Watts-Zimmerman paper along with their letter responding to this version. As you can see from their letter, they plan to reduce their response to fit the scope of this version.

I look forward to hearing how your reviewers react to this version.

Sincerely,

Germain Boer
Professor of Management

The Scientific Method and "The Market for Excuses": Some Comments

The paper on "The Demand for and Supply of Accounting Theories: The Market for Excuses" by Ross L. Watts and Jerold L. Zimmerman (hereafter referred to as WZ) contains some interesting concepts that are intuitively appealing to accounting researchers.* Their thoughts on how accounting theories develop raise many issues and questions of importance to accounting scholars. Unfortunately, however, the authors appear by their frequent references to "the supporting empirical evidence" and other suggestive language to have chosen to present their material as if it constitutes new theory, or something very close to that. Theories usually evolve from hypotheses which are tested by many researchers over time until enough evidence accumulates to allow researchers to say a theory has evolved.

Viewed either as a theory or as a verified hypothesis, the WZ thesis must of course rest on the method of science. Regrettably, however, the WZ discourse as presented fails the normal methodological tests. The purpose of this note is to identify the central fallacies and other methodological shortcomings of the WZ paper. In identifying these fallacies we have relied heavily on historical research methodology because WZ use a historical approach to gather evidence in support of their position.

However, their failure to acknowledge this reliance on historical methods leaves readers of their paper with no information about the alternative philosophies of how historical evidence can be used to support hypotheses. Such an omission may leave the reader with the impression that WZ are using a generally accepted methodology when in fact there is some debate among philosophers and historians on just how to use historical evidence. Some authors, such as Popper [1957] and Hempel [1942], argue that historical explanation is analogous to explanation in the natural sciences. Advocates of this viewpoint attempt to make deductive inferences, to predict and to provide causal explanations. They seek general laws of explanation for historical events.

On the other hand, there are philosophers and historians (for example, Collingwood, [1965], Dray, [1957], and Hexter, [1971]) who argue that science and history are so different that attempting to apply the methods of science to historical research is both questionable and fruitless. Members of this school of thought would reject the WZ approach because they would argue the WZ methodology is simply an inappropriate use of historical information. We do not intend to argue one position or the other. Nevertheless,

---

*Ross L. Watts and Jerold L. Zimmerman "The Demand for and Supply of Accounting Theories: The Market for Excuses," *The Accounting Review* (April, 1979) pp 273–305.

even if we accept their general approach, we can still identify a number of fallacies and methodological errors in their paper.

We have organized our comments into two categories: fallacies, and general comments.

I. FALLACIES

A. Fallacy Number 1: Argument from Presumptive Proof

Researchers commit this fallacy whenever they attempt to place the burden of disproof on the reader, and then argue that the reader's inability to disprove the assertion is itself evidence of the assertion. WZ commit this fallacy at least five times in their paper as the following quotations indicate:

Page	Statement
288	In that case, neither the public interest theory not our theory could explain the accounting literature. In essence we would be left without a theory of the literature. However, those who would argue such a scenario must then produce another explanation for, or theory of, the accounting literature.
291	We do not observe depreciation being treated as an expense prior to this century.
291	Yet, we do not observe any real concern with depreciation expense until the nineteenth century.
294	We do not observe the same concern in the U.S. at that time.
299	We do not observe this theory being generally advanced in the accounting literature prior to the Securities Acts.

In the first quotation WZ seem to suggest that the inability of researchers to develop alternative theories provides evidence to support their own. The fact that we cannot come up with an alternative theory adds no support whatsoever to their theory; it reflects our inability to develop an alternative theory—nothing more and nothing less. Their lack of observation of concern about depreciation until the nineteenth century, likewise, tells us nothing about accountants' concern with depreciation prior to the nineteenth century; it may merely reflect the fact that such concerns were not written about extensively prior to this time. The same criticism applies to the last two quotes. An author who states he has not observed something provides little information about the existence of these unobserved events. The author who describes in detail his search process, his sources, and the many different strategies he followed in seeking out the object he was unable to observe does provide his reader with some evidence of the nonexistence of these event. However, a simple statement that one has not observed the occurrence of an event provides no evidence to the reader for the nonexistence of an event. Not finding an issue discussed is quite different from finding that the issue was not discussed.

B. Fallacy Number 2: Post Hoc Ergo Propter Hoc

This fallacy is based on the false assumption that because two events stand in temporal succession they are therefore related. For example, WZ argue that passage of tax laws stimulated the depreciation discussions in both the U.K. and the U.S. because in both instances passage of tax laws preceded the appearance of the debates. Their assertion may be correct, but merely pointing out that the passage of tax laws preceded extended discussions of depreciation in both countries in no way shows that these laws caused the accounting interest in depreciation. The same is true of their comment that "The tax allowance of the depreciation deduction (1878) precedes the 1880s debates."

Their discussion of events surrounding the formation of the Securities and Exchange Commission provides another example of the *post hoc* fallacy. The authors in this discussion divide accounting literature into that published before passage of the Securities Acts and that published after the Securities Acts. They then attribute changes in the accounting literature to passage of the act. However, it may be just as plausible to argue that the social and economic events that gave rise to the Securities Acts also gave rise to the accounting literature, causing changes in this literature that lasted some time. If this were the case (and we are not arguing for this position) a review of the sequence of events could give one the impression that the Securities Acts caused the change in the literature.

In both the instances cited here WZ could have easily strengthened their arguments if they had looked at the comments of accountants contemporaneous with the passage of the laws. These comments might have supported the WZ position. Or, WZ could have looked at alternative explanations present in the social and economic forces of the time when the tax laws or securities laws were passed. For example, the securities laws were passed in the depths of the Great Depression, a period marked by thousands of company failures, numerous embezzlements of company funds, and severely depressed stock prices.

Such events may have had some impact on the accounting literature. The recent impact of the Equity Funding scandal on the accounting profession would seem to indicate that episodes of such behavior, as there were at the time the Securities Acts were passed, would also impact the accounting literature. For instance, the embezzlement at the Union Industrial Bank of

Business failures and admissions to prisons throughout the U.S. for embezzlement and fraud were as follows for 1929 to 1934:

Year	Business Failures*	Admission for Embezzlement & Fraud**
1929	22,909	1,391
1930	26,355	1,420
1931	28,285	1,503
1932	31,822	2,196
1933	19,859	2,048
1934	12,091	2,032

Sources:
*Historical Statistics of the United States: Colonial times to 1970, Bureau of the Census, U.S. Department of Commerce, U.S. Govt. Printing Office, 1975.

**Taken from the annual issues for the period 1929–1934 of Prisoners in State and Federal Prisons and Reformatories, Published by the Bureau of the Census, U.S. Department of Commerce.

Flint, Michigan, in 1929 has many parallels with the modern Equity Funding case [Galbraith, 1961, p. 139], and it may have influenced the thinking of accountants at the time of its discovery. The WZ omission of the fact that the Great Depression might have influenced the accounting literature is a serious one since this event alone, which happened to coincide with passage of the securities laws, may completely account for the changes in the accounting literature that WZ attribute to the passage of the securities laws. Unfortunately the WZ selection of an isolated event which precedes the literature changes of interest to them causes them to fall into the post hoc trap.

C. Fallacy Number 3: Confusion of Condition and Cause

Scholars define "cause" as some specific event which brings about another event called the effect. Conditions, on the other hand, are the set of related circumstances under which the cause-effect relation takes place. The cause produces the effect, whereas the condition provides the opportunity for the operation of the cause. The fallacy arises when a researcher confuses condition and cause or regards them as identical. For example, an economist who argues that economic prosperity in the United States is due to its democratic form of government may be overlooking the fact that the form of government merely provides the conditions for prosperity. Researchers who seek out the causes of past events face a particularly tough job of separating causes and conditions for they have to deal with a variety of causes, and trying to identify any one of them as the most important or key cause is a troublesome problem. Researchers who review past events can never examine all variables, and the nature of their research prevents them from ever concluding they have found the cause of an event. They can only assess the relative importance of the various factors on the event in question.

However, WZ choose specific factors and treat them as if they are *the* cause of an event. Consider this statement: "The timing of the depreciation debates in the U.K. also appears to confirm our hypothesis that political action caused the observed change in accounting theory." Maybe the political action was a condition instead of a cause, or maybe it plus some other factors influenced the event. Again, they say "The hypothesis that the dominance of the information objective was caused by the Securities Acts." An even stronger statement appears later where WZ say "Further, the justification caused the SEC to demand such theories." This statement would be hard to support even if the authors had presented evidence, but they cite none. WZ restrict their consideration of past events so severely that no elements such as economic conditions, social factors, or political forces can play a role in their hypothesis even if these were the predominant causes influencing the effects they are studying. WZ exclude all possible causal factors except those that fit the narrow scope of their hypothesis. They assume that all causation moves from government legislation to accounting theory development, and they mention no other possible causes.

D. Fallacy Number 4: Fallacy of the Declarative Question
This fallacy consists of the use of a declarative statement about what will be found in past events. It violates a fundamental rule that says questions should have an open end that allows the researcher a choice of alternative explanations for what he finds. A researcher who approaches the study of historical events with a simple affirmative proposition that "X was the case" is predisposed to prove it. He will usually find evidence to illustrate his expectations, if not to actually sustain them. If instead the researcher asks,

> "Was X or Y the case?" then he has an empirical advantage. And if he asks "Was X or not-X, Y or not-Y, Z or not-Z . . . the case?" and if he designs X, and Y, and Z in such a way that his own preferences are neutralized, and if he leaves the way open to refinements in the form of X_1, Y_1, Z_1, and if he allows for still other unexpected possibilities, then the probability of empirical accuracy is still further enhanced. [Fischer, 1970, p. 24].

By stating what they expected to find in past events and then finding events that support these expectations, WZ do not present evidence to support their hypothesis. They merely show examples of events that are consistent with their expectations. However, WZ did not unknowingly commit this fallacy; they did it openly. They admit their awareness of this problem, but they seem to lose their awareness when they write later pages. For example, after mentioning this problem in the early pages of the paper, they later make comments such as:

> The timing of the depreciation debates in the U.K. also appears to confirm our hypotheses. . . .

> The hypothesis that the dominance of the information objective was caused by the Securities Acts is supported not only by. . . .

> . . . . the only accounting theory that will provide a set of predictions consistent with observed phenomena is one based on self interest.

The first two statements are consistent with an open ended question that looks at all possible events—but this is not what WZ did. They stated what they wanted to find and reported instances that supported their hypothesis. The finding and presenting of these cases causes no problems; it is the WZ assumption that these events provide sufficient evidence for them to make the kinds of statements mentioned above that is the problem. Admitting that one has used a fallacious approach to looking at a problem does not make the approach correct, and it does not make valid the invalid results. Finally, the third statement is inconsistent with an earlier one: "Our objective is merely to present prima facie support for the hypothesis that accounting theory has changed *after* the introduction of government regulation." Selectively choosing only those phenomena that support a hypothesis does not enable a researcher to later use these same phenomena as evidence for the hypothesis.

II. GENERAL COMMENTS

A. Posner's Methods Versus the WZ Method

In justifying their ex post case study approach to looking at evidence to support their hypothesis, WZ cite a work by Posner [Posner, 1974] as an example of how this approach has been successfully used. It will be worthwhile to look at Posner's approach in some detail since WZ cite it as support for their methodology.

Posner looked at two theories of government regulation of the economy: the public interest theory and the interest group theory. His approach to looking at these theories differs significantly from the WZ method of looking at facts to support their hypothesis. At the outset Posner states clearly that he favors the economists version of the interest group theory: "I shall argue that the economists version is the most promising, but shall also point out the significant weaknesses in both the theory and the empirical research that is alleged to support the theory." [Posner, 1974, p. 36]. Compare this statement with the WZ description of what they plan to do in their empirical work: "Our objective is merely to present prima facie support for the hypothesis that accounting theory has changed *after* the introduction of government regulation." Notice how Posner considers evidence both for and against the theory he prefers, but WZ include only supporting evidence.

In reviewing the public interest theory of government regulation, Posner studied case studies and other empirical work that contradict the original assumptions of this theory. He then gives a reformulation of the public interest theory that has been offered in response to the criticisms of this empirical work, and goes on to show that this reformulation still does not adequately account for the empirical research findings. Posner's approach in attacking the public interest theory consisted of a literature review which identified cases that contradicted the theory (actually, he went far beyond a simple review of the literature and presented analytical arguments as well as the empirical data). Compare this approach to WZ. They did not gather evidence to contradict a theory, they gathered instances to support a theory. Gathering evidence to disprove what is generally accepted requires only a few clear cases contrary to the generally accepted idea, but to build a new theory requires more than a few cases confirming the theory. Posner's use of case studies in attacking the public interest theory does not provide adequate rationale for the WZ approach.

Nor does the way he uses case studies in looking at the economic version of the interest group theory. Since Posner states at the outset that he favors this theory, we would expect him to cite case studies that support the theory, which he does. He cites numerous cases of regulation that are explained by the economic theory in areas such as public utilities, common carriers, and airlines. However, Posner devotes four pages to a discussion of the shortcomings of this evidence.

Clearly, then, Posner looked at cases that supported the theory he preferred, but he did not uncritically accept them. He analyzes weaknesses in the evidence, points out difficulties in using the evidence to support the theory, and admits that serious questions remain. WZ offer little criticism of their evidence. In fact, at one point they appear to exclude the October, 1930, issue of the *Journal of Accountancy* from the accounting literature because it contained an article of a theory they said was not generally observed until after the Securities Acts of 1933–34. They justify this position by pointing out that the author of the article " . . . is not an accounting theorist; instead he is an employee of the New York Stock Exchange."

If this Posner paper is supposed to provide support for the WZ method of choosing events to support their proposed theory, it does so in a strange way. Posner used case studies, WZ used case studies, and there the resemblance ends. Posner cites and discusses at length cases that do not support the theory he prefers; WZ include cases that support their hypothesis or that support theories they reject. Any evidence contrary to their hypothesis receives no attention. We are puzzled by this reference to Posner; his paper provides no support whatsoever to the WZ method, his statements and conclusions are far more cautious than those of WZ, and he offers alternative explanations of events that do not match his preferred theory.

B. The Lack of a Theory Definition

Because the WZ paper deals with the demand for and the supply of accounting theories it does not seem unreasonable that they would provide a carefully structured definition of accounting theory so readers could see what WZ mean by this term. But their definition appears in a footnote on the first page where they define theory " . . . as a generic term for the existing accounting literature." Presumably "existing accounting literature" is meant to include all periodicals and books dealing with the subject of accounting. Yet two pages later they note that a diversity of interests prevents general agreement on accounting theory. Why should there be general agreement on the "existing accounting literature?" Surely WZ must be using some other definition. The one they may have had in mind is one used by Hendriksen in his book on *Accounting Theory:*

> . . . accounting theory may be defined as logical reasoning in the form of a set of broad principles that (1) provide a general frame of reference by which accounting practices can be evaluated and (2) guide the development of new practices and procedures. [Hendriksen, 1977, page I]

We don't know of course whether this is the definition intended by WZ, but it does seem to fit the context in which the term was used on page 275 of their paper.

Still another possible definition appears later in a statement about auditors: "Auditors would value information in the form of theories predicting how agency costs vary with accounting procedures." The apparent definition of theory here hinges upon its predictive ability, a characteristic not evident in earlier uses of the term. WZ add a fourth dimension to the term "accounting theory" when they seem to expand it to include the notion of justification or excuse. Because of the apparently differing definitions of "accounting theory," we found it difficult to follow their discourse. As a means of highlighting his definitional problem we prepared the following frequency distribution of the apparent definitions intended by WZ. We imputed the definition to the term from the context in which the term was used. Obviously our frequency distribution is not perfect, but it does seem to indicate that the definition of accounting theory varied from point to point throughout the paper.

Theory	Frequency
A	23
B	3
C	2
D	24
E	29

Key to theories

A. Definition similar to that of Hendriksen

B. Definition based on quantity of literature

C. Definition based on predictive power

D. Definition of theory as excuse or justification

E. Does not fit any of the above categories

Such variations in definition are confusing by themselves, and occasionally they seem to produce unusual results. Consider the paragraph beginning in the middle of the left column on page 283. The authors begin the paragraph using a definition of theory based on its predictive power. They argue that bureaucrats will use the theories that predict best "(i.e., the 'best' theories)" and that these theories will tend to predominate. In the last sentence of the same paragraph WZ cite several references which they claim are based on the premise that the best theories prevail. However, the term theory used in this last sentence appears to be one similar to that offered by Hendriksen. Arguing that the theories that best predict are the ones that predominate is different from saying that the theories that best provide a general frame of reference by which accounting practice can be evaluated [Hendriksen, 1977, page 1] will predominate. These are two different kinds of theories, yet WZ seem to treat them as identical.

Researchers can support, contradict or remain neutral on the WZ theory just by choosing the appropriate accounting theory definition. If the quantity of literature definition is used, we can cite a clear contrary example to their thesis by showing that approximately 23 accounting publications appeared in the two years prior to the formation of the Cost Accounting Standards Board, and approximately 28 appeared in the five years following its formation. This contradicts what they say we should find. However, if we use any of the other definitions of theory, we can say nothing about their hypothesis.

In the case of Medicare legislation we can show different results. In this case no accounting publications were listed in the *Accountants Index* prior to the enactment of Medicare legislation, but the *Accountants Index* shows 112 references alone in the 1967–68 edition approximately two years after the legislation became effective. Using theory definition B we support the WZ hypothesis, but any other theory definition leads to the opposite conclusion that Medicare legislation had no impact on accounting theory. Such vagueness of definition prevents researchers from making rigorous tests of the WZ theory.

C. Depreciation: Unobserved and Observed

As we noted in the beginning of our paper, the WZ inability to observe depreciation being treated as an expense prior to the nineteenth century provides little evidence for its omission from accounting records. Some references in the accounting literature indicate it was used far back in history. For example, Littleton states that:

> Depreciation was an old idea even in the nineteenth century. In his text of 1588, John Mellis credits "Implements of householde" account for the amount judged to be "consumed and worn", and debits "profit and loss" account for the same amount, "lost by decay of householde stuff." [Littleton, p. 83]

Littleton adds: 'The preferred theory and method of today are both very similar. As to theory, the consensus is that depreciation is a periodic expense. That was the idea in . . . examples from the sixteenth and seventeenth centuries." [Littleton, p. 83]

These comments by Littleton seem to indicate that the notion of depreciation as an expense has been in existence far longer than WZ suggest. Perry Mason in a 1933 article in *The Accounting Review* [Mason, 1933] gives three cases of depreciation recognition, one from the seventeenth and two from the eighteenth centuries. He also comments:

> If the records were available for inspection, one would expect to find evidence of some understanding of the phenomena of depreciation as far back in history as the origin of written records of business affairs. [Mason, 1933, p. 209]

These two citations do indicate that the depreciation concept and the recording of depreciation in the accounting records existed long before the nineteenth century even though WZ state ". . . we do not observe depreciation being treated as an expense prior to this century." The Littleton reference clearly suggests the idea existed as early as 1588 and the Mason article gives a specific case showing its recognition in the accounts in 1675.

III. CONCLUDING REMARKS

It might be argued that the first time a hypothesis is presented we should expect some problems in interpreting it because it is new, and we can accept this position. However, much of the imprecision in this paper seems to stem from the authors' avoidance of generally accepted standards of scientific research. There is nothing about the newness of a hypothesis that permits its author to avoid definitions of the key elements e.g., accounting theory, classical accounting literature. Nor does the newness of a hypothesis permit its authors to selectively choose only supportive evidence and then conclude that such evidence is sufficient to establish its truth. And newness provides no excuse for careless reasoning. It is regrettable that the WZ paper has so many flaws because it does deal with interesting issues of potential value to accounting researchers.

References

Collingwood, Robin G., *Essays in the Philosophy of History* (University of Texas Press, 1965).

Dray, William H., *Laws and Explanations in History* (Oxford University Press, 1957).

Fischer, David Hackett, *Historians' Fallacies: Toward a Logic of Historical Thought* (Harper & Row, Publishers, 1970).

Galbraith, John Kenneth, *The Great Crash,* 1929 (Houghton Mifflin Company, 1961).

Hempel, Carl G., "The Function of General Laws in History," *The Journal of Philosophy* (January, 1942), pp. 35–48.

Hendriksen, Eldon S., *Accounting Theory* (Richard D. Irwin, Inc., 1977).

Hexter, J. H., *The History Primer* (Basic Books, Inc., 1971).

Littleton, A. C., *Essays on Accountancy* (University of Illinois Press, 1961).

Mason, Perry, "Illustrations of the Early Treatment of Depreciation" *The Accounting Review* (September, 1933), pp. 209–218.

Popper, Karl R. *The Poverty of Historicism* (Beacon Press, 1957).

Posner, Richard A. "Theories of Economic Regulation," *Bell Journal of Economics and Management Science* (Autumn, 1974), pp. 335–358.

Watts, Ross L., and Jerold L. Zimmerman, "The Demand for and the Supply of Accounting Theories: The Market for Excuses," *The Accounting Review* (April, 1979), pp. 273–305.

Section I of *Reply to Boer and Moseley*
The Nature of Scientific Methodology

R. WATTS & J. ZIMMERMAN

In our article we explicitly stated what we consider a theory: a set of "principles advanced to explain a set of phenomena, in particular" . . . "sets of hypotheses which have been confirmed" (p. 273, fn. 1). That is a definition which is conventional in economics (e.g., Friedman, 1953, Part i) and in the physical sciences (e.g., Popper, 1959, p. 59). The objective of a theory is "to explain phenomena"; to predict phenomena not yet observed (see Friedman, 1953, p. 7). Phenomena "not yet observed" does not mean future phenomena, it Includes phenomena which occurred in the past, but on which you have not yet collected evidence. Explaining means predicting. The goal of science Is to produce theories which predict (see Braithwaite, 1953, p. 1; Poincare, 1952, Chapter 1, and Popper, 1959, Chapter III).

Logic plays a role in developing theories. Theories are based on assumptions and logic is used to derive propositions. However, given the logic of the theory is correctly developed, logic does not determine whether a theory is supported by the scientific community or not. Acceptance depends on the extent to which the empirical propositions (predictions) of the 'theory are consistent with observed phenomena (see Toulmin, 1953, p. 12; Friedman, 1953, p. 8; Popper, 1959, p. 109).

By their very nature theories are caricatures of reality. Assumptions are made which it is expected will capture the essence of the phenomena which is to be explained. As a consequence, theories typically do not explain all of the phenomena of Interest. This is true in the physical sciences as well as the social sciences. For example, current theories of physics cannot fully explain the existence of black holes. Further, the abstraction of theories also causes their predictions to not exactly fit the observed phenomena even in the physical sciences (see Toulmin, 1953, pp. 70–73).

In developing and testing theories scientists do not look at all the facts and come up with a general model. Such a procedure is logically impossible. In order to make a general statement, we have to ignore some of the facts particular to some observatIons. As Indicated above it is ThIs abstraction which leads to the Inability of the theory to explaIn, to perfectly fit, all observations.

Instead of looking at the facts (i.e., all the phenomena), scientists develop theories, make predictions and then look at the facts. The theories tell them which facts to look at. As Popper (1959, p. 59) puts it "Theories are nets cast to catch what we call 'the world': to rationalize, to explain, and to master It." Theories tell us what facts are relevant and what are not; where to fish. We have a classic example of this in physics. In investigating the structure of matter, physicists predicted the existence of quarks and then successfully looked for them.

A theory is tested by developing hypotheses and then comparing those hypotheses to the evidence. This usually involves many observations. If the observations are consistent with the hypothesis the hypothesis is confirmed. *Confirmation does not prove the hypothesis or the theory correct.* As Friedman (1953, p. 9) writes "If there is one hypothesis that is consistent with the available evidence, there are always an infinite number that are." A theory comes to be accepted after its hypotheses have withstood substantial empirical testing (see Popper, 1959, p. 109), i.e., have been confirmed in strong and numerous empirical tests.

In the fight for acceptance, a theory is almost always in competition with other theories. As Popper (1959, p. 108) writes, "We choose the theory which best holds its own in competition with other theories; the one which, by natural selection proves itself the fittest to survive." Competing theories are important in testing a hypothesis if no competing theories have been advanced we have no way of deciding what variables to control other than those indicated by the theory being tested (as indicated above there are an Infinite number of alternative possibilities). In that case no control other than that suggested by the theory being tested would be necessary. However, if competing theories exist, we use situations where the competing theories give us different predictions to test the theories.

It is important to note that scientists do *not* worry about the infinite number of estimated possible alternative explanations. They only concern themselves with theories which have been advanced and are sufficiently specified to be capable of explaining the phenomena of interest. The reason for this is apparent. Facts can only be organized and interpreted with the aid of a theory.

Because a theory's hypotheses are general propositions, those hypotheses are not rejected on the basis is of isolated observations which contradict a given hypothesis. As Popper (1959, p. 86) writes, "a few stray basic statements (observations) contradicting a theory will hardly induce us to reject it as falsified." Indeed, once a theory is accepted even contradictory observations which are reproducible will not lead to the theory's rejection if an alternative theory which explains more phenomena is not available. Newtonian physics is a superb example of this. Numerous systematic anomalies to Newtonian physics were observed before Einstein advanced his theories, but Newtonian physics was not rejected. In effect you stay with the "best" explanation until a "better" one is advanced (see Kuhn, 1970 for a discussion of the way In whIch one theory replaces another).

From the above it should be apparent that the test of a theory is not a simple matter of logic. For example, it should be clear that a theory is not rejected because of one contradictory observation.

Professor Germain Boer
Owen Graduate School of Management
Vanderbilt University
Nashville, TN 37203

Dear Germain:

The Scientific Method and "The Market for Excuses": Some Comments (2086)

As the reviewers of your manuscript are at odds, I am seeking further advice. I expect to be writing you again in four to five weeks.

Sincerely,

Stephen Zeff

Professor Germain Boer
Owen Graduate School of Management
Vanderbilt University
Nashville, TN 37203

Dear Germain:

The Scientific Method and "The Market for Excuses": Some Comments

On the basis of comments received from the reviewers, I have decided not
to accept your manuscript for publication in the *Review*. I am enclosing the
reviewers' comments. The reviewers are labeled 1, 2, and 3 so that you can
link the marked manuscript with the comments shown separately.

As you know, the initial two reviewers divided. Reviewer 1 recommended
rejection, while Reviewer 2 was favorably inclined toward the manuscript. I
obtained the reaction of Reviewer 2 to the comments of Reviewer 1, and I
thereupon sought the counsel of an editorial adviser. He may be an Associate Editor, Editorial Consultant, or another respected researcher. He is sent
the manuscript and reviewers' reports, all anonymously save for Associate
Editors. (He was also sent the reaction of Reviewer 2.) The editorial adviser
in this instance, Reviewer 3, recommends rejection, and I am accepting
his advice.

None of the three reviewers of 2086 was involved with 1942. As your
manuscript has been rejected in two versions, it is no longer eligible for
consideration by this journal.

Thanks for sending your paper to the *Review,* and I regret that the outcome was not favorable.

Sincerely,

S. A. Zeff

Comments on: "The Scientific Method and 'The Market for Excuses': Some Comments"

[Reviewer #1]

This comment attempts to raise a number of questions regarding the quasi-theoretical arguments and empirical evidence presented by Watts and Zimmerman (1979). As Watts and Zimmerman note in their reply, many of the issues raised in this comment appear to result from a fundamental confusion over the "scientific method" (broadly defined) and an unfamiliarity with the philosophy of science literature. As a consequence, the authors' remarks frequently obscure important definitional distinctions, raise tangential and peripheral issues, and lack the rigor and precision necessary for substantive clarification of Watts and Zimmerman.

The majority of the comments contained in this paper fall into one of two categories: *criticisms* which attempt to expose errors in Watts and Zimmerman reasoning or methods; and *extensions* aimed at suggesting how Watts and Zimmerman might have improved their theory and/or evidence. For example, the authors *criticize* Watts and Zimmerman by suggesting that Watts and Zimmerman are guilty of a logical fallacy ("Argument from Presumptive Proof"—paragraphs 6 & 7) and then proceed to argue that Watts and Zimmerman should have *extended* their theory by invoking (unspecified) socioeconomic factors to explain both regulation and the accounting literature. While some of the criticisms raised in this comment may indeed be valid, the arguments presented are generally opaque and unconvincing. At a minimum, the authors need to sharpen their own thinking on these points and to formulate cogent and rigorous arguments to buttress their criticisms. The suggested extensions, on the other hand, require more than improved clarity and precision in exposition. If these comments are to be relegated to a position above simple conjecture and hand-waving, they need to be formulated as rival theories and subjected to empirical refutation (e.g., see comments on paragraphs 8–10 below). Mere polemics are insufficient.

The following remarks summarize my chief concerns. Additional remarks are contained in the manuscript.

Para 1: Two points are bothersome here. First, by confusing *theory construction* (development) with theory *verification* and *acceptance,* the authors' paint an exaggerated picture of the role and importance of empirical evidence in Watts and Zimmerman's efforts. Secondly, the authors express a naive view of scientific progress—one which is in direct opposition to that outlined by major writers in the area (e.g. Kuhn). On the surface, these two points would seem to be of minimal importance since they could easily be corrected through careful editing of the manuscript. However, they are symptomatic of a fundamental unfamiliarity with scientific methods and the philosophy of science literature.

Para 2: The purpose of this "Comment" needs to be clarified. Do the authors intend to challenge the *arguments* Watts and Zimmerman invoke in deriving hypotheses and testable implications, the *inferences* Watts and Zimmerman draw from the data, or the data collection *methods* employed by Watts and Zimmerman? In other words, do the authors contend that Watts and Zimmerman are guilty of deductive and/or inductive "fallacies" (errors in reasoning) or poor empirical methods?

Para 3–4: This discussion of the "historical research methodology" is not germane to the paper, particularly the remarks contained in paragraph 4.

Para 6–7: "Argument from Presumptive Proof"—It is unclear in what sense Watts and Zimmerman have committed this fallacy. Several possible interpretations of the authors' remarks come to mind: (i) "presumptive proof" is the *only* form of empirical support Watts and Zimmerman marshall for their hypotheses; (ii) any theory which predicts that phenomenon X should *not* be observed is subject to this fallacy; or (iii) Watts and Zimmerman were remiss in not fully describing their data collection efforts (e.g. sentences 5 & 6 of paragraph 7). Although other interpretations are possible, of these three only the latter has any merit in the context of the Watts and Zimmerman paper.

Carefully reading of Watts and Zimmerman indicates that their hypotheses or testable implications typically exhibit the following general form:

> Since event E occurred at time t we *should not* observe X in periods prior to t and *should* observe X in periods following t.

Obviously, empirical evidence which runs counter to *either* prediction is evidence inconsistent with the hypothesis. Moreover, empirical evidence consistent with both predictions (including the inability to observe X in periods preceding t) is evidence which supports the hypothesis. There is no "fallacy" here, except perhaps in the sense implied by interpretation (iii), and if Watts and Zimmerman data collection efforts are indeed suspect then it is incumbent upon the authors to seek out the appropriate evidence rather than to merely speculate about the adequacy of Watts and Zimmerman's observations.

With regard to the Watts and Zimmerman quote in paragraph 6, the authors' remarks (sentences 1 & 2 of paragraph 7) suggest a fundamental confusion over the role of contradictory evidence in theory discrimination. Given two rival theories which purport to explain the same phenomenon X with reference to a set of observations A, the theory whose predictions are most frequently in accordance with the available evidence (data set A) is typically judged the better of the two. If the predictions of both theories fail to be supported by a *second* set of observations (data set B), this disconfirming evidence merely indicates that neither theory is complete. Disconfirming evidence of this sort does not provide a sufficient basis for choosing between the two theories under consideration, or for rejecting either theory. Obviously, what is needed in this scenario is a "new" theory whose predictions are consistent with all of the available evidence (data sets A and B). This seems to be the thrust of Watts and Zimmerman's original remarks.

Finally, the third sentence of paragraph 7 illustrates the authors' confusion over the nature of the phenomenon Watts and Zimmerman's theory seeks to explain. Note that the focus of Watts and Zimmerman is the *accounting literature* (an observable) and not "accountants' concern" (an unobservable).

Para 8–10: "Post Hoc Ergo Propter Hoc." The first two paragraphs raise the possibility that socioeconomic events coincident with the adoption of the regulations cited by Watts and Zimmerman may have been responsible for *both* the legislation and the emergence of particular streams of accounting literature. Teasing out direct causality in the presence of coincident events is obviously a difficult task, and the authors' conjectures here may indeed be valid. However, if this argument is to have substantive import the authors need to identify particular socioeconomic factors coincident with the adoption of specific regulations, and to conduct a *critical* experiment which pits the predictions of their socioeconomic "theory" against those of Watts and Zimmerman "regulation" theory. In the absence of a well articulated set of socioeconomic factors and a critical experiment, this discussion amounts to little more than speculation and hand-waving.

Watts and Zimmerman present a theory of the effects of regulation on the accounting literature. No attempt is made to isolate the particular sociological, political, or economic forces which may have been responsible for these regulations and consequently Watts and Zimmerman did not attempt to discriminate between regulatory and socioeconomic "causes" of the accounting literature. Nor should they be castigated for this omission.

Para 11–13: "Confusion of Condition and Cause." The point of this discussion seems to be that Watts and Zimmerman are (in the authors' opinion) guilty of attributing causality to "conditioning" (moderating) factors rather that to "*the* cause" of particular streams of accounting literature. The distinction between conditioning variables and causal variables in this context is specious. The authors provide no criteria for classifying a particular variable as "conditioning" or "cause", nor do they outline how one would test propositions of the sort identified in paragraph 12 ". . . political action was a condition instead of a cause . . ."

In the concluding sentence of this discussion the authors criticize Watts and Zimmerman because "(t)hey assume that all causation moves from government legislation to accounting theory developments, and they mention no other possible causes." *This is not a criticism at all!* It merely indicates that Watts and Zimmerman have attempted to formulate reasonably tight "theoretical" statements about the impact of regulation on the accounting literature and have appropriately restricted the domain of possible explanations of the phenomenon under study (the accounting literature) by limiting their hypotheses to regulation.

Para 14–15: "Declarative Question." The essence of this discussion seems to be that Watts and Zimmerman are guilty of articulating explicit hypotheses about what should (and should not) be observed in past events. It is apparently the opinion of the authors that explicit hypotheses "violate a fundamental rule that says questions should have an open end that allows the researcher a choice of alternative explanations for what he finds." In other words, hypotheses should either be avoided completely or stated in a vague and ambiguous fashion. This viewpoint is in such sharp contrast to the accepted methods of empirical science that further comment is unnecessary.

Para 16–21: "Posner's Method." As Watts and Zimmerman were careful to point out in their reply to an earlier version of this paper, the authors have misconstrued the extent to which Watts and Zimmerman rely upon Posner. Posner is not cited as a justification for the empirical methods used in Watts and Zimmerman, nor is such justification necessary. In short, the issues raised in this discussion have little direct bearing on the Watts and Zimmerman paper.

"Theory definition": The essence of this discussion seems to be that Watts and Zimmerman were remiss in not providing a clear indication of the phenomena addressed in their paper. Does the theory seek to explain particular pieces of accounting literature, trends or streams in the literature, accounting practice, or what? There is indeed some ambiguity and imprecision in Watts and Zimmerman's writing on this point. However, the authors' comments amount to overkill.

Para 6–27: "Depreciation." Given that the Watts and Zimmerman paper addresses the effects of regulation on the emergence of "streams" of accounting literature, it is irrelevant whether conventional depreciation methods were used by practising accountants prior to the nineteenth century since accounting practice is not the phenomenon of interest. Moreover, the existence of minor discrepancies between a theory's predictions and observations (an occasional paper on depreciation, for example) is generally insufficient to warrant rejection of the theory which attempts to explain *trends* or streams in the literature.

"COMMENTS" ARTICLE

1. There were several lines of criticism which I expected to find in the "Comments" article but did not:

a. The Fallacy of the Single Cause.
The WZ theory implicitly assumes that diversity of interests is the *only* factor preventing general agreement on accounting theory:

"We argue that it is this diversity of interests which prevents general agreement on accounting theory"

The implication is that if the personal interests of the various parties to the financial reporting process were not diverse, then agreement would be obtained. This would be true only if the problem were *solely* political. Corporate financial reporting attempts to represent a multi-dimensional reality in one-dimensional terms, and one who attempts to do such a thing is immediately faced with substantive philosophical problems which *are not themselves political*. In fact, isn't it the intractability of these *substantive* problems which allows the political process to have the wide play it has? To hypothesize that accounting theory simply responds to the demand for excuses ignores the very substantive problems confronting an *unbiased* attempt at wealth and income measurement. There is no logical principle from which one can infer that the cause of a surge in the accounting literature on a particular topic at any point in time is the same as the cause of our inability to get agreement on accounting principles. This distinction eludes WZ.

b. The Fallacy of One-Directional Tests.
WZ choose certain political events (SEC legislation, etc.), and then examine the accounting literature around them. They do not, however, choose certain accounting theory "events," e.g., the appearance of the efficient markets literature in accounting, the launching of a conceptual framework study, etc., and then look for the political or legislative event which spawned them. To borrow from auditing terminology when choosing (3) topics for investigation, WZ traced from the legisla-

tion to the literature, but not from the literature to the legislation. *If true, the self-interest hypothesis must stand under both directions of test. A one directional test is not adequate to support the thesis.* Due to the paucity of discussion on methodology, we do not know why the test was made in only one direction. *Of course, the tests in the other direction (from the literature to legislation) are more likely to uncover non-confirming evidence,* if there is any; hence, the failure to use such makes the results suspect.

c. There are standards-setters who have the task of determining what the accounting rules shall be. Don't they provide some of the demand for justifications? If the standard-setters are independent, how is their demand explained by "self interest" (in the sense "self-interest" is used in the article)?

2. It appears that the charge in Reply that the Littleton quotes were taken out of context by the Comments authors has merit. While that could be remedied by a rewrite, I would favor omitting Section "C. Depreciation: Unobserved and Observed." In my opinion, nothing of great substance would be lost by this deletion.

"REPLY" ARTICLE

1. The basic tone of the reply is "our article is an example of standard empirical research methodology and the authors of 'Comments' Just don't understand empirical research." I find the repeated references to the "lack of knowledge" of the Comments authors to be objectionable. A tasteful reply *shows* whether or not there is a lack of knowledge without asserting (and re-asserting) that there is.

2. At a more fundamental level, I find Section "I. The Nature of Scientific Methodology" to misrepresent the theory-building process and to lack directness in replying to the "Comments" paper.

First, there is the out-of-context reference to Fn 1. True, WZ explicitly stated what they considered to be a theory in Fn 1, but *(and they do not quote this part of Fn 1),* they then backed away from that definition, indicating that another definition would be used for the duration of the paper. What is the relevance of the citations in Reply (to Friedman and Popper) which show that the *rejected* definition was correct after all? I believe most of our readers interpreted Fn 1 as the authors of Comments did. Fn 1 should not be referred to out of context on page 1 of the Reply.

3. ". . . theories typically do not explain all of the phenomena of interest"

"In developing and testing theories scientists do not look at all the facts and come up with a general model"

While these statements are true, they do not provide justification for WZ's methodology (which is the point at issue). Obviously scientists can't look at *all* the facts before developing theories. This does not mean that they are free to use research designs which have little power to elicit nonconfirming evidence (c.f. 1b of my comments on "Comments"). Although, as WZ note, a theory can't explain everything, obvious incompleteness of the explanation for that portion of the phenomena covered by the theory (c.f. 1a above) and an abundance of counterexamples to the theory are taken *very seriously* by scientists. If someone criticizes methodology, the observations that no scientist starts with all the facts and all theories are incomplete are not valid defenses. The Comments paper, in my opinion, does not imply that scientists start with all the facts or that all theories are complete.

4. ". . . *our* theory tells us where to look for the evidence"
    Here again, WZ confuse "theory" with "research design." While a theory specifies the topic and hypotheses to be researched, it does *not* prescribe a research design. A theory, of course, identifies the phenomena of interest, but it doesn't tell the researcher *how* to look. The authors of Comments are critical of the manner of looking for evidence. "Our theory told us" is an invalid response to that criticism.

5. "Our situation is analogous to the physicists who predicted quarks and then went and looked for them"
    First, let's review what "our situation" (per the above quotation) is. WZ say "In our case, there is no literature on a theory of the accounting litera-ture," and on p. 9 they indicate they didn't have to control for other theories because there were none.
    The earliest physicists didn't predict quarks in their first attempt at theory building! This prediction came only as the result of a process of theorizing and testing which spanned hundreds of years. Eventually physics developed to the point where the existence of quarks could be derived as a *theorem* of physics. Quarks were the product of an abundant literature. They would not have been predicted otherwise.
    If it is true that there was no theory of the field at the time the "Excuses" paper was started, then there would seem to be little analogy to the case of testing a theorem from one of the most highly developed sciences. My real objection to the quarks analogy is not that it is wrong but that it is irrelevant to this section of the paper. The discussion of quarks appears under "Fallacy

of the Declarative Question" which is a fallacy *in the manner of posing questions* for investigation. The fact the physicists knew of quarks before testing is neither proof nor disproof that WZ formulated their questions in an optimum manner.

6. "Since no other theory of the literature had been advanced, strictly we had nothing to control"
  There are two types of controls in research design:

1. controls designed to assure that a hypothesis is posed in such a way that its test will distinguish between two competing theories.
2. controls mandated by the logic of experimental design (i.e., controls designed to assure that it is in fact the stated hypothesis which is being tested and not something else.)

As I understand Comments, the criticism is directed primarily to controls of the nature of 2) above. As I interpret Reply, the discussion is directed primarily to controls of type 1). This causes Comments and Reply to miss each other.

7. *Summary*
  The above is not a complete commentary on "Reply." It is intended only to show the basis for my opinion that Reply does not address the Comments paper directly enough. My suggestions would be:

1. To omit the general section on "The Nature of Scientific Methodology."
2. To rewrite the remainder, giving direct, succinct replies to the major points in Comments.

REVIEWER #2'S COMMENTS ON THE REVIEW OF REVIEWER #1

Reviews #1 and #2 were certainly at opposite poles. After consideration of review #1, I find myself in disagreement with its major points.
  Reviewer #1's style of criticism is to suggest that certain distinctions are very important, and then to argue that the authors of Comments overlooked those distinctions. In many cases, the distinctions the reviewer makes are not crucial distinctions in the context of the Comments paper he is criticizing.
  For example, take the distinction between *criticisms* and *extensions* (par. #2 of review #1). It is not accurate to characterize "Comments" as arguing for an extension of WZ's *theory*—it argues only for refinements (you may call this "extensions") to their *methodology*. Reviewer #1 even suggests that

criticisms of methodology are "hand-waving" unless they can "be formulated as rival theories and subjected to empirical formulation." I would
observe that many drama critics have never written a play. When the reviewer suggests that critics of methodology have an obligation to propose a
rival theory, he sets an unrealistic standard for criticism. The issue—which
is addressed in Comments—is whether WZ is methodologically sound, not
whether an alternative theory is better.

The distinction between theory *construction* and theory *verification*
which reviewer #1 makes also is a distinction which leads nowhere. The
reviewer *alleges* that the Comments authors exaggerate the importance of
empirical evidence in theory construction, but he gives us no hint as to the
reasons for this judgement. As I mentioned in my review, scientists take
known instances of non-confirmation very seriously *at the theory-building
stage.*

Actually, I find all the references to "theory" in these contexts out of
place. WZ have not put forth a "theory": they've put forth an hypothesis
and have pointed to some informal evidence which they believe supports it.
One hypothesis, however well documented, does not constitute a theory.

In making a distinction among *arguments, inferences,* and *methods,* the
reviewer questions whether the Comments authors are criticizing WZ's reasoning or WZ's empirical methods. I thought this point was clear in the
Comments manuscript—they're criticizing the reasoning by which the empirical methods were chosen. Empirical methods have to be justified on an
a priori basis. Had reviewer III taken the Comments piece as a piece of
criticism rather than as an *alternative theory,* this would have been clear.

To reviewer #1 W & Z have "appropriately restricted the domain of
possible explanations of the phenomenon under study." This would be true
only if WZ's topic was "the effects of regulation on the accounting literature." But that is not their topic. Their topic is a theory of the *determinants*
(plural) of the accounting literature. Since WZ defined their topic in that
way, I cannot agree with reviewer #1 that the exclusive focus on regulatory
matters means WZ have "appropriately restricted the domain of possible
explanations."

Review of "The Scientific Method and 'The Market for Excuses': Some Comments"

[Reviewer #3]

I have studied Ms. 2086, the reply thereto by Watts and Zimmerman, the comments of both reviewers, and Reviewer #2 comments on the review of Reviewer #1. It is my judgment that the manuscript simply misses the mark and is not worthy of publication. The comments of Reviewer #1 are comprehensive and incisive. I have not seen a better review of a manuscript. I find I have but a few observations to add:

1. Contrary to the judgment of Reviewer #2, I find the distinction which Reviewer #1 makes between theory *construction* and theory *verification* noteworthy. The authors of the manuscript are clearly concerned with the latter, yet Watts and Zimmerman explicitly state that their goal is the former: "Our objective in this paper is to begin building a theory of the determinants of accounting theory."

2. "Post Hoc Ergo Propter Hoc"—The following remark from Campbell and Stanley's *Experimental and Quasi-Experimental Designs for Research* is appropriate.

"The 'validity' of the experiment becomes one of the relative credibility of rival theories: the theory that X had an effect—versus the theories of causation involving the uncontrolled factors. If several sets of differences can all be explained by the single hypothesis that X has an effect, while several separate uncontrolled-variable effects must be hypothesized for each observed difference, then the effect of X becomes the most tenable." Watts and Zimmerman have formulated a single theory consistent with many observations. The authors have not. They merely mention "social and economic" events as rival hypotheses.

3. While Reviewer #2 has made some interesting remarks, they are applicable to the Watts and Zimmerman paper, not to the manuscript under review. It is apparent that this reviewer does not like the Watts and Zimmerman paper. This is not sufficient justification for publication of the manuscript. It's apparent, however, that Reviewer #2 could write an interesting comment on the Watts and Zimmerman paper. I encourage him to do so.

4. Reviewer #2 accuses Watts and Zimmerman of confusing "'theory' with 'research design' A theory doesn't tell the researcher *how* to look". It is Reviewer #2 who is confused. Watts and Zimmerman state ". . . *our* theory

tells us where to look for the evidence." Telling someone *where* to look is not the same as telling him *how* to look.

5. While I agree with the basic substance of the Watts and Zimmerman reply, I am appalled by remarks such as:

> "this claimed fallacy indicates another defect in their knowledge of empirical methodology . . ."

> "Part of [the authors'] problem is again their lack of understanding of empirical methodology . . ."

> "We didn't spell this out because we assumed that most readers understood empirical methodology. Perhaps we should have devoted some more space to these methodological issues."

> "The Littleton quotes provided by [the authors] shows how little care they put into reading our paper or their own source."

Not content with insulting only the authors of the comments, they then insult the readership of the *Accounting Review:*

> "it is apparent that [the authors'] criticisms suffer from a lack of knowledge of the methodology of science. It is regrettable that we did not anticipate that this may be a problem among the readers of the *Accounting Review.*"

What is regrettable here is that two people who consider themselves scientists should resort to insult and condescension because someone disagrees with them.

EPISTEMIC CRITIQUE 2

Editors' Introduction: Traditional epistemic concerns also dominate Lowe, Puxty and Laughlin's (LPL's) critique of the Excuses Theory. However, in contrast to the other critiques, historical (and mildly sociological) challenges also enter the fray. Thus they question whether Watts and Zimmerman's Excuses thesis "explains" British experience, and give greater play to historical inconsistencies in the Excuses theory. Once again, however, it is the intellectual tradition of this particular academy (in this case, the British branch) which dictates the nature of the challenge; we do not find much of the more radical critiques (see, for instance, Tinker, Merino, and Neimark, 1982) where history and sociology are used to investigate the origins of accounting thought, and elucidate its own politics of production.

THE WATTS AND ZIMMERMAN THESIS: THE MARKET FOR MYOPIA

E. A. LOWE, A. G. PUXTY, AND R. C. LAUGHLIN*

In a recent paper (Watts and Zimmerman, 1979) it was suggested that standard-setting is the result solely of a political process in which parties make representations based upon their needs with respect to wealth transfer; that they use accounting theories only to bolster their arguments, and not because of any genuine convictions regarding their validity: and that accounting theorists can therefore have no direct influence upon standard-setting, but because of the structure of the reward system in higher education, find themselves (albeit unwittingly) only following the political process rather than initiating thought. Such conclusions, if true, are evidently of crucial significance for the accounting theorist: because Watts and Zimmerman conclude that "not only is there no generally accepted accounting theory to justify accounting standards, there will never be one."

In order to demonstrate that the paper's conclusions do not hold it is necessary to demonstrate either that the evidence for its hypothesis is unsatisfactory, in which case the hypothesis remains just that, and no longer substantiated theory; or that the hypothesis itself is based upon faulty reasoning. Either will destroy the credibility of the conclusions. In this comment both will be demonstrated. First the credibility of the hypothesis design will be questioned. Then the evidence proposed will be examined and its relevance to the hypothesis challenged. Third we suggest that their conclusions, far from being obvious, lack clarity. Finally, a particular case is exam-

*Division of Economic Studies, University of Sheffield, Sheffield, England. The authors wish to acknowledge the helpful comments of Anthony Hopwood, John Arnold, Len Skerrett, Tony Tinker and anonymous referees, as well as those of Professors Watts and Zimmerman, on earlier drafts of this paper, which was presented at the 1980 Annual Conference of the Association of University Teachers in Accounting and greatly benefitted from the comments by participants.

TABLE 1

Step	The General Model	Watts and Zimmerman's Application of the General Model
1	Certain assumptions are made.	It is assumed that the economic model, dealing in demand and supply functions, is appropriate.
2	On the basis of these assumptions a logical progression of propositions is created which results in a testable hypothesis.	Using this economic framework the expected nature of the demand for and supply of accounting theories is analysed and conclusions reached concerning the likely juxtaposition of political processes and accounting theories.
3	The hypothesis is tested to see if it accords with observed facts.	Three case studies are given in which it is suggested that the predicted events occurred in the expected sequence.
4	If it does then the theory is not rejected.	Therefore the theory is considered upheld.

ined, that of the inflation accounting debate, to demonstrate that there is strong evidence against the theory.

The Theoretical Framework

Watts and Zimmerman approach their theory by the use of the hypothetico-deductive method. The structure of this method, and the way in which it is applied by them is set out in Table 1.

In this section it will be suggested that (a) their proposal to use an economic framework is unjustified and hence casts doubt upon the rest of the deductive process; (b) that the only possible justification of this, the positivist approach exemplified by the work of Friedman, is open to dispute; (c) that, even temporarily accepting the validity of their framework, they make unscientific proposals concerning the nature of proof; and (d) that such a framework, as used in the natural sciences, is of doubtful validity in the social sciences.

ECONOMIC FRAMEWORK

The introduction to the WZ framework is to be found on page 274. After giving detail of some earlier suggestions by other authors they continue:

> Our contribution to Zeff's and Horngren's ideas is to give them more structure so that we can make additional predictions about accounting theory. The source of that structure is economics. We view accounting theory as an economic good and examine the nature of the demand for and the supply of that good.

They use an economic framework to explain a political process but they do not justify this. Yet the use of a framework from outside a particular discipline needs justification. If a physicist were considering a proposition concerning subatomic particles, he would be expected to use the framework of physics, which has been shown in the past to be the appropriate one for reaching valid conclusions. To use any other framework would require justification. Watts and Zimmerman are purporting to explain a political process: yet the framework they use is not one from political science but one from economics. It may be valid: but its validity a priori needs to be discussed and justified. It cannot be sufficient to state that such a framework will be used without such a justification.

This is important because the selection of a framework is restrictive. Once a framework has been chosen, explanations which appear in other frameworks are excluded from consideration. If, therefore, two different frameworks explain the same phenomena (and they well might) then by selecting one of them and ignoring any other there will be no basis for judgement between the two: no basis for deciding which is better in terms of its explanatory power.

POSITIVIST APPROACH

The only justification which appears plausible for the choice of an economic framework lies in the Friedmanite positivist approach which dominates economic theory, under which the validity of prior propositions in a theory is of little importance, the validity of the theory being judged by its predictive power alone. This was put succinctly by Friedman in the following passage:

> Truly important and significant hypotheses will be found to have 'assumptions that are wildly inaccurate descriptive representa-

tions of reality, and, in general, the more significant the theory, the more unrealistic the assumptions (in this sense) . . . the relevant question to ask about the 'assumptions' of a theory is not whether they are descriptively 'realistic,' for they never are, but whether they are sufficiently good approximations for the purpose in hand. And this question can be answered only by seeing whether the theory works, which means whether it yields sufficiently accurate predictions. (Friedman, 1953, pp. 14–15).

This has been challenged by, among others, Nagel (1963) and Samuelson (1963) as a general proposition. It leaves unanswered the problem of the existence of two theories, both of which yield predictions which are the same, and accord with the apparent facts. Such situations are well-known from the work of Kuhn (1970). This is important in the present context because of the claims made by Watts and Zimmerman: that, because they claim their theory is borne out by the evidence, *therefore* an important conclusion can be reached (that "not only is there no generally accepted accounting theory to justify accounting standards, there will never be one." The authors recognize this situation:

> "Undoubtedly there are alternative theories which can also explain the timing of the accounting literature. The challenge is to those who would support those alternative theories to specify them and show that they are more consistent with the evidence than ours."

Such a proposal however requires a rigorous approach to evidence. It requires that, in principle, a theory presented should be testable. When we turn to Watts and Zimmerman's approach to the verification and refutation of theories, we find that they have failed to set to out their theory in a way which makes testing possible.

PROPOSALS FOR TESTING THE THEORY

The paper uses the approach to proof of the natural sciences. It is therefore appropriate to consider the extent to which, within this approach they themselves have chosen, their "theory" is a true theory. The nature of verifiable or falsifiable theories will first be considered, and then this will be contrasted with the approach in the paper.

The paradigm of natural science requires that the observed facts should accord with the predictions of a theory. If the facts are not in accordance with the theory then, assuming there has been no error in observation, the theory must be discarded and a better theory proposed: that is, an explanation which does predict the observed facts. There cannot be exceptions to a theory. Either it explains observed facts or it does not. According to Popper, a distinction must be made between a scientific and a metaphysical proposition. The demarcation is, he suggests, clear:

> "a system is to be considered as scientific only if it makes assertions which may clash with observations; and a system is, in fact, tested by attempts to produce such clashes, that is to say, by attempts to refute it. Thus testability is the same as refutability, and can therefore likewise be taken as a criterion of demarcation." (Popper, 1972, p. 256).

and

> "Only if a theory successfully withstands the pressure of attempted refutations can we claim that it is confirmed or corroborated by experience." (Ibid.)

It should not be assumed that this proposal is applicable only to deterministic systems: thus we might have the scientific proposition that fair coins will fall with $p = 0.5$ heads and $p = 0.5$ tails, and by testing this can be confirmed or refuted. The process is stochastic: the theory is a theory which is right or wrong concerning that stochastic process.

Upon turning to Watts and Zimmerman's paper the following statement is found:

> "One or two papers discussing a topic prior to the time the topic becomes politically active is not sufficient to reject our theory, just as one or two 'heads' is not sufficient to reject the hypothesis that a given coin is 'fair.' It is important to remember that as in all empirical theories we are concerned with general trends. Our predictions are for the accounting literature in general. . . . There are many interesting phenomena that this theory, at this stage of development, cannot yet explain. But this does not ipso facto destroy the value of the theory."

This statement contains three errors.

The first is that they are comparing the testing of a theory (which by its nature is supposed to have general validity) with the testing of a single instance *given that a certain theory is correct.* In the case of the coin, a "fair coin" is defined as one which will, in the long run, show roughly half heads, half tails: what is being tested is whether the particular coin in question is a member of "the set of fair coins." If the coin fails the test over a long period, this does not invalidate the theory of the behaviour of fair coins since there is no such "theory" but only a definition: it suggests only that the coin being tested is not a fair coin. On the other hand, in the case of the academic process of proposing normative theories, Watts and Zimmerman are considering the testing of a theory itself, in terms of its underlying tendency and its actual manifestation in observable events. They are suggesting that, if the observations do not correspond with the theory (as a general trend—we consider this point below) then the theory itself is rejected, rather than the particular instances under observation. The two cannot be compared: the analogy is false and hence fails as a justification.

The second error concerns the authors' attitude to refutation of their theory. They give no grounds for any critic to present evidence whereby their theory might be refuted. Their hypothesis is not subject to a crucial critical test; they claim that because they are "concerned with general trends" there may be exceptions to their theory. If therefore any evidence is presented to show that, in the case of a given set of facts, their theory was inapplicable, they propose that the evidence cannot invalidate their theory. According to Popper's criterion this means that their suggestion is not a scientific theory, but a metaphysical proposition. There are only two possibilities, therefore. The first is that they do take their proposition to be metaphysical. This is unlikely. The second is that they consider that they are dealing with a stochastic process (the nature of which is unspecified) and that, for example, on most occasions, (in principle quantifiable, say 90% of the time) their theory will hold, but in the other cases (say 10%) it will not. This is inadequate because they could object that any evidence which purported to refute their theory was part of the 10%. They might propose that, after a given number of instances of refutation their theory would be acknowledged to be invalid: but within the framework they give there is no basis for selecting the number of tests which would be acceptable as refuting the theory. Moreover, until the precise nature of the presumed stochastic process were defined by them, this could not be done. They do not define it precisely.

The problem here arises because WZ are proposing a precise theory for a general trend. They do not explain what a "general trend" is. We can only take it to mean a set of conditions which are likely to obtain in most cases under observation. This in itself might refer to two different matters. First, given a particular accounting issue concerning which there is political interest, the extent to which the precise conditions specified by their theory might hold—that is, the complete absence of academic interest before the political issue arises, for example. Support for this view is their statement in the opening lines of the last quotation above. If this is what is intended, then a particular case in which there are not one or two but dozens or even hundreds of publications before the political process commences would seem to disprove their thesis. In Part IV of this paper we give an example of just such a case, that of inflation accounting. Second, the idea of a general trend might be supposed to refer to whole cases as subjects, so that for most issues their hypothesis is true, and the market for excuses is the only process operating, but for other issues the hypothesis has no basis in fact. If this is so then the theory can have no predictive power whatever unless it is extended to explain why the occurrences and nonoccurrences occur. Unlike natural science, it cannot be adequate to ascribe the difference to random factors.

Thus one can go further in objecting to WZ's understanding of the nature of scientific testing. They claim that

> We are not purporting to have a theory that explains the behaviour of all accounting researchers or the acceptance, or lack of acceptance, of every published paper.

Their theory, as already quoted above, concerns general trends. It is quite evident that the authors are envisaging the process as similar to a natural science phenomenon: that there is an underlying trend which will not be observed in any individual instance, but which will come through in aggregate because of properties of the error term such as are assumed in regression analyses (for example, that of zero mean). This is however only an assumption, and it can be rebutted by evidence. In the case concerned the evidence is that the "error term" is not symmetrical about the mean simply because it is not a random variable in the statistical sense. It is, rather, the result of purposive action. Academics have goals; the actions they take will be in accordance with these goals. Hence the WZ proposition would only be acceptable if the general tendency their theory concerns were teleological (which of course it is: they posit academic goals in terms of matters such as self-advancement) and also that variations from these teleological processes were random. But the variations themselves are the results of goal-directed behaviour. Any a priori[1] assumption of a probability distribution is therefore untenable.

The third error in the passage cited is the implication that there is a similarity between the process of intellectual inquiry and the probability density function relating to a natural phenomenon. Intellectual inquiry is the outcome of human needs and human processes: it is most likely to be grounded in the scholar's search for truth which is carried out within the context both of the current debate upon a particular issue (part of which is the political process to which Watts and Zimmerman refer) and also within the context of the continuing growth of academic knowledge. The conditions of such inquiry are therefore not comparable to stochastic processes as exemplified by the coin analogy given.

PROPOSALS IN OTHER SOCIAL SCIENCES

This point is part of the more general point that social sciences are not in all respects the same as natural sciences. They differ both in the way phe-

TABLE 2

Academic Theory	Related Practitioners	Examples of Theories Relevant to Practitioners
Accounting Theory	Standard-setters	Capital asset pricing model; replacement cost accounting
Economic Theory	Government	Economic policy: for example, monetarism vs. neo-Keynesianism
Political and Social Theory	Politicians; pressure groups	Income distribution; individual freedom vs. state intervention
Developmental Psychology	Doctors and teachers	child-rearing and educational practice

nomena arise (through human action rather than natural causal relations) and in the consequent methodology applicable. This raises the problem that the process Watts and Zimmerman are analysing is a political process, which arises because of a posited relationship between intellectual inquiry and human political action. In this case the inquiry is the development of accounting theories, and the political process the setting of accounting standards. Yet this is only one example of the more general case in which the results of the investigations of social scientists might be supposed to have implications for practical action. Examples are given in Table 2.

Relationships Between Theories and Practical Action

According to Watts and Zimmerman, standard-setters do not take notice directly of accounting theories, but only of political protagonists who use the theories as excuses. This makes a statement therefore both about the eventual decision-makers, and the interested parties: that they are concerned with self-interest rather than true belief in principles. If this were generalised to other social sciences, the proposition would be that, for example, political parties which wished to form governments would "hold" beliefs which were in fact never based upon true belief but only upon calculations about likely electoral popularity. Similarly, (for example) the accepted state of education practice would be the result not of consideration of research findings, but of lobbying self-interested pressure groups. If the reader of this paper is to take it seriously therefore he must suspend all his experience of personal human relationships. He must moreover suspend belief in the models of man proposed in the social scientific and philosophical literature over a long period of time. Most models of human action suppose that values and attitudes come before action (cf. Rokeach, 1973). Most models of people allow them various interests and beliefs. They see both good and bad in people and acknowledge that some will be honest, some dishonest. Some will value truth, others will not. But the only motives which WZ allow to the parties in the political process are those of self-interest, of the utilization of Accounting standards to achieve wealth increase. Similarly, the only interest allowed to the academic who writes upon a topic is the self-interest which arises from wishing to enhance his reputation, visibility and status, and thereby attract benefits such as research funds. There is no room in the model for any academic to research an area and publish simply because he feels the subject is inherently interesting. This cannot happen according to the model, because if it did, then writing on a subject would appear before it became politically significant. WZ claim that it does not. Whether WZ's own work, and that which they support (Zimmerman, 1980) is caused by political interests is not clear, It cannot be argued that it is "different" because it is not putting forward a normative theory, because what is at stake is the motivation for research by an academic, not the kind of research he carries out.

But if the problem of self-interest is great for the model of the academic, then it is even greater for the standard-setters themselves. In section II of their paper WZ suggest that all parties in the political process, including the regulators (standard-setters) are rational, but that the regulators will accept a theory on the basis of excuses because of transaction costs: because investigating the validity of the excuses is costly and

> if people do not investigate the validity of theories, it is because they do not expect such investigation to be worthwhile. If the expected benefits of investigation to an individual are small, he will make only a limited investigation.

No doubt this is so, under these conditions. But WZ insist upon the empirical verification of this set of proposals. It is certainly hard to find in the case of the FASB. Long periods of time, a number of permanent staff, and long analytical discussion documents precede the issuance of an exposure draft. If these are "limited" it is difficult to envisage a "full" investigation.

Watts and Zimmerman's Evidence

It is not at all clear whether Watts and Zimmerman intend that theirs is a theory which should apply only to the United States, or is more generally applicable. On the one hand the vast bulk of their examples during their detailed argument is taken in the U.S. context (see, for example, their references on pp. 280–281 alone to antitrust legislation, affirmative action, then S.E.C., the Federal Revenue Acts, the Interstate Commerce Commission, the F.T.C. and the U.S. Congress). The structure of the relationship between the academic profession and political interest groups also appears to be very much a United States phenomenon. Yet on the other hand, when they come to give their evidence, they refer frequently to the United Kingdom in the nineteenth century. It must be assumed therefore that their theory is supposed to hold when certain conditions are fulfilled, wherever they are fulfilled.

But this raises a more difficult and quite extraordinary point in relation to the situations discussed in WZ's evidence and the political/academic structure they describe in their theoretical development earlier. Critical to their discussion of the supply of accounting theories is the set of pressures on the academic accountant.

> The consumers ("vested interests") determine the production of accounting research through the incentives they provide for accounting theorists. The greater the prestige and articulation skills of an accounting researcher, the more likely practitioners, regulators and other academics will know his work and the greater the flow of both students and funds to his university. Researchers have non-pecuniary incentives to be well-known, and this reputation is rewarded by a higher salary and a plenitude of research funds.

And this is developed in a footnote:

> Even though we have argued the existence of close substitutes, all researchers will not be earning the same compensation. Higher compensation will accrue to the most prolific, articulate and creative advocates—to those who are able to establish early property rights in a topic and thus must be cited by later theorists.

and later

> Practitioners (and) regulators are more likely to read or hear of the output of an accounting researcher if it bears on topics of current interest. As a result, the researcher who is motivated by pecuniary and non-pecuniary factors will tend to write on the current controversies in accounting.

It is clear from these passages that the authors envisage a structure in which researchers are employed by universities, since it is the reward structure of universities, rewarding those who become well-known, which determines the incentive of the researcher. Until the end of the nineteenth century there were no accounting researchers in the universities of either the United States or the United Kingdom. The first business school in the former, The Wharton School of Finance and Economy, was not set up until 1881, taught accounting (bookkeeping) first in 1883 on an ad hoc basis, and was not followed by any greater number of universities until after the turn of the century (Allen, 1927; Lockwood, 1938). In the United Kingdom progress was even slower: the first full-time Chair in Accounting was not created until 1948. It is essential to Watts and Zimmerman's hypothesis that such a structure should exist, since the conclusion they reach concerns the actions of accounting theorists. When their evidence is perused the following is found:

ON RAILROAD LEGISLATION:

There is no doubt that the development of railroads both in the US and the UK affected the accounting literature on the nature of depreciation, including the question of charging depreciation as an expense . . .

This literature existed at least by 1841 in the UK . . . and by 1850 in the US."

ON INCOME TAX LEGISLATION AND THE DEPRECIATION LITERATURE:

In that decade (the 1880s) we observe a spate of UK journal articles and textbooks on the question of depreciation for corporations in general."

In two of the three examples given as evidence by WZ, therefore, we find that the conditions they posit for their theory to hold do not in fact exist! Whatever the mechanisms which were acting, therefore, they are not mechanisms which concerned the academic and his needs for recognition through writing on topical subjects in a way which furthered the interests of politically-motivated groups.

The attitude to evidence of the third example given by WZ is no less extraordinary. It is proposed that the shift to the information objective and to the search for accounting principles is the result of a political act: the enactment of the 1933–1934 Securities Acts in the United States. Their treatment of this leads to a number of points.

First, there is once again the problem of culture: is this intended to explain the experience of research in countries other than the United States or not? There is no comparable legislation to the Securities Acts in, say, the United Kingdom: moreover, to claim that there is or is not is rendered difficult if not impossible by the precise definition of a political issue. How can it be defined other than in terms of its consequences: and if this is done, then since the consequences include the literature the argument becomes self-fulfilling. We shall return to this point shortly. U.K. academic research developed at the London School of Economics in the 1940s and 1950s. No similar piece of legislation or other political act seems evident to the writers as possibly explaining this.

Second, there is the definition of a political act just referred to. In Section IV of this paper we present evidence which we suggest shows that the academic literature in the inflation accounting debate preceded the political interest over the issue, but followed a rise in the inflation rate. We accept the latter as causing the interest in the subject. For WZ's thesis to survive this evidence it is therefore necessary to claim that the rise in the inflation rate was itself a political issue (indeed, WZ have claimed just this[2]). To claim this is however to broaden the definition of a political issue beyond that which might normally be expected, and certainly beyond the normal usage of the expression.

Certainly, inflation is a matter of concern to those involved in the political process, and there is no doubt that political action follows from rising rates of inflation. But WZ's theory is a theory of accounting. It is a theory in particular of the relationship between a political debate within the accounting world—such as a standard setting process—and the development of an academic literature which under WZ's conditions might be deemed to be excuses. The excuses can only be excuses for a proposal to be credible. The rise of the inflation rate (for example) cannot be seen in this way. Political proposals follow such a rise. The more general matter which arises from this is that, if any event which is in any way linked to the political process is described as "political" for the purpose of WZ's theory, then it will merely become self-fulfilling. Nobody, and certainly not the present authors, would claim that accounting theories (or any others) spring from nothing more than the creative process of the academic thinker. Their antecedents may be many, including particularly intellectual tradition in a subject. But to attempt to muster all these antecedents under the heading of "political issues" would be to say nothing at all which is new.

The lack of definition of a political issue thus makes their theory highly tendentious. To claim, as they do, that all searches for accounting principles can be seen as the result of the Securities Acts is to dismiss the particular processes which have led to the various schools of thought developing within that search. They claim that their theory is concerned with prediction: but since the rise of any future theory can be described as "part of the search for accounting principles" and hence the result of these Acts the lack of specificity in this claim makes the potential for prediction virtually zero.

The Lack of Clarity in the Resultant Conclusions

The final point concerns the imprecision of the Watts and Zimmerman conclusions and to demonstrate this it is necessary to analyse their final words in full. They are as follows:

> . . . the only accounting theory that will provide a set of predictions that are consistent with observed phenomena is one based on self-interest. No other theory, *no normative theory currently in the accounting literature (e.g. current value theories) can explain or will be used to justify all accounting standards*, because:
>
> 1. accounting standards are justified using the theory (excuse) of the vested interest group which is benefited by the standards;
> 2. vested interest groups use different theories (excuses) for different issues; and
> 3. different vested interest groups prevail on different issues.
>   While a self-interest theory can explain accounting standards, such a theory will not be used to justify accounting standards because self-interest theories are politically unpalatable. As a consequence *not only is there no generally accepted accounting theory to justify accounting standards there will never be one.* (Emphasis in the original.)

This passage is confused because the expression "theory" is used in two different ways. It is used for prescriptive theories for accounting: it is also used for "descriptive" theories of theories—which is what the WZ thesis purports to be. To clarify this, we suggest that a theory of a theory be described as a metatheory. If this is done, however, and one attempts to rewrite the above passage, difficulty arises precisely because of the lack of clarity of thinking in the original. According to WZ, their metatheory explains the accounting standard-setting process. Other theories can only be used to justify particular accounting standards. Evidently the first appearance above of the word theory should read "metatheory." It is not clear how one should read the next two appearances of the term, because the passage is confused as between metatheories which explain agreement processes and theories which prescribe good accounting practice. This can be seen in the juxtaposition of "can explain or will be used to justify." According to them, a metatheory would explain, a theory would "justify" (being an excuse). There is no possibility at all of a "normative theory" being able to explain accounting standards, because that is not the function of normative theory—at least, not as the expression "normative theory" has been used in this paper.

The crux of the paper's argument lies in its final sentence. It will be seen that this sentence is misleading, because it is phrased in terms of "justifying" accounting standards. The idea of justification is one which Watts and Zimmerman have themselves created. Accounting theorists do not create normative theories to justify standards, and it has never been suggested that they do. Some theories may require standards: others my not.

A Counter-Example: The Case of Inflation Accounting

In many ways enough doubts have been cast on the WZ thesis to leave the analysis at this point. Questioning both the structure and evidence of a theory is usually quite enough to dismiss the claims made. However, to reinforce the poverty of their thesis we shall consider how well the WZ model looks when applied to an important area of accounting thought and writing: the inflation accounting debate, particularly in the United Kingdom but also, to an extent, in the United States of America due to the close linkage between the two countries.

Our explanatory model in diagrammatic form is presented in Figures 1 and 2. However, before looking at this in detail it is necessary to discuss two preliminary matters: firstly concerning the claims of this explanatory model and secondly a reminder of Watts and Zimmerman's central conclusions.

On the first point it is important to appreciate both that it is a partial model of accounting reality and a possibly insufficient one according to WZ to refute their claims. It is partial since its application is meant to cover only the inflation accounting debate and not the whole of accounting thought: nor, even for this does it claim necessarily to have captured all the complex variables. This in its own way casts doubt on the WZ thesis since it suggests that the institution of accounting may be much more complex than WZ seem to suggest. In addition the model may be an insufficient basis to refute the claims of WZ for the reasons stated above concerning the absence of a scientific basis on which refutation is possible—the inflation accounting debate could be classified as in the class of the one or two papers! Yet the inflation accounting debate is of considerable importance in accounting thought and the proposed model looks sufficiently different from the diagrammatic presentation of the WZ thesis (Figure 1) to seriously question and doubt the validity of their thesis.

As our second preliminary point it is necessary to restate the central and general claims of the WZ thesis. These are basically twofold and are summarised by WZ in the following two quotes. Firstly:

> The predominant function of accounting theories is now to supply excuses which satisfy the demand created by the political process; consequently accounting theories have become increasingly normative.

In sum this has a timing and motivational aspect to it. Theories are generated after an issue becomes politically active and such theories are created as a bolstering "excuse" for a particular political standpoint on the issue in question.

secondly:

> . . . the only accounting theory that will provide a set of predictions that are consistent with observed phenomena is one based on self-interest. No other theory, no normative theory currently in the accounting literature (e.g., current value theories) can explain or will be used to justify all accounting standards, because:
>
> 1. accounting standards are justified using the theory (excuse) of the vested interest group which is benefited by the standards;
>
> 2. vested interest groups use different theories (excuses) for different issues; and
>
> 3. different vested interest groups prevail on different issues.
>   While a self-interest theory can explain accounting standards, such a theory will not be used to justify accounting standards because self-interest theories are politically unpalatable. As a consequence *not only is there no generally accepted accounting theory to justify accounting standards, there will never be one.*
>   (Emphasis in the original.)

As discussed above this passage is confused because the expression "theory" is used in two different ways. What we can say though is *if* theories are generated after an issue becomes politically active, *if* such theories are created as "excuses" and *if* different vested interests of different parties dominate on different issues from a self-interested viewpoint *then* WZ's final sentence in the above quote follows. However, if any of the "if" clauses is in doubt then the conclusion does not follow at all. Our model of the inflation accounting debate casts doubt on the validity of at least the first two of these "if" clauses, if not all three.

In order to understand more clearly the difference between Watts and Zimmerman's model and the one proposed here, we shall give a brief exposition of each. WZ's original model is given in Figure 1.

A particular issue arises (say WZ). As a result, the legislative body or bodies are called upon to make a pronouncement about the "best" way of dealing with the issue in terms of accounting regulations. We suppose there are two parties whose wealth will be affected by the direction the legislation takes: since each wishes to maximize his wealth, we suppose that each party will advocate the use of that accounting method which will have that effect. These two parties to the political process therefore search for accounting theories to legitimate their positions, theories which are expressed in terms of general wellbeing rather than specifying that they will enrich that party. The sources of accounting theories are accounting academics. Each party therefore is attracted to a theory not in any way because it is intrinsically satisfactory, but because it is in his economic interest. The theories themselves arise not in a vacuum but subsequent to the issue's arising, since it is in the interests of academics to discuss topical matters. As competing theories arise they are seized by the competing parties to buttress their positions (theories at$_2$ and at$_3$) the theory which finally becomes the accepted one therefore does not arise because it is intrinsically appealing—there is no such thing as a "right" theory—but because it is in the interest of a particular party to a political process who is able through that political process to persuade the legislative body that their particular solution bolstered by a supporting theory is desirable. The law (see Figure 1) which follows from the process is therefore the outcome of the political process directly and is not affected by the theories themselves. When we turn to Figure 2 it will be seen that this is based upon Figure 1 but with significant differences. These are basically threefold concerning:

1. The Issue and the Law Standard
Unlike WZ's view (or rather absence of view) the issue on which a law or standard is to be set does not arise somehow by itself. It is connected through a complex network to what we call a "societal dynamic need." This is many respects is something of a "black box" for the purpose of this model since we do not claim to be certain of the process involved which generates the issue (although some thoughts on what it could be are presented in the following section). However, the important point is that an issue does not arise in a vacuum; it has its own causes which may have no connection whatsoever with the self-interest of the standard-setter. Equally the law/standard once set feeds into this societal black box playing a part in the formulation of new issues.

2. Accounting Theory Generation (at$_1$ to at$_4$)
Accounting theories (at$_1$ to at$_4$ in Figure 2) are generated before the issue becomes politically active but are once again connected through a complex

FIGURE 1
A Diagrammatic Presentation of the WZ Thesis

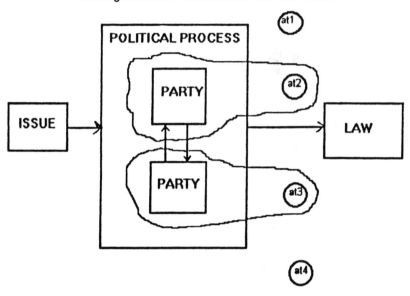

FIGURE 2
An Explanatory Model of the Inflation Accounting Debate

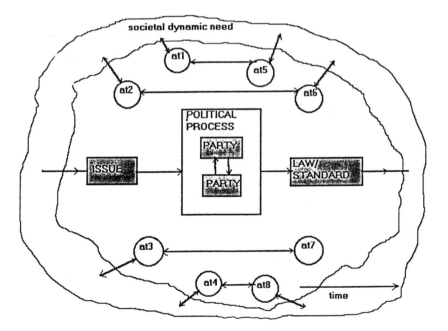

network to a societal need. These theories become both an appreciation of the issue (subsequently to be of interest to the standard-setter) and a suitable theoretical solution to it.

3. Accounting Theory Generation (at₅ to at₆)

3. Accounting Theory Generation (at_5 to at_6)

Accounting theories (at_5 to at_8 in Figure 2) are generated after the issue becomes politically active. Such theories are clearly related to the political process in some way and are used by the parties but not necessarily in an "excuse" capacity. However, such theories are also related to previous accounting theories (amplification of and development of ideas) and to the societal need in terms of further revelation of the issue and its necessary solution.

We now consider the evidence concerning the comparative validity of this model and WZ's original.

The U.K. and U.S. Inflation Accounting Debate: Evidence for an Alternative Thesis

The three major differences between WZ's explanatory model and our own as applied to the inflation accounting debate are as follows:

1. EVIDENCE FOR THE GENERATION OF THE ISSUE

We suggest that an issue becomes a political issue when the parties who have power to set standards (primarily the professional bodies) make moves to produce such standards on the issue in question. In the inflation accounting debate this could be legitimately assumed to be around 1963 in the U.S. with the publication of the Accounting Research Study No. 6 and around 1968 in the U.K. with the publication of the research monograph by the Institute of Chartered Accountants in England and Wales (I.C.A.E.W.) entitled "Accounting for Stewardship in a Period of Inflation".

Before this time the issue of inflation had been brought before the various professional institutions but rejected in various Bulletins and Recommendations. In 1949, in the U.S., the Accounting Research Bulletin No. 33 which was reinforced by Bulletin No. 43 in 1952 dismissed out of hand that there was an issue as such which required changes in accounting bases. In the U.K. in 1949 the Institute Recommendations N.12 reinforced again in 1952 by N.15, took the same view.

Undoubtedly there was pressure on both the powerful Institutes to take a different view. For instance in the U.K. both the Institute of Cost and Works Accountants (as it was then) and the Association of Certified and Corporate Accountants issued monographs pressing for changes. In the U.S.

as Zeff (1972) points out there were some considerable internal pressures on the contents of Bulletin No. 43 such that it was only just carried. However, despite these pressures the respective Recommendations and Bulletins stood until around 1963 and 1968 as mentioned above when the research monographs were published.

Since then the issue and its solution in terms of standards have taken a long and tortuous pathway. In 1969 the U.S. statement No. 3 was published—a somewhat lesser view than an Opinion—by the A.I.C.P.A. However, in 1974 the Financial Accounting Standards Board published a Standard on Inflation Accounting which was ratified and made compulsory by the Securities Exchange Commission in 1976. In the U.K. in 1973 Exposure Draft No. 8 was issued which became provisional Standard No. 7 in 1974. The standard was provisional due to the involvement of the British government through the Sandilands Committee which published its report in 1975. As a result the Accounting Standards Committee revoked P.S.S.A.P. 7 and published Exposure Draft No. 18 in 1976 which was subsequently rejected. As a result the temporary "Hyde Guidelines" were published and instituted in 1977 while Exposure Draft No. 24 was being prepared. This was finally published in 1979 and has since become Statement of Standard Accounting Practice No. 16.

Recounting what has actually happened is obviously only half the story, the important question remains: why was the issue not "politically active" until 1963 in the U.S. and 1968 in the U.K.? The question is complex but cannot be answered solely by the "self interest" thesis of WZ. A more reasonable, but not a fully comprehensive answer, is connected with an increase in domestic inflation rates which casts doubts on the adequate depiction of reality expressed by historic cost accounts. During and immediately after the second World War inflation rates on both sides of the Atlantic were at an all time high. For instance in the U.K. in 1947 and 1948 the percentage rate of change of the Retail Price Index was 6.7% and 7.8%. These rates, as Mumford (1979) points out, were "Unprecedented in Britain in peace time in this century." (p.98). It was, we postulate, as a reaction to this rise in the inflation rate and as Mumford (1979) points out, to a composite fall in stock market prices that the potential of the issue was brought before the respective Institutes. Equally we would maintain the reason it was not taken as an issue at this time was due to the profession's (genuine) belief that historical cost based accounts were "objective" and thus the only satisfactory basis for audited accounts and for tax purposes. We would maintain that the Institutes' staff were well aware of what happened after the first World War when inflation was high initially and then deflation occurred—such a memory transposed on to the period following the Second World War would explain the Institutes' reactions of non involvement.

Similarly a realization that deflation did not occur and an appreciation

TABLE 3

INDEX OF RETAIL PRICES (US)			
1957	3.5%	1966	3.0%
1958	2.6%	1967	3.0%
1959	0.8%	1968	3.6%
1960	1.6%	1969	5.5%
1961	0.8%	1970	5.9%
1962	1.6%	1971	5.0%
*1963	1.6%	1972	3.0%
1964	0.8%	1973	5.2%
1965	1.5%		

TABLE 4

INDEX OF RETAIL PRICES (U.K.) (Monthly Average)			
1962	1.6%	1971	9.4%
1963	2.0%	1972	7.1%
1904	3.3%	1973	9.2%
1965	4.8%	1974	8.5%
1966	3.2%	1975	24.2%
1967	2.5%	1976	16.5%
1968	5.4%	1977	15.8%
*1969	5.4%	1978	8.3%
1970	6.4%		

that inflation was here to stay and needed to be faced was probably the motivating force behind the U.S. and U.K. Institutes' decisions to see the matter as an issue in 1963 and 1968 respectively. *As support to this claim* Tables 3 and 4 trace the percentage rise of consumer prices six years before the Institutes' see inflation as an issue and ten years after—all giving support to the steady consistent increase in inflation during these periods.

2. EVIDENCE FOR THE GENERATION OF ACCOUNTING THEORIES BEFORE THE ISSUE BECAME POLITICALLY ACTIVE

The WZ thesis would imply that we would expect the inflation accounting literature and consequent theories to appear after 1963 in the U.S. and 1968 in the U.K. Obviously since the literatures of the two countries are so intertwined the most important year looks like 1963 when the issue at least became politically active in the U.S. Thus the expectation following the WZ argument would be negligible publications ("one or two") on inflation accounting before 1963 and a massive increase after that date particularly in the more formative stages say up to 1968 or 1969. However, no such evidence exists. The contrary appears to be true. WZ claimed that a literature review of this kind was rendered difficult for reasons of expense and bias, as well as changes in terminology (footnote, p. 289). We dispute this. As to the first, we see no "obvious cost" of this exercise using the source we do (the A.I.C.P.A. Accountants Index). As to the second, whatever bias there may be in the taxonomic process of the Index's compilers it is not evident that it might be one which would materially affect the validity from the point of view of this hypothesis. Linked to this is the third problem: and again, it is hard to see how any change in terminology regarding inflation accounting might affect the matter. We have therefore considered as a preliminary test a comparison for the periods 1953–1958 and 1963–1968. The results as given in Table 5 suggest that for inflation accounting and allied areas there were approximately as many publications in one period as another. According to the theory there should have been next to none in the earlier period (since the political issue had been dropped and no excuses were therefore necessary). In fact there was a very substantial number. In addition to this, most of the classics in this area (for example, Sweeney, Canning, Bonbright, McNeal, Edwards, Paton, Baxter) appeared before this time. All the fundamental principles had already been developed. To claim, as WZ do (again, in private correspondence) that such work was a result of legislation (the Securities Acts yet again) is unacceptable for reasons we have already outlined. We suggest therefore that all these theorists were concerned with this problem because they saw it as important both conceptually (to place accounting on a firm foundation) and practically (because they had seen the results of both hyperinflation and slow but long-term inflation over many years). They could not be supplying excuses because there were no possible users of such excuses.

3. EVIDENCE FOR THE GENERATION OF ACCOUNTING THEORIES AFTER THE ISSUE BECAME POLITICALLY ACTIVE

Certainly from 1969 to the present day there has been a massive increase in publications on inflation accounting. However, there is little evidence to support the view that these publications have been called for and used by the professional parties involved in the formulation of the standards. Most of this literature appears to be a mixture of a reaction to accelerating inflation (see Tables 3 and 4) or development of previous inflation accounting theories and a massive number of comments on suggestions and thoughts on what the professional bodies are proposing.

Such a view is also substantiated if one looks at the professional pronouncements which appear not to need theoretical bolstering for their suggestion. For instance the U.K. Sandilands Report (1975) by the Government

TABLE 5

PUBLICATIONS ON INFLATION & ALLIED AREAS No. of Articles/Books	
1953 & 1954	68
1955 & 1956	27
1957 & 1958	67
TOTAL	162
1963 & 1964	50
1965 & 1966	60
1967 & 1968	58
TOTAL	168

committee waited until chapter 10 before introducing a discussion on some of the theoretical literature on Replacement Cost Accounting. The Committee concludes:

"We do not consider that some of the more rigid forms of replacement cost accounting which have been suggested to us in evidence are suitable for general application by all companies, and in particular we do not think that the concepts of capital maintenance normally associated with replacement cost accounting would, if strictly applied, meet the requirements for information of users of accounts. However, we do believe that certain forms of replacement cost accounting as applied in practice by a number of companies come close to meeting the requirements of users which we set out in chapter 5. Our own proposals in chapters 12 and 13 have many' similarities' with these forms of the replacement cost technique."

Thus the Sandilands Committee gave more cognizance to actual examples of replacement cost accounting than any theoretical underpinnings. But even here the Committee are independent and unabashed in their recommendations requiring no bolstering or support for the position they take. Equally when looking at Exposure Draft 24 and Standard Accounting Practice 16 there is virtually no mention of any supporting theories which are claimed to give respectability for the proposals that are put forward. Thus WZ's view that accounting theories are generated after an issue becomes politically active and are created to supply excuses for political standpoints looks extremely dubious.

A possible more realistic proposition which comes from looking at the professional pronouncements is that accounting theories on inflation produced before the early 1960s have had some considerable effect on the formulation of the institutional suggestions. For instance it is interesting to note that accounting theories produced before the 1960s have basically been in two schools of thought: the replacement cost school and the stabilized index linked school. It is even more interesting to note that on both sides of the Atlantic a form of replacement cost accounting is present standard accounting practice and the only viable alternative proposal has been an index linked suggestion (Exposure Draft 8 and Standard Accounting Practice 7 in the U.K.).

In addition, as Stamp (1981) has pointed out, the development of both the "value to the firm" concept and the problem of the gearing adjustment have been theoretical issues which have been extensively considered in the U.K. literature but hardly at all by U.S. theorists. If the inflation rate increase is taken as the political event sparking off the literature, then there is no explanation at all for why such differences of emphasis grew between countries (for example both Baxter's and Stamp's contributions to the "value to the firm" concept preceded the practical interest taken in the idea by the Sandilands Committee).

Thus contrary to the somewhat inept role WZ give to accounting theories it may well be the case that, based on the inflation accounting debate, it can be concluded that accounting theories create the broad boundaries in which professional institutions can specify solutions to important issues. However, *this is not claimed to be a general theory*. As stated at the beginning of the fourth section, we do not claim for this theory any generality whatever. The development of a theory of academic developments and political issues similar to the rigorous approach WZ take is, it is suggested, inappropriate to the nature of the subject. To replace their "positive theory" by another which was similar but more sophisticated would nullify the purpose of this analysis. We have been concerned to demonstrate merely that WZ's thesis cannot hold up either logically or empirically, and that there are therefore no grounds either for claiming that there will never be a generally-accepted accounting theory, or that academic work is nothing more than the unwitting (at times), supply of excuses for political protagonists.

Notes

1. We stress that we are not claiming that the variations cannot form such a distribution: but that there is intuitive evidence that they need not, and that evidence must be proposed to rebut the presumption that they do not.
2. In private correspondence.

References

Allen, C. E. (1927): "The Growth of Accounting Instruction Since 1900," *The Accounting Review*, vol II, (1927), pp. 150–166.

Friedman, M. (1953): *Essays in Positive Economics* (University of Chicago Press, 1953)

Inflation Accounting Committee (Chairman F.E.B. Sandilands) (1975): *Inflation Accounting* (H.M.S.O., Cmnd. 6225, 1975).

Kuhn, T. S. (1970): *The Structure of Scientific Revolutions* (University of Chicago Press, 1970).

Lockwood, J. (1938): "Early University Education in Accountancy," *The Accounting Review,* vol. XIII, No. 2 (1(138), pp. 131–144.

Mumford, M. (1979): "The End of a Familiar Inflation Accounting Cycle," *Accounting and Business Research,* No. 34 (Spring, 1979), pp. 98–104.

Nagel, E. (1963): "Assumptions in Economic Theory," *The American Economic Review,* Supplementary Volume No. 53 (1963), pp. 211–219.

Popper, K. R. (1972): *Conjectures and Refutations* (Routledge and Kegan Paul, 1972)

Rokeach (1973): *The Nature of Human Values* (Free Press, MacMillan, 1973).

Samuelson, P. A. (1963): "Discussion of 'Problems of Methodology,'" in *American Economic Review* Supplementary Volume No. 53 (1963), pp. 231–236.

Stamp, E. (1981): "Commentary on 'The British Contribution to Income Theory,'" in *Essays in British Accounting Research,* ed. M. Bromwich and A. G. Hopwood (Pitman, 1981), pp. 30–32.

Watts, R. L. and J. L. Zimmerman, (1979): "The Demand for and Supply of Accounting Theories: The Market for Excuses," *The Accounting Review,* Vol. LIV, (April, 1979), pp. 273–305.

Zeff, S. A. (1972): *Forging Accounting Principles in Five Countries: A History and an Analysis of Trends,* (Stipes Publishing Company, 1972).

Zimmerman, J. L. (1979): "Positive Research in Accounting," in *Perspectives on Research,* eds. R. D. Williams and T. H. Nair (University of Wisconsin Press, 1980), pp. 107–128.

REPLY TO LOWE, PUXTY AND LAUGHLIN

ROSS L. WATTS AND JEROLD L. ZIMMERMAN

1. Introduction

Lowe, Puxty and Laughlin (1980), (LPL) claim the methodology we use in Watts and Zimmerman (1979) (the "Excuses" paper) is inappropriate. Further, they claim that even if our methodology were sound, our own evidence and the evidence they present contradicts our model. Both claims are demonstrably false. However, structuring a cohesive reply to LPL's claims is difficult because the LPL paper is poorly organized and confused in many of its claims. Nevertheless, we shall structure our reply to their two-pronged attack under the headings of methodology and evidence.

The attack on our methodology is the most important because the nature of the attack, by implication, constitutes art attack on most of the finance and economics based empirical research in accounting that has grown up in the last 15 years, and indeed, on much of the empirical research in economics and finance. Further, the issue of methodology cannot be separated from the evidence issue, because despite LPL's claims otherwise, their assessment of the evidence depends on their view of methodology, in particular their view of the methodology of social science. That view is at variance with both the evidence on that methodology and the views of many philosophers of science. Hence, we address the methodology issue first (Section 2).

LPL's claims on evidence are investigated in Section 3. LPL's assessment of our evidence and particularly their alternative model and their claims that the evidence they present supports their model and refutes ours are extremely poor. It is gratuitous to call their "alternative approach" a model because it is not sufficiently specified to be able to derive testable implications, let alone test them. The evidence LPL present is eminently consistent with our model. The only contrary "evidence" consists of assertions.

In their prescriptive postscript and in their conclusion LPL reveal what really bothers them about our "excuses" paper. One reason LPL do not like our model is that it portrays individuals as acting in their self-interest. They do not want to allow any theories based on self-interest because such theories legitimize self-interest actions (see p. 17). Such a position which "apriori" precludes a substantial set of possible theories from consideration purely on normative grounds can only be described as *anti-intellectual.*

A second reason LPL do not like our model is the prediction we make in the last sentence of our paper, that there never will be generally accepted accounting theory to justify accounting standards. They interpret that prediction as suggesting an accounting academic cannot influence policy decisions and are concerned that academics will stop trying to influence those decisions. They are afraid academics will stop "searching for truth" (p. 10). While we are flattered that LPL think we could have such an impact, we shall see that LPL's interpretation of our prediction is purely their own. While our model does suggest that academics do not have a major impact on policy decisions, the model does suggest they have a marginal effect. Nor does our model imply accounting academics should or will stop attempting to model accounting phenomena ("searching for truth" is too pretentious). Those who are sufficiently self-deluded to think their research will have a major impact on the world are not likely to believe our model. Those more modest will be satisfied with marginal effects and will be rewarded (our model does allow demands for understanding the world as well as for "excuses"—see below).

Our prediction plays a central role in LPL's criticisms. They end to view it as a logical conclusion. It is logical, given our assumptions about relative costs, assumptions which we believe capture the essence of the phenomena now. However, it is not a necessary result of a self-interest model or of our model in general. In an uncertain world those relative costs may change.

2. Methodology

LPL's attack on our methodology is very confused. It begins with criticisms, which LPL themselves partially answer. They are the familiar criticisms of many non-economists; that we cannot justify the assumption of an economic framework; and that such a framework is restrictive. Any theory, even that of the natural sciences, is by its very nature restrictive (see our attached section on the nature of scientific methodology from another paper). The issue is how to restrict and the most important criterion is predictive-ability. Others are free to make different assumptions and produce different theories. The determination of which theory is accepted in the scientific community will depend heavily on the theories' relative predictive-ability but will be affected by other criteria such as plausibility.

LPL show that they know part of our answer to the first criticism. They provide a quote from Friedman (1953) which gives the predictive-ability criterion. We are aware that (as recognized in the philosophy of science literature) other criteria play a role in determination of the theory which wins acceptance but those criteria are not reasons for rejection of a model for adopting a particular set of assumptions, per se. The criteria are for choice among theories. What then is LPL's criticism?

Apparently it is that other models with different assumptions *may* yield the same predictions (see the bottom of LPL's page 4). Of course, that's true. As Friedman (1953, p. 9) puts it "If there is one hypothesis that is consistent with the available evidence, there are always an infinite number that are." We never pretend otherwise in our paper. We explicitly recognize one alternative theory (the "public interest" theory) and implicitly recognize that there are others (p. 288). Further, we explicitly state (p. 288) that "Our objective is merely to present prima facie support for the hypothesis that accounting theory has changed *after* the "introduction of government regulation."

It is not our role as researchers to put forward all the possible alternative theories consistent with the evidence. That is clearly an impossible task. In the progress of normal science (see our attached summary of scientific methodology) our only responsibility is to empirically discriminate our model from others which exist in the literature and are well enough specified to test. No such well specified model existed, so we chose to extend the "public interest" model implicit in much of the literature and used it as the alternative model. We find that the evidence is consistent with our model and is inconsistent with our version of the public interest model. We make no more claims than that in our paper. We don't claim our model is the "truth." In fact, we expect our model to be modified as further tests are forthcoming (see the top of page 290).

In essence, LPL's first criticism is not a criticism, it is a confused way of putting forward the proposition that alternative theories can exist. As we have seen, we do not deny the possibility of developing such theories in the paper, in fact we recognize that possibility. Further, we fulfil our responsibility under normal science to discriminate against existing empirically testable theories. What then bothers LPL? It appears to be the prediction we make at the end of our paper (see the bottom of LPL page 4). That prediction is purely in the context of our model and we don't pretend otherwise. We don't deny that it is probably possible to develop another model consistent with our evidence which does not yield that prediction. There is no fault in our methodology or prediction, the problem is LPL don't like our prediction; theirs is an emotional response.

The second part of LPL's attack on our methodology is more than just a lack of understanding that empirical accounting researchers know and operate under scientific methodology, it is an attack on much of the empirical work in finance and economics. The first criticism in this attack is that stochastic processes are inapplicable to social science theory. The criticism rests on the proposition that the outcome of the toss of a fair coin and the outcome of aggregate human behavior are different things. We agree. Ross Watts and Jerry Zimmerman are different people, that doesn't mean we can't be treated as two observations in a sample of accounting researchers. The crucial issue is whether modelling the outcomes of human behavior using probability distributions yields predictions which can be tested and are useful. For example, failures of corporations are the outcome of human behavior and are modelled using probability distributions. If the frequency of failure of firms each years is .05 and we present a model which is able to predict which firms fail each year with a .999 frequency of success who cares that human actions are not the same as coin tosses? We suspect most businessmen and indeed most people wouldn't, they would just use that model.

The second criticism in the attack on empirical methodology in the social sciences is that our model cannot be refuted because it is "concerned general trends" and is stochastic. The reason is that we have not specified a formal level of significance. As LPL's criticism reads all stochastic models must "a priori" state the level of accuracy of its predictions. Clearly that position is absurd, researchers typically have conventions as to statistical significance to avoid that very problem. Although it is not stated that way, we could be charitable, and interpret this criticism as a complaint that we did not perform formal statistical tests. However, that charge lacks force because we openly admitted that we did not perform such tests (p. 288, 2nd column) and do not pretend otherwise.

The third criticism in the attack on the methodology of empirical work in social sciences is a variation on preceding criticisms. It is that our model cannot have an error term because the human actions are purposive, so that the error terms themselves are not error terms but are the result (presumably) of omitted variables. There are two answers to this question. One is that we could assume that human actions are purposive on average but there are random deviations. Then LPL are back to questioning our assumptions (see the first criticism in this section). The second answer is more telling in its revelation of LPL's ignorance of empirical methodology. In order to construct a model which explains more than one observation (as explained previously) we have to abstract from reality. Necessarily variables are omitted. Attempts to explain *all* observations would quickly exhaust all degrees of freedom so that such explanations are unlikely to predict on data other than that which is used to develop it.

The fact that variables are omitted is *not* a reason to reject a model. All theories have omitted variables and are to some extent misspecified even those in the natural sciences. As a consequence, mots theories do not perfectly predict including theories in the physical sciences. There are numerous examples. For example, until relatively recently the theories of aerodynamics predicted that the bumble bee would not fly. Also, at the present time theories of physics cannot fully explain the existence of black holes. These examples do not cause those theories to be rejected. As we have indicated, the acceptance of a theory crucially depends on its predictive power vis-à-vis other theories, not vis-à-vis the criterion of perfect prediction. Basically, the philosophy is—if it works, use it. This is not to say that omitted variables and misspecification are unimportant. They are important because they suggest ways that a "better" theory can be developed.

LPL conclude their criticisms of methodology by claiming that the methodology of natural scientific testing is inapplicable to human social processes. They state that a vast literature exists on the subject and it can be read in any basic book on the philosophy of social sciences. The implication is that this literature supports their claim and any person who has looked at the philosophy of science literature would recognize that point. We have read some of the philosophy of science literature (see the attached section on the topic) and can state that the implication is false. While there are those in the literature whose position supports LPL's, there is also substantial support for the position that the methods of natural science are also applicable to the social sciences (for example, Popper and Hempel)[1].

The essence of LPL's argument that natural science methods cannot be applied to human behavior is that while the behavior of natural phenomenon is such that laws can be proposed to predict the phenomena under certain circumstances, human behavior need not be of that kind. Perhaps some human behavior cannot be predicted, but it is also apparent that a substantial portion of human behavior is such as to enable us to make successful predictions using the methodology of the natural sciences. Many examples can be given, even in accounting. Consider annual earnings. Both annual earnings numbers and stock prices effectively follow a random walk. If asked to predict whether the change in a firm's stock price will increase over the next year, our best prediction would be no change (ignoring, for purposes of the example, the drift term) However, if we were told that the firm's earnings increased for the year, we would predict an increase in the stock price. Over a large number of trials, the prediction errors would be significantly less for the prediction conditional on the knowledge of earnings than for the unconditional prediction. That result is well-known and has been reproduced in many time periods and various countries. Many other examples can be given (e.g., bankruptcy predictions, bond rating predictions, predictions as to selection of accounting procedures, etc.).

The above predictions are clearly useful and are used by financial analysts, lending institutions (e.g. credit scoring models), etc. Should we abandon a methodology which yields useful results purely because it *may* not be able to be used to predict *all* human behavior? Do we throw out something that works in some situations, because it *may* not work in every circumstance? Obviously, the answer is no! We do not have physicists abandon their methodology because they cannot fully explain black holes. Yet, in essence LPL's arguments against empirical methodology imply physicists should abandon their methodology for that reason.

Regardless of what LPL think methodology *should* be, the methodologies that survive will be the ones which produce useful theories. Prediction and explanation of phenomena will be demanded and theories which provide them will survive. Even in accounting there is a demand for such theories (see p. 278 of the "excuses" paper—the information demand). If a methodology does not produce predictive theories, it will only survive to the extent it produces theories useful in other dimensions (e.g., "excuses" for political action).

In summary LPL's criticisms of our methodology are confused and indicate a lack of understanding of both empirical methodology and its fruits (the predictions we are able to make successfully). Further, it is apparent that LPL have not fully pursued the implications of their arguments. Finally, there is some evidence that our prediction, as to the use of accounting theory, bothers LPL more than our methodology.

3. Evidence

LPL begin their discussion of our evidence by asserting that we apparently consider accounting unique among the sciences. LPL make the claim that they have not observed any other science in which there has been proposed (as we have for accounting) "the twin propositions that theory cannot in itself affect beliefs, but can only be used as a set of excuses" (LPL, p. 8). Unfortunately, LPL have not read our paper very carefully, because if they had they would realize that we do *not* make those propositions anywhere in the paper.

First, in our theory of accounting, if theories did not affect beliefs, they would not be used as excuses in the political process (given such use is costly). What we argued was not that theories did not affect beliefs of voters, etc., but that because of costs in the political process, the most successful theory in terms of influencing beliefs of voters would not be the theory which explained or predicted the best (which we expect would be a self-interest theory). Consequently, self-interest theories would not be used to justify accounting standards.

Second, we did not argue that theory can *only* be used as excuses. We explicitly recognize that there is a demand for theories which predict (the *information demand*, "excuses" paper p. 279). What we stated was that with the growth of government intervention the justification demand "has come to eclipse" (p. 282) the other demands. That means that the justification demand surpasses, overwhelms or casts into shadow the other demands, it doesn't make them cease to exist. As we have indicated above, we do see predictive theory being developed in accounting. We would agree such theory can influence the beliefs of academics and accountants, but we explicitly argue such theory (if self-interest based) will not be effective in swaying the beliefs of voters in general and hence the outcome of the political process.

Given LPL's confusion as to our propositions it is little wonder that they think our propositions are unique. However, our propositions, as we stated, are not unique to us or accounting. George Stigler in the article we quote on page 286 makes a very similar argument to ours about economics (see Stigler, 1976). Also several other prominent economists have read our paper and in correspondence have indicated that they consider it also descriptive of economics. Indeed, our theory doesn't just apply to economics and accounting, we would also claim it applies to sociology, political science and the other social sciences. LPLs "evidence" that our theory doesn't apply in those areas is absurd. It consists of statements and assertions such as "many working class within the United States are poor; according to the WZ theories they would espouse those political theories which appeared best for them, such as socialist policies which redistributed wealth in their favor. Yet a socialist party has never been successful in the American context." (LPL, p. 8). Our theory does *not* imply that workers necessarily perceive socialist policies will redistribute wealth in their favor. Even if it did, it does not necessarily imply a socialist party would be the natural consequence.

LPL's next criticism of our evidence concerns our use of the railroad literature in the U. K. and U. S. and the depreciation literature in the U. K. as evidence on our theory when at those times no academics existed. We do not see any problem in this use. The supply side of the model is described in the paper in contemporaneous circumstances. We clearly imply that the demand for excuses applies across time and countries and state that supply adjusts to demand. If academics do not exist to supply the excuses, others will (e.g., academically inclined practising accountants).

The next criticism of our evidence (LPL p. 10) is that the timing of the depreciation debates says nothing about causality. We agree, we never stated that it did. Causality can only be inferred with a theory. What we argue is that the timing is *consistent* with the implications of our theory and to that extent confirms our theory. Our theory yields the causality.

LPL continue on from the causality statement which is familiar to any beginning researcher to the argument they have made before, that other hypotheses could explain the timing. As we indicated above, of course they could and we don't deny they could. We expected most readers of the *Accounting Review* would be familiar with the proposition that if one hypothesis is consistent with the data an infinite number can also be consistent. We fulfilled our responsibility to normal science by trying to specify an alternative hypothesis when none existed.

In concluding the section of their paper on our evidence LPL again reveal that they did not read our paper very carefully. They state: "According to Watts and Zimmerman's thesis, if the opposite had been beneficial to railway corporations (that is, the omission of depreciation from accounts as an expense) then today we should not be allowing depreciation either, however logical it may be. *We find this so improbable as to be unacceptable.*" (emphasis added, p. 11). If LPL are suggesting that we wouldn't be allowing depreciation for all companies, they forget the tax law effect we postulate which also would lead to allowance of depreciation. If LPL are referring to railroads they are very poor predictors *and* they didn't read the paper we wrote. LPL's prediction came true for railroads in the U.S. The fact that the Interstate Commerce Commission adopted a policy which didn't allow depreciation expense is well known and documented and is referred to explicitly in the "excuses" paper (p. 293). The Commission allowed a policy which was more advantageous to the railroads.

Their section on our evidence not only makes us wonder whether LPL read the paper, it indicates that they do not understand that accountants know something about scientific methodology (see the "causal" issue above). Further, the evidence they offer (e.g., assertions about socialist parties) makes it clear they are not empiricists.

LPL continue on to propose an alternative model and then claim to demonstrate that their model is more consistent with the evidence than ours. Unfortunately LPL's model is extremely vague and doesn't begin to be well enough specified for tests to be conducted which discriminate between their model and ours.

A major innovation in LPL's model is the addition of a blob to the figure they claim represents our theory, a blob they call "Societal Dynamic Need". What these needs are and how and when they arise are not specified. The addition has no predictive context, it can fit any issue arising. LPL fail to specify this process despite their criticism that we do not specify how issues arise in our model. While we don't make such specification in the "excuses" paper, the explanation is implicit in our theory of the political process and is addressed in some of the articles we reference. Issues arise when the relative costs and benefits of certain political actions occur. For example, mine legislation tends to follow major mine disasters (see Watts, 1977, for further discussion).

A second innovation in LPL's model is the feedback of the law and accounting theory into the nebulous societal process. This feedback can cause rules to be overturned. We do not consider this an innovation. Our model does allow for this interaction. As the relative costs of political action change rules are changed. In fact, in Watts and Zimmerman (1980) we even use our theory to successfully predict the voting of the Accounting Principles Board on issues such as the investments tax credit example given by LPL. The LPL model doesn't provide any predictors.

The third and final innovation LPL claim to provide in their model is a direct connection between accounting theories and "societal need" (which is undefined and is not modelled). Again the linkage is not specified in any way which makes it possible to test, except for the LPL claim that the theories of Chambers and others preceded changes in practice (and presumably standards). These claims show the lack of care with evidence and a lack of careful reading of our paper which is epidemic in LPL's paper. They ignore the fact that we explicitly argue that theories such as Chambers are the consequence of regulation, regulation which *precedes* Chambers' work (see the bottom of column 1, page 299 of the "excuses" paper).

The evidence LPL offer which they claim is consistent with their model and not with ours appears to be eminently consistent with ours. The timing of the literature's concern with inflation fits perfectly, it tends to follow substantial increases in the U. K. inflation rate which itself is a political issue. Why it is an issue can be explained by our model. "Societal need" is not an explanation, it is tautological. We only have LPL's statement that lobbying on inflation accounting in the U. K. does not line up with wealth effects. Every empirical researcher knows that finding no results are very easy to obtain, especially if the study is poorly designed and executed. Also, the Jenkins statements are exactly what our model would predict.

LPL's idea of evidence amounts to nothing more than casual assertions. They do not carefully specify their model—so that it can be discriminated from ours. Their methodology suggest a lack of concern with describing phenomena.

4. Summary and Conclusions

In LPL's Prescriptive Postscript (their section VI) and their Conclusion they show why they are not concerned with careful analysis and empirical testing. They do not like the way human nature is portrayed in our models as "invariably selfish and hypocritical." (LPL p. 17) and consequently they are going to reject our model whatever the evidence. Further, LPL are concerned that the "'description' of events can affect the events themselves thus acting as legitimation devices". (LPL p. 17). Apparently the researcher is not to try to describe the world as much as to come up with theories which portray the world as it *should* be. If we follow that approach we'll have as many theories as people have visions of brave new worlds, and *no* way to choose among them. LPL's approach would be amusing except it proscribes a subset of theories purely on the basis of LPL's tastes. In that, it is anti-intellectual.

LPL's conclusion reveals another reason they do not like our model. They do not like our implication that the products of accounting research are not likely to have major impact on the world. They do not like the idea that as a consequence of researcher's efforts the world is not necessarily becoming a better and better place to live in as a consequence of researchers' work. They do not like the prospect that at the end of their fairy tale everyone may not live happily ever after.

Notes

1. We don't agree with arguments which appeal to authority, but we were curious, given LPL's use of authority and our knowledge of the literature, as to exactly what LPL's authorities on the philosophy of science stated so we attempted to obtain and read those authorities (Pratt, 1978 and Keat and Urry, 1975). One of those authorities (Pratt) was not in the University of Rochester Library. The other (Keat and Urry) was indexed under Marxist philosophy but the only copy had apparently been stolen. Not having time to obtain the books through interlibrary loan we asked the chairman of the University of Rochester philosophy department (an eminent philosopher whose area of speciality is the philosophy of science) whether he knew of the two books. The chairman replied that he didn't know of the books or the authors.

References

Friedman, M. (1953), "The Methodology of Positive Economics," Part I of *Essays in Positive Economics,* reprinted by the University of Chicago Press, 1966.

Keat, R. and J. Urry (1975), *Social Theory as Science* (Routledge and Kegan Paul)

Lowe, E., A. Puxty and R. Laughlin (1980), "The Watts and Zimmerman Thesis: An Evaluation", unpublished paper, University of Sheffield.

Pratt, V. (1578), *The Philosophy of the Social Sciences* (Methuen)

Stigler, G. (1976), "Do Economists Matter?", *Southern Economic Journal* (January, 1976), pp. 347–363.

Watts, R. (1977), "Corporate Financial Statements, A Product of the Market and Political Processes", *Australian Journal of Management* (April, 1977), pp. 53–75.

Watts, R. and J. Zimmerman (1979), "The Demand for and Supply of Accounting Theories: The Market for Excuses", *Accounting Review* (April, 1979), pp. 273–305.

———(1980), "Auditors and the Determination of Accounting Standards," unpublished paper, University of Rochester, December 1980.

Professor S. A. Zeff, Editor
The Accounting Review
Jesse H. Jones Graduate School of Administration
Rice University
P O Box 1892
Houston, Texas 77001
USA

Dear Steve

We have now received the response from Watts and Zimmerman to our comment. We are alarmed however that they have not responded to the comment we submitted.

The comment (under a slightly different title) was given at the AUTA Annual Meeting, and at the time a copy was sent to Watts and Zimmerman. At the time they did not respond to this. Subsequently, we polished and strengthened the manuscript in the light of comments received before submitting it to you.

We feel that WZ's response should be to the manuscript we sent, and not to an earlier attempt. Can we ask therefore that their response to our comments reflects this?

[Yours sincerely]

Editors' Note: The original letter sent to Professor Zeff cannot be found, and the exact wording cannot be assured. The above letter is a reconstruction necessary to understand the letter that follows from Professor Zeff. It is based on the authors' recollections of the correspondence.

APRIL 24, 1981

Professor E. A. Lowe
Division of Economic Studies
The University of Sheffield
Crookesmoor Building
Sheffield S10 1FL England

Dear Tony

On returning to my office, I found a letter dated March 30th from Ross Watts. He writes that while your proposed Comment is "a little more polished" than the manuscript to which he and Zimmerman replied, he sees insufficient difference in content between the two to warrant the preparation of a new reply for review purposes. Therefore, I suggest that we press ahead with what they have supplied, and you may wish to attach a brief note to your proposed Comment indicating any correlations between their reply and your Comment which may not be obvious to a reviewer. Send me three copies of the Comment (on one side of each sheet only) and your check for the submission fee. When these are in hand, I will send it out for review.

Naturally, you should modify your Comment in the light of what is persuasive from the Watts and Zimmerman reply.

Enjoyed seeing you in Dundee.

Sincerely

Stephen A. Zeff

JUNE 5, 1981

Professor S. A. Zeff, Editor
The Accounting Review
Jesse H. Jones Graduate School of Administration
Rice University
P O. Box 1892
Houston, Texas 77001
USA

Dear Steve

We have now received a letter dated March from Ross Watts saying essentially what he said to you: that he does not feel it is necessary to modify their reply to our comment. We have considered their reply and do not feel that any alteration in our comment is necessary.

I accordingly enclose the comment and correspondence together with a brief note (as you requested) guiding a reviewer through the differences between their reply and what is relevant. We hope he will not be too confused!

Best wishes

Yours sincerely

Professor E. A. Lowe

Review of Manuscript: The Demand for and Supply of Accounting Theories: A Comment

1. The disagreement between Watts and Zimmerman (WZ) and the authors of this comment (LPL) seems to rest on two differences in assumptions. I will consider these in turn.

2. WZ assume accounting theory is an economic good; LPL do not. WZ justify this assumption by appealing to positive economics, citing Friedman; LPL reject the appeal, citing Kuhn, Nagel and Samuelson. It is simply not possible to choose between the two approaches on any other than epistemological basis. Neither approach can be "proven" correct from first principles.

3. The second difference is that LPL assume, or assert, that there cannot be exceptions to a theory. As a corollary we have the argument that intellectual inquiry on a macro scale cannot be thought of, or considered, as a stochastic process. WZ, on the other hand, are looking for "general trends", that is to say, anecdotal evidence, which is consistent with their theory. If some of this found, (and three data points are, evidently, found), then the theory is to be accepted, at least provisionally.

4. There is thus a basic and irreconcilable difference between theory verification as viewed by LPL (failure to refute a hypothesis) and by WZ (general agreement between the hypothesis and the data, or at least some of the data).

5. I believe that all other major disagreements between WZ and LPL follow from these differences in assumptions (but see comment 7). Unfortunately, tests of the validity of either pair of assumptions are not intuitively obvious, at least to me. It seems a resolution will not be reached easily.

6. This comment does not address some specific details of the WZ paper. To give just two examples:

   a. the weaknesses in the chain of deduction that leads from "prima facie support for the hypothesis that accounting theory has changed *after* the introduction of government regulation" to the "self-interest" theory of the sociology of accountants.)

   b. the fact that WZ expect more from a normative theory (explain or justify all accounting standards) than they do from their own; see comment 3, above).

7. The LPL comment does, however, make an interesting point: academics,

they say, did not really exist for accounting until after the events that WZ cite as evidence for the hypothesis that academics act in their own interest in supplying theories. If this is so, the "supply side" of the theory falls apart.

8. My overall impression is that since the comment is based on broad differences in assumptions, the authors did not think it necessary to deal with many specific issues on a detailed level (but see comment 7). In this regard, the comment is too long for the points it makes, and incomplete. It could be shortened along the lines I've suggested in my notes on the paper itself. I also suggest that the authors organizer the exposition around the differences that underlie their comment.

Comments on Manuscript: "The Demand for and Supply of Accounting Theories: A Comment

The criticisms of Watts and Zimmerman's (WZ) paper which the authors of this comment raise are essentially twofold. First, the theoretical underpinnings of WZ are attacked as inappropriate for explaining the phenomenon of interest. Secondly, one segment of the empirical evidence presented by WZ is argued to be inconsistent with the WZ hypotheses. Although both criticisms may have some merit, the authors do not build a convincing case for either point. The remaining portions of the manuscript consist of loosely structured comments concerning a number of tangential issues; e.g. reactions to 'positivist' theory construction, concerns over the distinction between 'theories' and 'meta-theories', etc. In short, the comment does not made a substantive contribution to our understanding of WZ.

The following comments address a number of the specific points raised in this paper.

1. Relatively unambiguous criteria for evaluating this manuscript are provided on page 1 where the authors express their intent to demonstrate that (a) "the evidence for (WZ's) hypothesis is unsatisfactory", and (b) that "the hypothesis itself is based upon faulty reasoning." When the manuscript is evaluated according to these criteria it is found to be seriously lacking. No logical fallacies are identified, alternative explanations consistent with the evidence are not proposed, nor is the evidence cited by WZ shown to be inconsistent with their original hypotheses.

2. The purpose served by Table 1 is unclear and the authors' choice of terminology is misleading e.g. the use of "testable conclusions" rather than the more common "implications", "propositions", or "assertions"

3. Page 2 argues that WZ's "proposal to use an economic framework is

unjustified and hence casts doubt upon the rest of the deductive process. Apparently the term 'unjustified' is to be interpreted literally since the authors express concern about the absence of an elicit justification for WZ's economic analysis of a political process. It would have been interesting had WZ provided a detailed discussion contrasting the advantages and disadvantages of economic modelling vis-à-vis alternative frameworks. The absence of an explicit justification, however, does not alter the viability of their approach, and to demand justifications of this sort would impose unnecessary constraints on all research. If the economic analysis of WZ is indeed inappropriate in this context, this fact should be borne out by the data.

4. In commenting on the absence of a justification for the economic framework used by WZ, the authors state that: "If, therefore, two different frameworks explain the same phenomena (and they well might) then by selecting one of them and ignoring any other there will be no basis for judgement between the two; no basis for deciding which is better in terms of its explanatory power." Similarly, in commenting on the positivist approach to theory construction, the authors state that the use of 'unrealistic' assumptions 'leaves unanswered the problem of the existence of two theories, both of which yield predictions which are the same and accord with the apparent facts."

The concern raised by these comments in unclear. On the one hand, the authors may be expressing concern about the existence of alternative theories which are consistent with the empirical evidence cited by WZ. If that is the point, it is incumbent upon the authors to elucidate and test an alternative theory. On the other hand, the authors could be taking issue with WZ theory because it rests upon 'unrealistic' assumptions; yet, here again it seems incumbent upon the authors to propose (and test) a rival theory based upon more 'realistic' assumptions. Merely to assert, rather than empirically demonstrate, the inadequacy of a theory is insufficient.

The authors seem to confuse 'realism' with 'observability' throughout much of this discussion. Theories frequently contain predictions about observable phenomena derived from relationships hypothesised to exist among unobservable constructs. Those constructs may or may not have observable referents, nor is observability of crucial importance in this context. The critical test is whether the predictions of the theory, predictions about observable phenomena, accord with the facts (i.e. empirical reality). If a 'rival theory' can be articulated—based upon a different set of more 'realistic' assumptions or upon an alternative 'framework—then the rival theory has empirical importance only to the extent that it explains the same phenomenon previously explained by the original theory and predicts some new phenomena. The critical test or crucial experiment then lies in which theory's predictions about the new phenomena best fit the data. If two theories "yield predictions which are the same" then for all practical purposes the two are identical and one's preference between them becomes a matter of personal taste. No empirical test can discriminate between them.

5. A critique of the positivist school is provided on page 3 with the major criticism centering on the role of 'realistic' assumptions in theory construction and testing. The authors paint an exaggerated picture of the "irrelevance" of descriptively valid prior propositions (i.e. assumptions) to theory construction within the positivist school, and fail to link this 'criticism' to the WZ paper. Merely providing references to earlier work does not produce penetrating insights about the point under contention; namely the adequacy of WZ's theoretical formulation for explaining the development of the accounting literature.

A second problem with this discussion is that the linkage between the authors' arguments concerning realistic (descriptively valid?) assumptions (paragraph 1 of this section) and their statements concerning theory discrimination in the later paragraphs is quite unclear.

6. Under the heading "Proposals for Testing the Theory", the authors provide a discussion of largely unrelated and irrelevant issues. When one distils the authors' remarks, two major points emerge. First, it Is asserted that WZ's testing criteria are so vague and ill-defined that it is difficult (if not impossible) to identify classes of data which would serve to refute the theory. Secondly, the authors take issue with the unit of analysis about which the WZ theory makes predictions.

As to the first point, I quite agree that testing criteria need precise identification if the WZ theory is to be subjected to meaningful empirical refutation. In the absence of specific testing criteria, virtually any set of data can be construed as consistent with the theory, in which case the theory becomes little more than a metaphysical proposition in the sense suggested by Popper. What the authors have not convincingly demonstrated in this discussion is that the hypotheses identified by WZ fall into this category—is there no set of data which would serve to refute these hypotheses? Or is it simply the case that WZ were negligent in failing to identify such a data set?

As to the second point, it is unclear whether the authors take exception with WZ's unit of analysis or simply confuse the phenomenon WZ seek to explain ("general trends") with other phenomena which the authors' would have liked WZ to explain ("individual pieces of research"). Additional comments on both of these points follow below.

7. I find several of the passages in the section on "Proposal for Testing the Theory" particularly perplexing. Consider, for example, the following:

i) "The paper uses the approach to proof of the natural sciences." To what alternative mode of proof is the 'natural science approach contrasted? Do the authors' mean to imply that the 'natural science' approach precludes an error theory; i.e. all observations must be in accord with the theory's predictions since "there cannot be exceptions to a theory"? If that is the case, the authors are imposing an unusual definition for proof in natural science and in other disciplines. All scientific theories implicitly allow exceptions since some observations may be inconsistent with the theory's predictions solely as a result of measurement/observation error.

ii) "It is therefore appropriate to consider the extent to which (WZ) 'theory' is a true theory." "True" in what sense—conformance with the definitional distinctions of Popper and other philosophers of science, conformance with observations, or what?

iii) "they are comparing the testing of a theory (which by its nature is supposed to have general validity) with the testing of a single instance given that a certain theory is correct". The substantive content of this passage escapes me. I am not sure what is meant by the reference to conditional testing (i.e. the testing of a single instance given. . .), nor is it clear what interpretation should be ascribed to the notion of "general validity".

8. Considerable attention is devoted to discussing the WZ 'fair coin' analogy, although the purpose of this discussion remains unclear. Throughout these comments there seems to be a general confusion between definitions (i.e. what we mean by a "fair coin"), testing criteria (i.e. under what circumstances would we consider a particular coin to be a "fair coin"), hypotheses (i.e. coin A is a "fair coin" while coin B is not), and theories.

For example, the authors state: "If the coin fails the test over a long period, this does not invalidate the theory of the behaviour of fair coins, but suggests only that the coin being tested is not a fair coin." This statement confuses theories with definitions in a manner reminiscent of Popper distinction between theories and metaphysical propositions. No empirical evidence would invalidate the "theory" of the behavior of fair coins because there is no theory, only a definition.

The next several lines link this fair coin discussion to WZ's theory, but once again confusion runs rampant. The WZ approach to theory testing is described in the following terms: "if the observations do not correspond with the theory . . . then the theory itself is rejected, rather than the particular instances under observation." The authors argue that since this approach is inconsistent with that described in the fair coin example the analogy fails, although the implications of this conclusion are not specified.

The point of the fair coin analogy seems to have been misconstrued—it has nothing to do with rejecting theories or particular instances under observation. Rather WZ are pointing out a fundamental difference between predictions about aggregate behavior (e.g. general trends) and those which concern individual cases (e.g. the outcome of a particular coin toss).

9. Page 6 contains the following: WZ "claim that it is not subject to crucial, critical test; that, because they are 'concerned with general trends' there may be exceptions to their theory. If therefore any evidence is presented to show that, in the case of a given set of facts, their theory was inapplicable they propose that the evidence cannot invalidate their theory".

Apart from the fact that explicit citations to the WZ paper are noticeably absent, the remarks again demonstrate a confusion between predictions about general trends and predictions about individual, isolated events.

The point at issue here seems to concern the proper 'unit of analysis' for testing WZ's theory; not the number of tests required or how many failures are necessary to cause rejection of the theory. WZ argue that their theory is concerned with prediction about 'general trends in the literature' rather than individual articles. Granted, how one operationally defines 'general trends' in this context remains problematic, it is nevertheless possible to refute WZ by identifying a general trend inconsistent with specific predictions. Individual, isolated research papers are not to be considered as evidence refuting the theory's predictions because the theory makes no claims about the factors which govern such phenomenon. More precise theories could well be constructed to explain both general trends *and* individual cases, but to date such theories have not been forthcoming.

10. I am not certain what useful purpose the "error term" discussion on page 7 serves. Apparently, it stems from an inability to recognize or accept the focus of WZ's theory. I have similar problems with the authors' unusual use of statistical termInology in this discussion—random variable, random distribution (does this mean a distribution that is sometimes uniform, occasionally normal, and sporadically poisson?), and probability density functions. What seems to be at the heart of these remarks is that WZ fail to include explicit statements about the individual altruistic goals of accounting researchers, choosing instead to rely upon economic arguments as a way of describing aggregate behavior, The authors apparently find this approach abhorrent; although they do not demonstrate its inconsistency with the empirical evidence.

11. The section entitled "Proposals in Other Social Sciences" is without substantive content. Can you provide definitive and convincing support for

the assertion on page 8 that the phenomena of interest to social scientists are sufficiently different from those studied in the natural science so as to demand fundamentally different research methodologies? Economic and quasi-economic models have a long history of application to describing aspects of individual and aggregate behavior even though those models are devoid of references to "true beliefs" in the sense in which the authors use the term. The discussion which concludes this section is particularly confused, as my marginal notations indicate.

12. Page 10 develops a potentially interesting weakness in the evidence cited by WZ as support for their theory. The authors point out that the accounting literature to which WZ refer predate the formal establishment of university accounting programs, hence the "conditions (WZ) posit for their theory to hold do not in fact exist!" While the authors may have a telling point here, the evidence marshalled as support is inadequate. Even if one takes a narrow view of the term "accounting researchers", employing it as synonymous with academic accountants, the authors still must identify the individuals responsible for this early literature and convincingly demonstrate that those individuals had no university affiliation during the period(s) in question.

13. The points raised in the final section of the comment are irrelevant, reflecting matters of editorial style rather than substantive concerns.

Professor E. A. Lowe
Division of Economic Studies
The University of Sheffield
Crookesmoor Building
Sheffield S10 1FL England

Dear Tony

The Demand for and Supply of Accounting Theories: A Comment

On the basis of comments received from the reviewers, I have decided not to accept your manuscript for publication in the *Review*. I am enclosing the reviewers' comments. The reviewers are labeled 1 and 2 so that you can link the marked manuscripts with the comments shown separately.

Reviewer 1 felt that, while your manuscript does contain some interesting points, there is not enough of a substantive contribution to the literature to warrant eventual publication. reviewer 2 recommended rejection. On a reading of the reviewers' comments, there simply is not sufficient reviewer support for pursuing the editorial review process further.

Thanks for sending your paper to the *Review,* and I regret that the outcome was not favorable.

Sincerely

Stephen A. Zeff

EPISTEMIC CRITIQUE 3

Editors' Introduction: Most research in accounting "fudges" the relationship between positive accounting research and the Excuses Theory. Positive accounting theory is an outgrowth of the relativism of Watts and Zimmerman's Excuses Theory. Once it is accepted that no absolute ground or foundational authority exists for normative statements—that all theories are arbitrary (relativistic) excuses or apologies—then (it is argued) the best researchers can do is to replicate reality exactly "in theory". This is the empiricist project of positivist accounting: to focus on "what is" and to abandon "subjective" concerns about "what should be". Unfortunately, this is positivistic philosophical position is based on a false dualism: that we can describe without making theoretical (and thus normative and value laden) commitments. Paul Williams' critique—again from a traditional philosophical position from within the North American academy-drives home this inconsistency in positive accounting work. The modest truth of Williams' position is plain to see with the hindsight of 1994, when positive accounting researchers have now abandoned the more extreme implications of their positivism. They now begrudgingly acknowledge that financial reporting does not merely describe history, but actually changes economic (and social) conditions (through bond covenants, etc) thereby raising once again the thorny question prompted by Williams' critique: "What criteria (norms) should guide financial reporting, disclosure, and corporate accountability?" But the truth of Williams' critique is of secondary importance to us—and the editorial process of The Accounting Review. At the time of its submission, Williams' manuscript was subversive of the orthodoxy: theoretical change has been subsequently tolerated by the mainstream, but in a manner controlled by their own excuses.

JULY 13, 1987

 **American Accounting Association**

Professor William R. Kinney, Jr.
Editor: *The Accounting Review*
Graduate School of Business Administration
The University of Michigan
Ann Arbor, MI 48109

Dear Professor Kinney:

Enclosed are three copies of a manuscript titled "The Logic of Positive Accounting Research" which I am submitting for editorial consideration by *The Accounting Review*. The paper is a comment on the methodology of positive accounting research. It is not under consideration by any journal. Thank you for your consideration.

Sincerely,

Paul F. Williams
Associate Professor
North Carolina State University

PFW:sr

Enclosures

SEPTEMBER 22, 1987

 North Carolina State University

Professor Paul F. Williams
North Carolina State University
School of Humanities and Social Sciences
Department of Economics and Business
Box 8109
Raleigh, NC 27695-8109

Dear Paul:

On the basis of comments received from the reviewers and my own review, I have decided not to accept your manuscript for publication in the Review. Neither reviewer recommends acceptance and I cannot find sufficient grounds for disagreement. I am enclosing the reviewers' comments (labeled A and B) and B's marked manuscript copy.

B is the more favorable of the two reviewers and believes that you have a subtle but potentially important point to make. B also believes that the point is well disguised by unnecessary and confusing exposition.

I have tried to follow the argument and tried to match the claims against the empirical work in Table 1. It is hard to do since many of the studies do not (as you claim) have an accounting measure on the dependent variable side. Others have one accounting choice (e.g., depreciation method) explained by size as measured by (accounting) sales. Do you mean to suggest that another size measure such as number of employees or number of units produced (or "value" of units produced) would yield different answers?

Reviewer B may be correct about the point made. However, a paper that better explains the point would seem to be an essentially new paper.

Thanks for sending your paper to the Review. I regret that the outcome was not favorable.

Sincerely,

William R. Kinney, Jr.

THE LOGIC OF POSITIVE ACCOUNTING THEORY

PAUL WILLIAMS

ABSTRACT

This paper is a "method-illogical" comment on positive accounting research (PAR). PAR consists of tests of positive accounting theory. PAR is a relatively small but growing body of important accounting literature. The discussion in this paper is aimed at demonstrating that as positive accounting researchers have translated the theoretical language of positive accounting theory into an empirical language which permits experimentation they have transformed positive accounting theory into a tautology. In effect they have put dependent variables on both sides of their equations. This makes accounting practice its own explanation which is not the improvement in our understanding envisioned by positive accounting theory. In addition the paper includes the demonstration that any plausible argument that is available to defend PAR against the accusation that it is tautologous fails. This leaves the results of PAR, in any substantive sense, uninterpretable and thus unbelievable.

Introduction

Positive accounting research (PAR) has produced a sizeable body of literature (see Table 1 for examples) consisting of reports on experiments investigating the accounting procedures choice problem. The researchers performing these experiments have been informed by what is called positive accounting theory; specifically, the application of Jensen and Meckling's (1976 agency theory to explain managers' (and others') choices of accounting procedures. These choices may be either actual choices of procedure or preferences for procedures revealed through lobbying standard setting bodies.

The purpose of any accounting theory, according to positive theory's more prominent proponents (Watts and Zimmerman, 1986, p. 2), ". . . is to *explain* and *predict* (emphasis in original) accounting practice". Positive accounting theory provides teleological explanations of accounting choices rooted in the purposes of managers.[1] Simply stated, these purposes of managers, as inially described by Watts and Zimmerman (1978), are reducible to economic self-interest. That is, when choosing accounting procedures managers consider only the effect of the procedures on their wealth; choices are wealth-maximising given the constraints imposed by other wealth-maximizing agents (eg., shareholders, bondholders). Further, it is presumed that mangers maximise their wealth if they choose those accounting procedures that maximise the value of the firm and/or maximise manager compensation via compensation agreements tied to accounting numbers. The list of wealth costs is familiar, eg. political costs, bookkeeping costs, taxes, contracting costs.

The type of study with which this paper is concerned is identified as positive accounting research since all studies of this type involve testing positive accounting theory. The purpose of this paper is to demonstrate that these PAR studies are all plagued by a fatal logical flaw which makes PAR incoherent. The logical problem is created when the theoretical language of positive accounting theory is translated into the empirical language of PAR. The result of the translation process is to place dependent variable on both sides of the PAR equations; experimentally positive accounting theory is made tautologous.

This paper is both a comment and to an extent a polemic. It is a comment by its demonstration of the logical problem with PAR which may help account for PAR's modest results and by its suggestion of the minimum to be done to make PAR believable.[2] The paper is polemical to the extent that its demonstration of the incoherence of PAR represents an intellectual embarrassment for accounting research, something that frequently occurs with the substitution of form for substance. What this paper is not explicitly concerned with is the "philosophy of science" underlying positive theory; positivist assertions are purposely taken at face value.[3]

The remainder of the paper is in three sections. The next section will describe how the logical problem is created. That will be followed by a section which describes the ways in which the problem is now implicitly being escaped and which demonstrates that all of them fail. The final, brief section consists of some conclusions.

The Problem Explained

The logical problem with PAR will be explained through the use of the following set of logically related statements, in syllogistic form, which describe the logic informing PAR:

Theoretical Premise (TP):	Managers' economic self-interests determine managers' choices of accounting procedures.
Factual Premise (FP):	Accounting procedures that managers choose determine accounting measures.
Theoretical Conclusion (TC):	Managers' economic self interests determine accounting measures.

The premise labelled TP is the statement of positive accounting theory. If positive accounting theory is true then TP is believable.[4] Positive accounting researchers clearly behave as if they are willing to come to a belief in TP since the hypotheses tested and the models built are attempts explicitly directed at establishing the truth-value of TP.

The premise labelled FP is a factual premise which may or may not be believable. Anyone trained in accounting should agree that the choice of an accounting procedures determines, ceteris paribus, at least some accounting measures. For example, the choice of a depreciation procedure affects the measure of total assets and net income and consequently numerous ratios that may convey economic information about a firm. Without the modifier "that managers choose" FP is true by the very nature of accounting. The addition of "that managers choose" to the premise may make FP false. For the time being it will be assumed that FP has truth-value. The justification for this comes directly from observing the behavior of positive researchers. If it is trivially true that choices of accounting procedures determine accounting measures and if positive researchers have thus far focused principally on management as the most important choosers of procedures, then one must be willing to believe that managers' choices are not insignificant determinants of accounting measures. For example, if a manager chooses a depreciation procedure ad libitum she has determined some accounting measures. If the choice of accounting procedures is exclusively the domain of management then management does indeed determine all accounting measures. Later in the paper the assumption of the truth-value of FP will be relaxed and the implications for PAR of FP being true and FP being false will be indicated. The theoretical conclusion would seem to be believable if both TP and FP are believed.

The very essence of PAR is providing the empirical evidence necessary to justify belief in TP. To do so requires the experimenter to alter the language of TP so that is has empirical meaning. Since managers' economic self-interests are not directly observable, and perhaps not even capable of being spoken about, experimenters define certain "economic variables" which they believe can eventually be operationally defined and they substitute those variables for managers' economic self-interest. With this substitution TP becomes the modified premise labelled TP-1:

TP-1: "Economic variables" determine managers' choices of accounting procedures.

Once "economic variables" have been substituted for managers' economic self-interest, positive researchers can begin to move from a conceptual to an observational language. This is accomplished by identifying "nameable economic variables" which by the logical arguments provided by positive theorists are linked to managers' economic self-interest. A familiar example follows.

One "nameable economic variable" is "political costs", linked to economic self-interests via an argument similar to the following. Large proportions of managers who decide accounting procedures have ownership interests in the firms they manage. Making managers owners is one tactic shareholders apparently employ to optimally contract for managers' services. Any manager's individual wealth is thus directly linked to the value of the firm, and almost anything that threatens to diminish that value adversely affects the wealth of the manager. Any firm's value can be lessened by direct government regulation or other form of political interference, ie. by "taxing" the firm with political costs. Thus managers in choosing accounting procedures would act so as to minimise the expected value of these costs.

Such arguments linking "nameable economic variables" to managers' economic self interest are certainly plausible. They mst be so for experimentation to proceed (see Watts and Zimmerman (1986) for the arguments linking other "nameable economic variables" to managers' economic self-interests).

By identifying "nameable economic variables" positive researchers have again altered the language of TP. Substituting "nameable economic variables" for "economic variable" in TP-1 the new premise (labelled TP-2) now reads:

TP-2: "Nameable economic variables" determine managers' choice of accounting procedures.

After "nameable economic variables" have been enumerated and linked to managers' economic self-interests it becomes necessary to identify proxies for these "nameable economic variables" in order to define them operationally.[5] Continuing with the "political costs" example, the proxy substituted for this "nameable economic variable" is firm size. This substitution is based on the assumption that larger firms are more visible and thus more likely to be subjected to regulation. Some "nameable economic variables", eg. leverage, need no proxy before they can operationally defined;

they serve as their own proxies. The language of TP has again been altered with the substitution of "proxies" for "nameable economic variables" so that TP-2 now becomes TP-3 which reads:

TP-3: "Proxy economic variables" determine managers' choices of accounting procedures.

Now the experimenter needs but one more step in order to complete the translation of TP into a premise with empirical content. This is accomplished by identifying "measures" for the "proxies." In most instances these "measures" are accounting measures. Table 1 contains a list of the measures for proxies used in a selected number of positive experiments.

In every study save one over 50 per cent of the measures were "accounting measures," i.e., based on the accounting numbers reported in the financial statements of firms in the samples. It is the use of these "accounting measures" that creates a serious logical problem for PAR. The logical problem arises in the final step of the translation process when "accounting measures" are substituted for "proxy economic variables" in TP-3 to create a new premise. This new premise is now one with empirical content and it is accordingly labelled Empirical Premise (EP) and reads:

EP: "Accounting measures" determine managers' choices of accounting procedures.

This empirical premise is indeed the one tested by positive researchers. In the probit, logit. or OLS regression models informed by EP to test TP, it is in the most instances indeed some "accounting measures" used as the independent variable to predict the dependent variable which is some managerial choice of accounting procedure.

The problem is revealed when the empirically meaningful EP is substituted for the theoretically meaningful TP in the original set of statement to yield an empirical conclusion:

Empirical Premise (EP):   "Accounting measures" determine managers' choices of accounting procedures.

Factual Premise (FP):   Accounting procedures that managers choose determine accounting measures.[6]

Empirical Conclusion (EC):   Accounting measures determine accounting measures.

Clearly something has been lost in the translation. The sense of EC is clearly other than the sense of TC.

TABLE 1

EXAMPLE OF PAR STUDIES		
Authors	**Dependent Variables (AM2 Type)**	**Independent Variables (AMI Type)**
Watts and Zimmerman (1978)	1. Support or Not Support GPLA	1. Depreciation Expense + Mkt. Value* 2. Net Monetary Asset Position + Mkt. Value* 3. Sales X Effect of GPLA on income* 4. Sales + Total Sales in SIC Group X GPLA effect* 5. Compensation Plan: Yes or No 6. Regulated: Yes or No
Hagerman and Zmijewski (1979)	1. Inventory Method 2 Depreciation Method 3. Pension Method 4. ITC Method	1. Total Assets* 2. Sales* 3. Beta 4. Fixed Assets + Sales* 5. Concentration Ration* 6. Compensation Plan: Yes or No
Dhaliwal (1980)	1. Oil and Gas Development Cost Method	1. Sales (Control Variable)* 2. Debt/Equity*
Salamon and Dhaliwal (1980)	1. Disclosure of Segmental Data	1. Total Assets* 2. New Capital Issues: Yes or No
Bowen, et al (1981)	1. Capitalisation of Interest	1. Compensation Plan: Yes or No 2. Dividends + Unrestricted R/E* 3. Current Interest + Interest Expense* 4. Net Tangible Assets + Long Term Debt* 5. Sales* 6. Unrestricted R/E: Yes or No*
Holthausen (1981)	1. Abnormal Return, Proxy for Depreciation Change	1. Forecast Error EPS + Stock Price* 2. Compensation Plan: Yes or No 3. Impact of Dep. Change on EPS + Stock price* 4. Book Value of Public Debt + (Stock Price X Shares)* 5. Book Value of Private Debt + (Stock Price x Shares)* 6. Inventory of Payable Funds + (Stock Price X Shares)* 7. Book Value of Public Debt + Book Value of Private Debt + (Stock Price X Shares)*

TABLE 1 (continued)

EXAMPLE OF PAR STUDIES

Authors	Dependent Variables (AM2 Type)	Independent Variables (AMI Type)
Leftwich, et. al. (1981)	1. Frequency of Interim Reporting	1. Net Property + Firm Value* 2. Mkt. Value of Stock + Book Value of Current Liabilities, Long Term Debt and Preferred Stock* 3. Book Value of Bank Loans, Public and Private Debt + Firm Value* 4. Book Value of Preferred Equity + Firm Value* 5. Outside Director 6. Frequency of reporting in 1937 7. Stock Exchange Listing
Zmijewski and Hagerman (1981)	1. Income Strategy	1. Compensation Plan: Yes or No 2. Concentration Ratio* 3. Beta 4. Log of Net Sales* 5. Gross Fixed Assets + Sales* 6. Total Debt + Total Assets*
Chow (1982)	1. Hire External Auditing	1. Mkt. Value of owners' Equity + Book Value of Debt* 2. Debt + (Measure defined in 1 above)* 3. Number of Accounting Measures used in Debt Covenants 4. % Management Ownership 5. Stock Registration: NYSE or OTC
Dhaliwal, et. al. (1982)	1. Depreciation Method	1. Owner Controlled: Yes or No 2. Total Assets* 3. Debt + Equity*
Kelly (1982)	1. Reaction to SFAS #8	1. Compensation Plan: Yes or No 2. Debt + Equity* 3. Total Consolidated Assets* 4. % Management Ownership 5. Foreign Sales + Total Consolidated Sales*
Kelly (1985)	1. Lobby on SFAS #8	1. Foreign Sales + Total Consolidated Sales* 2. Total Debt + Total Assets* 3. % Management Ownership 4. Total Assets*

*Denotes an Accounting Measure

The Empirical Conclusion reads the same in either direction; it is tautologous. It can be inverted with no alteration of its meaning. If TC is inverted it reads:

> YC (inv): Accounting measures determine managers' economic self-interests.

This would seem to contradict the direction of causality implied by positive accounting theory. It also now makes the theoretical statements tautologous. The unaltered factual premise states that managers determine accounting measures and by TC (inv) accounting measures determine managers' economic self-interests, so managers determine their own economic self-interests, which is a proposition positive theory starts out with. It appears that in the process of defining an experimental language for positive accounting theory the theory has been made circular.[7] Empirical tests of the theory boil down to testing which accounting measures correlate with which accounting measures. Some will, as anyone aware of the codetermined nature of accounting numbers would predict.

That PAR has been and continues to be done indicates that positive accounting researchers must believe that there is a plausible escape from the circularity. Implicit in the behavior of positive accounting researchers is the strategy that they have followed to escape the obviously circular EC and assert that their results speak to the theory. The strategy will be described and shown to fail in the next section.

Escaping the Circle

Note that in the Empirical Conclusion "accounting measures" as subject of that sentence was not enclosed in quotation marks as it had been in every previous instance. This raises the obvious suspicion that a semantic trick was required to assert EC as it was originally written. That is "accounting measures" as the subject of the sentence means something different from "accounting measures" as object. If EC is rewritten as:

> EC': Accounting measures-1 (AM1) determine accounting measures -2 (AM2) and AM1 means something other than AM2, then EC is meaningful and not inconsistent with TC.

This is the strategy that positive researchers have obviously followed. In every positive study of management accounting choice the dependent variable, which is equivalent to AM2 in EC', is some observed *choice* about an accounting measures, e.g., depreciation method, inventory method, capitalisation of interest. It measures managerial behavior; AM2 informs the researcher about what accounting actions management took.

Accounting measures, the nouns, which are equivalent to AM1 in EC', say something about the independent variables (the predictors). AM1 has a different meaning than AM2. To the positive researcher AM1 has *economic* meaning. It informs him about managers' economic self-interests, not, like AM2, about managements' behaviors. For example, as AM1 "total assets" means "high or low political costs." It informs about managers' motives. It does not mean, as it would if it were AM2, "management has in the past chosen accounting alternatives to deflate the amount reported assets," a management behavior. By asserting the different semantic content of each of the "accounting measures" appearing in EC, the positive researcher may be confident that the circle is broken.

To contend that AM1 and AM2 mean different things is merely as assertion that is sufficient for the person with an incredulous willingness to believe. But if logical consistency is required of positive researchers then the strategy does not work. The remainder of this paper is devoted to demonstrating the logical inconsistencies in the beliefs informing the positive researcher who adopts the AM1 = AM2 strategy described above. The strategy will be assessed under two different conditions: first, under the condition that the Factual Premise has truth-value; and, second under the condition that it does not.

IF FP HAS TRUTH VALUE

If FP is believable, that is, managers' choices of accounting procedures do, to a significant extent, determine accounting measures, then managements' behavior will play a significant role in explaining existing accounting practice. This possibility must motivate to some extent the attention that management has received in PAR. If FP is true two conclusions about the strategy are possible depending upon what interpretation one gives to self-seeking managerial behavior and its likely consequence for accounting practice.

One interpretation of self-seeking behavior is that it implies management is manipulative, that it is in some sense willing to lie.[8] That means that management chooses accounting procedures so as to tell a story that is beneficial to it. If existing accounting practice is determined to a significant extent by such a manipulative management then how can economic meaning be ascribed to AM1? There is so obvious a reflexivity; managers are manipulating those variables to misrepresent the "economic" facts.[9] How can one then interpret those variables as containing information of economic substance? Accounting measures in such circumstances can convey nothing more than information about managements' past choices of accounting procedures. This point can be illustrated with a simple example from positive theory. Sales and Total Assets are accounting numbers used to measure political costs. Positive theory predicts that, ceteris paribus, firms that are "larger", measured by Sales or Total Assets, will have higher potential political costs and their managements will, therefore, choose income reducing accounting procedures. This strategy is deemed rational because of the assumed importance of profits (namely "excess profits") as an event prompting the imposition of increased political costs. How can managers choose income reducing procedures without affecting either Sales or Total Assets? By the arithmetic of the income equation managers can reduce income by decelerating the recognition of Sales revenue or accelerating the recognition of expenses which in turn decelerates the growth of Total Assets. If some managers are effective manipulators of accounting measures and if the process of managerial selection of accounting procedures is ongoing, there is no way using just reports to shareholders or the SEC and data tapes to know whether accounting measures say something say something about the relative political costs of firms, i.e., are AM1, or simply the relative effectiveness of managers as manipulators of accounting numbers, i.e., are AM2. Some managers for one reason or another lie better than others.[10] It would seem that if convincing tests of positive theory are to be made under the assumption of successfully manipulative managers then the measures on the independent variables must be purged of measures produced by those managers, if that is possible. Otherwise there is no reason to take PAR results seriously.

The other interpretation of managerial self-seeking behaviour is that it is not manipulative, or is not successfully manipulative. This is equivalent to granting to the positive researcher his assertion that accounting measures used as independent variables have AM1 meaning. Thus managers' choices of accounting procedures produce accounting measures that have an economic interpretation; they tell the researcher something about what managers' economic self-interests are. Therefore regardless of the motives of managers, they are somehow guided to choose accounting procedures that have economic interpretations that are not just informative about their own behaviour (AM2); they are also AM1. But this interpretation leaves the definitions of "accounting measures" in the Empirical Conclusion still equivalent and the tautologous nature of that conclusion is undisturbed. It is an unconvincing argument in defense of the positive researcher's strategy to assume the truth of EC in order to prove it false! By assuming accounting procedures chosen by managers invariable produce AM1 type measures, the positive researcher cannot maintain the AM1-AM2 distinction—the semantic trick is one he is playing on himself.

A further devastating implication of granting AM1 status to accounting measures is the apparent loss of self-interest as an *explanation*. If the accounting procedures chosen by managers produce accounting measures that are believed by researchers to be reliable indicators of economic constructs then it can be said that in a very real sense the choices of managers are "honest."[11] Since managers' past choices are used as measures of independent variables and those measures are assumed to be "honest" measures, then self-interest and honesty become indistinguishable. It is impossible to discern without psychological testing of individual managers whether their accounting choices are motivated by economic self-interest or by a desire to tell the truth, at least to positive researchers. An "honesty" theory of accounting practice is just as plausible as a "moral hazard" one.

Perhaps another way of stating the above conclusion will add some clarity. Experimentally positive theory states that managers' choices of accounting procedure are functionally determined by accounting measures of managers' economic self-interest, i.e.:

Managers' current choices = f (accounting measures).

But the accounting measures are believed to *measure* in an economically meaningful way the economic variables that tell the researcher about managers' economic self-interest, so:

Managers' current choices = f (accounting measures that are "true")

where "true" merely means that the researcher believes them to convey knowledge about economic phenomena motivating managers. That is, the measures are AM1 type.

The assumption that the Factual Premise is true permits the following statement:

Managers' current choices = f (managers' past choices which produced "true" measures)

An experiment confirming this relationship that "true" accounting measures predict managers' current choices, i.e., coefficients of the variables are statistically significant, would imply that managers' behaviours are consistent with their economic self-interest but it also implies that their current choices will produce "true" measures in the future. This last implication must be assumed because if current choices don't produce "true" measures, any subsequent experiments will demonstrate that managers are economically irrational. This is so because measurement error of the independent variables has been induced by managers if they don't choose "true" measures. If the experimenter continues to believe the future measures are "true" her future experiments will indicate that economic variables don't predict managers' behaviors. If the experimenter wants to believe he has conducted a meaningful experiment he must have some confidence that the experiment could be performed for the *next* accounting choice and yield similar results. The only way this confidence is justified is if she believes the choice she has just investigated leads to "true" measures just as she implicitly assumed all previous choices led to "true" measures. She must believe that economic rationality is not interspersed with periods of irrationality. But if managers' choices always lead to "true" measures then whether economic self-interest or a desire to accommodate positive researchers motivates managers in their accounting choices becomes moot. How does one tell the difference *empirically?* Appeals to the common archetype of businessmen as thieves who work in the daylight just will not do.

In conclusion the assumption that Factual Premise is true makes PAR implausible. If managers manipulate numbers it is very doubtful those numbers are interpretable as conveying information that informs us about managers' economic self-interest. If the accounting numbers are "true" then the theory is tautologous and whether managerial self-interest is explanatory is undecidable with models that include accounting measures.

IF FP HAS NO TRUTH VALUE

The other condition under which to consider the positive researcher's denial of the circularity of PAR is that of the Factual premise having little or no truth-value, i.e., managers' choices of accounting procedures only weakly determine existing accounting practice. This defense of the strategy that AM1 and AM2 mean different things is a more plausible defense than under the condition that FP is true, but other beliefs on the part of the positive researcher are required which create equally damaging logical problems for PAR.

The assumption that management does not substantially determine accounting practice (FP is not true) implies that there are other participants who are involved. The creation of accounting practice is a multi-participant process (a social one). Positive researchers could argue that these other participants through their joint behaviours create accounting measures which have economic interpretations, a "markets-produce-the-truth-argument". The researcher thus relies on these others as providing the assurance he needs to ascribe economic meaning to his independent variables. This reliance on the other participants has two possible implications.

The first is that this reliance on participants other than management implies that the process does not really require management participation. Accounting measures would be the same whether management chooses one accounting procedure or another.[12] This must be asserted for if the measures would not be the same we are back to FP being true and the defense fails for the reasons given in the previous section. But if positive accounting theory is an explanation of accounting practice, and accounting practice produces accounting measures, and if accounting measures to be of the AM1 type must be produced by a process not materially affected by management behaviour, why are the choices of accounting procedure made by management important? The obvious answer is that, by assumption, they aren't! The important behaviour for understanding existing accounting practice would appear to be the behaviours of all those other participants except management, for it is they that apparently produce the AM1 type measures, that positive researchers use to test their models of managements' behaviours. This "other process" seems to be what a theory of accounting practice should be about.

The second implication devolves from the likely response to the preceding discussion. What if FP is neither strictly true nor strictly false? That is, managements' choices do have an effect on accounting practice, but the nature and magnitude of that effect is determined by the choices and actions of the other participants. This process could still be a process driven by economic self-interests, couldn't it? What the positive researcher is doing by focusing on managers' choices is conducting a partial test of positive theory.

But can one logically conduct partial tests? The answer is of course no. Substitute for "managers" any other participant you want; who it is is purely arbitrary. As long as one is using accounting measures to evaluate the economic self-interest of that participant, the same logical problems previously elucidated hold. To believe accounting measures are of the AM1 type still requires the researcher to make the same "ceteris paribus" assumptions as when managers were the object of study. Characterising positive theory as a multi-participant interactive process doesn't permit escaping the circularity. Such a theory is not meaningfully testable at the margin unless some other measure of economic self-interest independent of accounting practice can be devised.[13]

Conclusion

The conclusion of this paper as a comment is a rather simple one. It is that a theory about accounting practice can not be convincingly tested by, in effect, resorting to accounting practice itself as its own explanation. The cavalier use of accounting measures to represent the presumed *independent* economic self-interest of the individuals putatively producing those very measures in the service of their interest is not particularly good science. Whether such independent measures are available is at this point in time speculative. They may not exist and if they do it may require some hard work to find them. For those persons interested in continuing to do PAR that work should be a first priority.

The conclusion of this paper as a polemic is also a rather simple and disconcerting one. PAR has been "going-on" now for about a decade without anyone noting or admitting so obvious a logical incoherence to it. As a commentary on the status of accounting science it doesn't induce optimism. The ethics of science require an attitude of self-criticism, of rebuke rather than self-congratulation, of doubt rather than hubris. The incoherence of PAR may merely be a symptom of accounting becoming an intellectually closed society where how you know is far more important than what you know. The malady is caricatured well by Abdel-Khalik (1986) who provides an amusing, but all too depressingly true, cartoon account of the young accounting researcher, enslaved by his computer, desperately searching for correlations among accounting numbers. McCloskey (1985, p. 52) says it best:

> Little wonder that youths in science are drunk with methodology: 'Ale, man, ale's the stuff to drink/For fellows whom it hurts to think/ . . ./ And faith, 'tis pleasant till 'tis past:/The mischief is that 'twill not last.' One can understand the attraction of methodological formulas immediately potable. A textual critic equipped with the formula 'the more sincere text is the better' or an economic with 'the statistically significant coefficient should be retained' is ready for work. That his work will be *wrong* (emphasis added) bothers him less than that he will not get the stuff out at all unless he possesses, as he is inclined to say *some* (emphasis in original) methodology. Output man, output's the stuff to get,/So deans and chairman will not fret.

Notes

1. Managers are obviously not the only persons involved in the process of determining accounting practice. The argument to be developed in this paper will initially focus on managers. Later in the paper the introduction of other participants into the process will be discussed and the implications described. At this point the fact that accounting practice involves numerous participants is not central to the arguments. It is also not within the purview of this paper to consider the issue of the causal status of motives. That is a problem for positive accounting theory; this paper is concerned only with a problem of positive accounting research.
2. If one does not adhere rigidly to the notion that statistical significance means real significance (ie. alters permanently one's belief's about the world), then it isn't unreasonable to argue that PAR has produced no support for the theory.
3. The epistemology informing positive accounting theory has been roundly criticised. For an excellent discussion of the anachronistic nature of the dominant accounting epistemology see Arrington (1986).

4. The term "true" is not to imply eternal truth but merely "believable until something better to believe comes along".

5. The issue of selecting better or worse proxies is a problem in its own right but is not particularly germane to the issue at hand. The "proxy problem" being considered in this paper goes beyond the goodness or badness of proxies to the issue of the appropriateness of even considering something as a candidate.

6. The factual premise is not altered by the translation. Its truth or falsity is not affected by the behavior of the positive researcher.

7. Another interpretation is that the process is made recursive, but if that is admitted the whole structure of positive accounting theory crumbles. Positive theory takes managers' economic self interests as the immutable given; these interests originate within the managers themselves and are not caused by anything but Man's presumed fundamental nature. But if managers choose accounting measures which in turn determine managers' economic self interests the process is dialectic and which is causing which and where it will all end up is anybody's guess. The assumed causal agent in positive accounting theory is also problematic, but, as previously noted, beyond the scope of this paper.

8. Lying is here meant to imply only that management purposely does not communicate its full knowledge of some circumstance. It implies nothing about motives; the intent may be evil or good. See Bok (1978) for a discussion of the morality of lying.

9. One might argue there are no economic "facts" conveyed by accounting numbers. The response to this is if there is no extant idea of communicating reliable economic data then manipulating accounting measures makes no sense. For example, the notion of income smoothing is irrational unless one believes something of economic significance is being communicated other than that management is acting to smooth income.

10. There is the old ethnic joke about a certain nationality of businessmen who maintain three sets of books: one for share-holders, one for the government, and the real one. If positive researchers were testing positive theory on firms domiciled in this nation, from which set of books would they obtain measures of their independent variables?

11. Management may be trying to tell lies to shareholders, creditors, the IRS, and the SEC, but positive researchers, by their unquestioning acceptance of accounting measures as independent variables, act as if management is at least telling them the "truth".

12. Here "same" does not mean identical. "Same" implies immaterial difference where immateriality is decided by the positive researcher.

13. Two additional implications of this interactive process argument are rather interesting. Does positive theory predict that the accounting measures produced by this process serve as AM1 type measures of the economic self-interests of each and every type of participant? To use accounting measures to test the theory in total would still require that such be the case. Also, if the accounting measure so produced are of the AM1 type what advice can positive researchers give to a policy maker who asks them what to do? If the researchers want to continue

doing their experiments (for which many are paid large sums of money) they had best response, "Keep doing what you're doing now". That may be very sound advice.

References

Abdel-Khalik, A., "The Computer Held Hostage, Day 1001: A Research Story," *Issues in Accounting Education* (Fall, 1986), pp. 207–229.

Arrington, C., "The Rhetoric of Inquiry and Accounting Research," unpublished Working Paper (The University of Iowa, 1986).

Bok, S., *Lying: Moral Choice in Public and Private Life* (Pantheon Books, 1978).

Bowener, R., J. Lacey, and E. Noreen, "Determinants of the Corporate Decision to Capitalise Interest," *Journal of Accounting and Economics* (August, 1981), pp. 151–179.

Chow, C., "The Demand for External Auditing: Size, Debt and Ownership Influences," *The Accounting Review* (April, 1982), pp. 272–291.

Dhaliwal, D., "The Effects of the Firm's Capital Structure on the Choice of Accounting Methods," *The Accounting Review* (January, 1980), pp. 78–84.

———, G. Salamon, and E. Smith, "The Effect of Owner Versus Management Control on the Choice of Accounting Methods," *Journal of Accounting and Economics* (July, 1982), pp. 41–53.

Hagerman, R., and M. Zmijewski, "Some Economic Determinants of Accounting Policy Choice," *Journal of Accounting and Economics* (August, 1979), pp. 141–161.

Holthausen, R., "Evidence on the Effect of Bond Covenants and Management Compensation Contracts on the Choice of Accounting techniques: The Case of the depreciation Switchback," *Journal of Accounting and Economics* (March, 1981), pp. 73–109.

Jensen, M., and W. Meckling, "Theory of the Firm: Management Behaviour, Agency Costs and Ownership Structure," *Journal of Financial Economics,* vol. 3 (1976), pp. 305–360.

Kelly, L., "Corporate Lobbying and Changes in Financing or Operating Activities in reaction to FAS No. 8, *Journal of Accounting and Public Policy* (Winter, 1982), pp. 153–173.

———, "Corporate Management Lobbying on FAS No. 8: Some Further Evidence," *Journal of Accounting Research* (Autumn, 1985), pp. 619–632.

Leftwich, R., R. Watts, and J. Zimmerman, "Voluntary Corporate Disclosure: The Case of Interim Reporting," *Journal of Accounting Research* (Supplement, 1981), pp. 50–77.

McCloskey, O., *The Rhetoric of Economics* (The University of Wisconsin Press, 1985).

Salamon, G., and D. Dhaliwal, "Company Size and Financial Disclosure Requirements with Evidence from the Segmental Reporting Issue," *Journal of Business, Finance and Accounting* (Winter, 1980), pp. 555–568.

Watts, R., and J. Zimmerman, "Towards a positive Theory of the Determinants of Accounting Standards," *The Accounting Review* (January, 1978), pp. 112–134.
———, ———, *Positive Accounting Theory* (Prentice-Hall, 1986).
Zmijewski, M. and R. Hagerman, "An Income Strategy Approach to the Positive Theory of Accounting Standard Setting/Choice," *Journal of Accounting and Economics* (August, 1981), pp. 129–149.

"The Logic of Positive Accounting Research"
Comments to the Author(s)

This paper is a commentary on whether (in the author(s)' opinion) the premises underlying positive accounting research are "logical". The author(s) begin by considering the theoretical underpinnings of positive accounting research and conclude that empirically, positive accounting theory is a tautology. Thus, according to the author(s), this whole line of research is lacking in any substantive contributions.

Two major deficiencies underlie this paper. First, it is basically an opinion piece. The reader must accept the author(s)' interpretations and definitions to agree with their conclusions. Little substantiation for their allegations is offered. For example, the author(s) do not take any one positive accounting research study and trace its conceptual foundations through its empirical development to demonstrate where or how the tautology arises. If, in fact, the tautology does exist, it would be enlightening for the author(s) to consider how it could be addressed (within the context of the research study being reviewed). Nor do the author(s) refer to previous research on positivism or the philosophy of science. For an example of this approach, the author(s) are referred to Charles Christianson, "The Methodology of Positive Accounting", the *Accounting Review*, January 1983. This article should have been at least referenced in the present paper.

Second, the author(s) loosely use the method of logical argument to demonstrate the tautology of positive accounting research. This method needs to be applied more rigorously. That is, the premises and arguments should be developed using the methods common to logic. As it is currently written, the paper consists of confusing statements containing twists of words. And it is these word twists the author(s) use to reach their conclusions! While the author(s) state they are not concerned with the philosophy of science underlying positive theory (page 2), it is not clear this can be ignored in a critical analysis of the development of the framework of positive accounting research.

Other observations are as follows:

1. On page 2, the author(s) refer to "PAR's modest results". These should be described and the author(s) should specifically show how the alleged tautology is responsible for these results.

2. The definition of truth in footnote four is a bit amusing: "believable until something better [in who's opinion?] comes

along". This is a troublesome definition since much of the paper is written in terms of what is or is not (in the author(s)' opinion) "believable".

3. Emotional language is unnecessary: "intellectual embarrassment"; "incredulous willingness to believe"; businessmen as thieves who work in the daylight"; "cavalier use of accounting measures"; "self-congratulation", "hubris", "intellectually closed society"; and the potshot in footnote 13.

4. No substantiation is given for what the author(s) consider to be the "logic informing PAR". Again, these premises and conclusions are the author(s)' opinions. For example, some might argue that the theoretical premise is a maintained hypothesis, with empirical tests aimed at examining managers' behaviour assuming their economic self-interests determine their accounting choices. Indeed, much of the research examines how different implicit and explicit contracting environments create different self interests and thus different accounting choice motivations. Yet the author(s) claim researchers attempt to establish the "truth-value" of the premise.

5. The modified premises TP-1 through TP-3 and the empirical premise are really nothing more than the operationalisation of theoretical and conceptual ideas. There is nothing new in the author(s)' observations. The substitution of works economic self interest → economic variables → nameable economic variables → proxy economic variables → accounting measures is not adequately explained. Yes, accounting measures may surrogate for managers' self-interest, but only because they are used to enforcing an explicit or implicit contract that affects managements' self-interest. Indeed, the author(s) state the problems with their paper on page nine: "clearly something has been lost in the translation".

6. The use of the term "determines" in the premises is disturbing. It would be more appropriate to say influences. In a sense, the use of the term "determine" creates the tautology in that most researchers admit they are using proxies to examine influences on accounting choices.

7. It is quite possible that "accounting measures determine accounting measures" without this being a tautology. For example, management may already be using accelerated depreciation and not want to further lower net income through an

accounting procedure thus so elect to use FIFO inventory valuation. What the author(s) observe as being "circular" is really nothing more than dynamics and relatedness of the system.

8. It is also quite plausible that managers manipulate accounting measures (eg. sales or total assets) such that the measures reported reflect both economic substance and past accounting choices. This is endemic in the process by which accounting measures arise. This "problem" might not emerge if, for example, only outside independent auditors could choose the firm's accounting procedures. It is not clear in the author(s)' argument why this "problem" means there is no reason to take PAR results seriously".

9. The whole discussion regarding the distinction between AM1 and AM2 (pages 12–19) is very confusing and unenlightening. It is here where the author(s) seem to be playing word tricks. The premise underlying positive accounting research is that managers' current accounting choices are influenced by the status quo as represented by accounting measures, whether "true" or not. It is not at all clear how the author(s) reach the conclusion based on these arguments that "the assumption that Factual Premise is true makes PAR implausible".

The Logic of Positive Accounting Research: Comments to Author

In general, this is a well-argued and original paper, which deals with an issue of significance to accounting research. It argues that at the empirical level PAR is tautologous, ie. that PA researchers seek to explain accounting choices by reference to accounting choices, that is, accounting measures.

The argumentation is subtle and complex and so rather demanding on a reader. To a large extent this is necessitated by the topic, and indeed is probably one reason why the issue has not been dealt with previously. However, there is considerable scope for shortening and tightening the paper. The following comments relate mostly to tightening the paper.

Detailed comments:

1. Is it your paper which is "method-illogical?". It seems rather that this paper concerns the method-illogicality of PAR. Also, unless this paper is intend for the Comment section of the A/R, it is best not to describe it as a "comment".

2. PAR is a "relatively small but growing body of . . . literature". This seems an understatement (on p.1 PAR is referred to as a "sizeable body of literature).

3. Many readers of the A/R would not be familiar with the term "teleological". Could it be omitted; or a substitute such as "causal" substituted?

4. This paragraph seems superfluous and as such distracts from the line of argument in the paper. Same applies to footnotes 2 and 3. Also this paper does not suggest "the minimum to be done to make PAR believable"—p.20 "states whether such independent measures are available is at this point in time speculative". Could the paragraph be omitted without loss of content? I think so.

5. P.4 discusses a very simple point and needs to be condensed. How much of the encircled part of p. 4 could be eliminated without losing the thread of the argument? All of it?

6. The alternative use of "he" and "she" in the paper is distracting. Also p.16.

7. Since this discussion relates to a syllogism, is not "logically

follows" more precise in this context than "would seem to be believable".

8. This is one of the crucial points of the paper, but clumsy expression weakens the sense of it.

9. Is footnote 6 necessary? The reader can see that FP has remained the same as on p.3.

10. Clarify and summarise here to recapitulate for the reader: "content has been lost in the translation" of *what* (the theoretical premise?) into *what* (the empirical premise or conclusion?).

11. Either explain this sentence or omit it. Does it add anything if elucidated?

12. Is this a case of the author inferring beliefs from behaviour? Does it follow that because "PAR has been and continues to be "done" that "PA researchers believe there is a plausible escape from the circularity"? Perhaps they are not aware of the circularity. Pointing out this circularity seems to be the original contribution of this paper.

13. Following on from the above point (12) does the section on *Escaping the Circle* address "strategies that they (PAR's) have followed to escape the obviously circular EC", or are these possible strategies that might be adopted to evade the charge of tautologousness? Are there any PAR's who have recognised the problem, followed these strategies, and/or consequently asserted "that their results speak to the theory"?

14. This reference to reflexivity needs explanation. But the concept of reflexivity is a complex one. Could the reference be omitted without significant loss of content or sense?

15. An important point is being made here, but poor wording obscures it.

16. "Some managers for one reason or another lie better than others". This sounds pejorative, and so detracts from the argument. Also footnote 10 is colloquial and adds nothing to the point that is being made.

17. Could the wording of this paragraph be improved? It seems confusing. In particular, the following sentence is confusing: "It is an unconvincing argument in defense of the PR's strategy to assume the truth of EC in order to provide it *false!*" What is

meant by "false" here? As I understand this paragraph, it would be clearer without this sentence. If this reflects a misconception on my part it may be attributable to the wording of this paragraph.

18. "The semantic trick is one he is playing on himself". Let the arguments speak for themselves (if I may use such a gross personification). When a cogent argument has been made, a personal jibe detracts from it. The argument is there; that is what convinces the reader. This same comment applies at various points throughout the paper, eg. pp.11, 20, 21, f 'note 10 on p.26.

19. It might be worthwhile to remain the reader succinctly of what is meant by "AM1 status"—the distinctions here are subtle and easy to lose.

20. "But if managers' choices always lead to "true" measures then whether economic self-interests or a desire to accommodate positive researchers motivates managers in their accounting choices become moot". This sentence takes up the point mentioned on p.14/15, but it is confusing. Is the author seriously positing a theory about management desiring to tell the "truth" to positive researchers? If not, as is I presume the case, the point of this paragraph needs to be made more cogently.

21. "Whether such independent measures are available is at this point in time speculative. They may not exist. . ." What about the independent variable proxies which did not rely on accounting measures in Table 1? On p.7 it was stated that only "over 50 per cent of the measures were 'accounting measures'."
    The author needs to take up this issue rather than glossing over it. Can he/she suggest alternative proxies? If not, why not? What are the implications of the answer to this for future research? If existing proxies are inadequate does this suggest the need for alternative data sources and/or research methods, for example participant observation studies or case studies, in which the researcher directly observes managerial choice-making?

22. Whilst I am in sympathy with the sentiments of McCloskey, it is a long and difficult quote and perhaps overdoses the point. A sentence or two in the author's own words about the resources devoted to this research may be as effective. Zeff (A/R, Jan 1983, pp.129–134) sounds a similar note to that of McCloskey in relation to accounting research.

POLICING ACCOUNTING: THE SOCIOLOGY OF KNOWLEDGE AS PRAXIS

POLICING ACCOUNTING: THE SOCIOLOGY OF KNOWLEDGE AS PRAXIS

TONY PUXTY AND TONY TINKER

Over the past century journals have become the accepted form of disseminating academic knowledge. By knowledge we mean the broad range of social understandings and meanings that extends from popular literature to the natural sciences. Hence we refer not just to the results of systematic investigation into the processes of the natural or social worlds, but also to critiques of, and commentaries on, other works, "literary" or not,[1] as well as to analytic knowledge in journals of mathematics and logic.

As journals have flourished, the refereeing process has crystallized. For most journals, the editorial structure now consists of an editor, and possibly associate editors guided by one or more referees. The referee(s) is not told the identity of the author(s), who is likewise unaware of the identity of the referee's identity. The editor eventually makes a judgement based on the paper itself and the referees' comments. In the *Accounting Review*, as Williams and Rodgers (1992) point out, this process was not formalized until 1967, and even for the highest-status journals in many other fields it is still not the norm.

Although the purposes of the refereeing process are often unstated, the process itself is usually considered to be a means of ensuring the quality of the journal's contents. The generally accepted position can be summarized by suggesting that the process

1. acts to refine and improve researchers' ideas by requiring authors to improve their papers' as regards clarity of exposition, logical reasoning, statistical testing procedures, and data sources. This supposedly enhances the quality of research for the academic community and the wider public

2. saves the members of the research community the time and trouble of sifting through the extensive output of working papers, conference papers, occasional papers and so on, then having to discard what they judge to be the poor ones. The referees thus serve the research community by increasing the efficiency of its processes[2]

3. puts an *imprimatur* on accepted papers, so that there is a grading process. This is further refined by journal rankings, prizes, and so on. This also signals to the community which papers should receive more attention.

There is also a less explicit agenda to the journal process. It

1. permits a powerful minority to decide counts as valid knowledge
2. permits ideological formations in accounting departments to reproduce themselves by selecting for tenure persons committed to a particular approach to knowledge, so that it becomes institutionalized as the only legitimate approach to knowledge-creation for any one who wishes to advance in the accounting research community
3. creates status systems that are similarly self-perpetuating since only those who have passed the initiation test by showing themselves committed to a particular ideology are permitted to participate in the policing process in the next generation
4. impacts on society both because of this ideological police is then given the task of teaching the next generation of students, most of whom will become practitioners not academics, and is hired to give expert testimony in the juridical or political arena. Both of these are material consequences.

The notion that proposed additions to the stock of knowledge have to be scrutinized before publication may be linked to the proposition that knowledge is something more than ideas in investigators' minds. On the contrary, it is said, by becoming crystallized in published and thus widely-disseminated form, and hence exposed to critical appraisal by the research community as a whole, the stock of knowledge comes to constitute a body of knowledge in its own right. This is, of course, Popper's (1979) proposal of a World 3, which consists of knowledge in libraries and other permanent media that is something beyond the personal stock of knowledge in the minds of individual investigators but, in contrast, gains its tentative validity from its ability to defeat the attempts to refute it that will be made as a result of the normal commitment to knowledge found in the scientific community.

We raise the specter of Popper because his name is frequently invoked by those involved in positivist research (cf Watts and Zimmerman, 1986, chapter 1) and because what is permitted to become part of World 3 is important. In other words, *if a knowledge-claim appears in a journal it is tentatively good knowledge; if it is rejected from the journal it is implicitly invalid knowledge.* If it later appears in a journal of less status in the acknowledged rankings then it is implicitly second-rate knowledge. Thus we have guardians not just of what may be admitted into a status system, but of what is greater or lesser knowledge. Entry into the pantheon *defines* knowledge.

The argument here is not that journal processes are inherently flawed. However, we do wish to interrogate particular systems of policing since, if ideological gatekeepers control what constitutes knowledge, theirs ideology becomes the prevailing ideology; and if the community of researchers and guardians is then self-perpetuating through social mechanisms of reproduction, we have a system in which that ideology is sustained and elaborated and has the power to exclude from community's shared beliefs criticism and alternative knowledge.

We interrogate work within the Popperian framework by critiquing Popper's own program in the context of the refereeing processes to be found operating in the course of this book. We acknowledge that many of those involved are Popperians in name only (cf Hines, 1989, Christenson, 1983, Lowe et al., 1983), but we frame our critique through Popper's work because it is the chief framework acknowledged by apologists for positive accounting. We do so for one further reason. Mainstream accounting research has shown a marked reluctance to acknowledge that any criticism of its fundamental tenets exists, and acts as if there were none. There is no sustained response to the extensive array of criticisms.[3] We have to turn to Popper himself who, claiming to demonstrate the weaknesses of approaches opposed to his own, has at least attempted to confront them.

Thus in the next section we turn to Popper's program for the development of knowledge and subject it to conceptual criticism. We also provide evidence from the processes in the academic accounting community to argue that, even were his program to have some potential validity (which we deny), it does not and cannot work in practice because of the institutional frameworks that operate against it.

The Popperian Program

In the earliest work he wrote in English[4] setting out his ideas on the nature of knowledge production and validation, Popper offers criticisms of those who viewed knowledge as a social artefact. After preliminary comments in a chapter entitled "The Sociology of Knowledge," he explicates what he saw as the subject's Hegelian roots and distinguishes between two variants, which he calls Marxism and sociology of knowledge, thus suggesting that the latter does not encompass the former. He begins his specific attack as follows:

> Marxists, in a like manner, are accustomed to explain the disagreement of an opponent by his class bias, and the sociologists of knowledge by his total ideology. Such methods are both easy to handle and good fun for those who handle them. But they clearly destroy the basis of rational discussion, and they must lead, ultimately, to anti-rationalism and mysticism.

Popper is setting up a straw man. Marx himself was ambivalent about whether ideological processes resulted in a class view (that is, different views by different classes—cf the *Preface to a Critique of Political Economy* and *The Eighteenth Brumaire*) or a fundamentally homogeneous view, which was molded by the needs of the ruling classes (cf the *Preface* again, and *The German Ideology*).[5] Most Marxists since Lukacs and Gramsci, although acknowledging the key significance of class as a determining variable, have offered a far more subtle and complex analysis of ideology than as some monocausal epiphenomenon resulting from (generally economic) interests.[6] Because of this, in what follows we will distinguish between the categories proposed by Popper and refer loosely to the sociology of knowledge as SK which, we suppose, encompasses a number of variants including Marxist analysis.[7]

In the passage quoted, Popper argues that SK "clearly" destroys the basis of rational discussion and leads to antirationalism. His grounds for this claim appear to be that SK argues that a person's knowledge is molded by her socialization, and that this necessarily either destroys or damages her ability to seek and recognize truth. Popper appears to have missed the bulk of the critical literature over the past fifty years, including critical accounting.[8] We and our colleagues in critical accounting have indicated the ways societal processes can direct whole communities to ideological activities and research programs (see, for example, Tinker et al, 1982; Lehman and Tinker, 1987; Cooper et al, forthcoming; Cooper, forthcoming). In general, this *opposes* ideology to good scientific practice. Popper appears to believe that SK thesis boils down to a 'single ideology' thesis, from which only a small body of social analysts sees itself as exempt. As we show, the dialectical method is argued to be necessary because critical theorists do not believe this of themselves, or of anyone else.

From this point Popper becomes more specific. He says, he will allow himself some fun criticizing the methods of SK. He turns the "socioanalysts" against themselves, he tells us, by pointing out that it must be an inescapable feature of their own ideology to believe that they are the "body of the elect which alone was capable of objectivity" (p.216). This, it seems, undermines their argument since it constitutes a logical paradox (that is, we assume, that if ideology is all-encompassing then sociologists of knowledge must be subject to it, in which case they cannot recognize it; by recognising it they show it to be false). The situation is the precise opposite of that depicted by Popper. A wide bank of research, from ethnomethodology to the Frankfurt School, is grounded in the proposition that knowledge is socially constructed, and that to interrogate this social knowledge it has been necessary be devise methods that recognize the investigator's subjectivity while at the same time seeking a means of transcending it. But "transcend" here does not mean the once-and-for-all dissolution of the problems of either subjectivity or ideology; it is, rather, a method that (unlike positive accounting) continually recognizes its own limitations *through* the investigative process. It is for this reason that we insist on the dialectical approach to knowledge which immanently subjects every knowledge claim to critique, and, in effect, demands that each knowledge claim vitiate itself through this process. In particular, we reject absolutely the proposition that critical theorists claim to be capable of objectivity. On the contrary, we maintain that no body of knowledge can be objective, Marxism included. Chief among the virtues of the Marxist form of analysis is its dialectical method, and we have sympathy with Allen's (1975, p.62) quotation from Lukacs:

> Let us assume for the sake of argument, that recent research had disproved once and for all every one of Marx's individual theses. Even if this were to be proved, every serious 'orthodox' Marxist would still be able to accept all such modern findings without reservation and hence dismiss all of Marx's theses *in toto*—without having to renounce his orthodoxy for a single moment . . . orthodoxy refers exclusively to *method*. It is the scientific conviction that dialectical materialism is the road to truth and that its method can be developed, expanded and deepened only along the lines laid down by its founders.   *(Lukacs, 1971)*[9]

In writing what he did, it is Popper, we suggest, who lacks the capacity for self-criticism.

But then, Popper tells us, he has more serious objections. The sociologist of knowledge, its seems, "looks upon science or knowledge as a process in the mind or 'consciousness' of the individual scientist, or perhaps as the product of such a process." Popper himself acknowledges that the individual scientist may well be partial—his expression—and not objective, in the defense of a particular theory or interpretation of an observation. But, according to Popper, this does not matter because the problem is resolved through scientific method.

> And, ironically enough, objectivity is closely bound up with the *social aspect of scientific method,* with the fact that science and scientific objectivity do not (and cannot) result from the attempts of an individual scientist to be 'objective', but from the *friendly-hostile co-operation of many scientists.* (p.217)

There are two aspects of this method, we are told. One is that "the scientific attitude means criticizing everything, and they are little deterred by authorities" (p.218). The other is that scientists try not to talk at cross-purposes; they try to share a language, and to express their ideas in ways that "can be refuted (or else corroborated) by such experience. This is what constitutes scientific objectivity." However, he issues a warning later in the paragraph "Only political power, when it is used to suppress free criticism, or when it fails to protect it, can impair the functioning of these institutions, on which all progress, scientific, technological, and political, ultimately depends." (p.218)

On this basis, we may subject Popper to analytic criticism, but also to synthetic criticism by examining the controversies discussed in this book as exemplars. It is clear that for the most part Popper's processes require the dissemination of knowledge through some publication process; and hence the validity of the Popperian empiricist method depends crucially on his claims as to the value of the processes concerned and the extent to which they are consistent with his picture of the committed scientific community. We now consider these claims in the context of the processes to be found earlier in this volume.

Popper refers to the "friendly-hostile co-operation" of investigators. However, in the discourses quoted in this book, the social conditioning, and economic interests of, those who engage in these discussions, lead them to be anything but cooperative. We observe overt friendliness in the exchanges (the frequent use of first names rather than surnames is indicative in correspondence between the editor and various respondents), and hostility in much of the virulent language complained of both by Foster and by reviewer #3 of Boer and Moseley's response. However to "criticize everything", as Popper suggests, is not the same as to subject all knowledge-claims to the same intensity of criticism. We leave it to the reader to judge whether reviewers #3 and #4 subjected the original WZ manuscript to the same level of critical scrutiny to which the Boer and Moseley manuscript was subjected, (especially when contrasted to WZ's Reviewer #2) to whether the editor's willingness to accede to WZ's appeal to permit their ideas to be opened to the forces of the marketplace of ideas[10] was matched by a corresponding willingness to expose the various commentators' views to that same marketplace. Libertarian market exponents were granted this privilege, not their critics.[11]

We conclude that the reviewing process evidenced in these exchanges does not satisfy Popper's first criterion of the scientific attitude. The approach taken by the referees is, on the contrary, conditioned by the personal histories and the social context of mainstream, markets-based accounting academia; and this results in asymmetries of criticism, whereby tendentious statements are permitted to go unchallenged because they are part of the shared paradigm of author and referee.[12]

We turn next to Popper's contention that scientists "share a language". Careful perusal of the debates in this volume suggest otherwise. On the contrary, much of the dispute arises around the extent to which the disputants do share a language. To take one example, WZ in their response to Foster appear to believe he was seeking econometric evidence: "Reviewer #2 has no perspective when it becomes necessary to trade-off substance and testing by formal econometric techniques. . ." and Foster responds: "Not once in my review did I mention econometric techniques. Not once in my review did I suggest one had to use such techniques to address issues of substance". As a second example, a reviewer of the Boer and Moseley response observes that "The authors . . . describe four logical fallacies, each with a catchy title and each taking one or two typed pages to describe. I think that fallacies A, B, and D are really the same issue". Boer and Moseley clearly do not think so; and these are thus *different readings* of the same words despite careful scrutiny, which amounts to a different language as to what constitutes the boundary between one point and another.

We then turn to Popper's next condition: that scientists express their propositions in a way that can be refuted. As Lowe et al and Boer and Moseley point out, this is what WZ decline to do. They describe their theory as a general theory, as a result of which one or two contrary instances will not be admitted to disprove it. WZ in their reply to Boer and Moseley make the following claim:

Because a theory's hypotheses are general propositions, those hypotheses are not rejected on the basis of isolated observations which contradict a given hypothesis. As Popper (1959, p. 86) writes, "a few stray basic statements (observations) contradicting a theory will hardly induce us to reject it as falsified." Indeed, once a theory is accepted even contradictory observations which are reproducible will not lead to the theory's rejection if an alternative theory which explains more phenomena is not available. Newtonian physics is a superb example of this. Numerous systematic anomalies to Newtonian physics were observed before Einstein advanced his theories, but Newtonian physics was not rejected.

However, Newton did not express his theories as "general" in the sense that he was satisfied that there might be contrary observations that would not bother him. He was precise in formulating his ideas; on that basis, the experimter/observer could be sure when a contrary observation had been made. As Boer and Moseley point out, the imprecision of the language used by WZ does not permit of this.

Finally we turn to Popper's remark, quoted above, about political power. Popper is making this point because of the context in which the passage appears—a book in which he attacked, over the course of two volumes, Plato, Hegel, and Marx for their tendencies to suppress what he saw as proper critical attitudes (inter alia). He was concerned that government interference in free scientific speculation and study would stifle progress—the problem of Lysenko and the insistence on "official" genetics in Stalin's Soviet Union was well-known at the time the book was written. No overt government control in US or UK society prevents free criticism in academic journals; and hence we may suppose that those who view these states as pluralist will assume that there can be academic discourse can without political interference.

This is not so. Popper's definition of "political interference" appears to narrowly, include only state or government interference. Yet in a capitalist state, the power to intervene in the accumulation of knowledge, especially when the accumulation process clearly transgresses capital's desire to limit discourse to those it believes to be nonthreatening, leads to numerous instances of the exercise of the power to silence debate. For example, in the UK, higher education institutions, professional institutions, and accounting firms that fund research have, in the recent past, attempted to suppress dissident voices (Jack, 1993,[13] Puxty et al, forthcoming). This attempted censorship of the free flow of ideas contradicts any proposition that there is a principled scientific community free from external political pressures, or that there is a marketplace for ideas separate from the societal power structure. In the broader sense, given that funding in accounting research so frequently comes from audit firms or national funding bodies that are part of the capitalist state, there are financial pressures to conform, and general tendencies to decline to support or refuse to publish critical research. All of these pressures in effect represent the use of political *and* *economic* power to silence informed debate.

However this is only the process at the societal level. At the level of the individual journal as considered in this book, the political pressures to suppress certain kinds of debate, and certain kinds of evidence, are still more salient. They arise, from the fact that those who have obtained power within the structures of academia (Williams and Rodgers, 1992) having shared views, the result of shared backgrounds and their putative economic interests suppress those features of knowledge production that conflict with their own views. *The very process of refereeing lends itself to this kind of abuse.* This is not to say that all refereeing activities are thus tainted, and it is certainly not to claim that there is any conspiracy to exclude certain terms of discourse; but rather that, when there are gatekeepers who have the power to suppress arguments that are inconvenient to them, it may be expected that they will take the opportunity to use the political power provided by their positions to suppress them. The established journals have always been the intellectual property of a power elite that is committed to the ideology of the market (for an especially virulent advocacy of the virtues of the market and the American way see Paton's writings later in life; see also Merino, 1993, Oakes and Arnold, forthcoming, and Tinker, 1985). This cadre has acted both to maintain the fiction of free debate—there is a permanent section in TAR for comments—while at the same time suppressing fundamental criticism, by selecting editors and referees who can be trusted to find grounds to exclude criticism that might undermine their common worldview.[14]

Popper's argument for the dissemination of ideas the scientific community where they can face the scrutiny of other scientists thus fails with respect to accounting at two levels. First, it fails in conception by neglecting to consider that the political processes of which he writes are not to be found only at the level of the state's power structure, but that they permeate the organs supposedly charged with disseminating research so that it might face informed criticism. Putative knowledge, under the Popperian scheme, must be placed in the public arena so that the process of criticism may proceed. As we have now argued, the structures of the establishment generally operate to prevent this.

Second, Poppers process fails in the accounting arena because the power structures of the high-status journals change their grounds of objection so as to reject papers criticizing the dominant paradigm (such as agency theory) while at the same time restricting their objections to economics-based empiricist papers to the quality of the evidence.[15]

This defense of the status quo is not limited to accounting. An interesting parallel is found in psychology, which has also nailed its colors to the mast of the classical scientific method of hypothesis testing through empirical analysis. However, in contrast to accounting, the research process in psychology has been willing to turn its method's searchlight upon itself to consider refereeing the processes and the extent to which referees might be able to free themselves from an unconscious defense of the status quo:

> In Mahoney's experiment, journal referees gave a high rating to relevance and methodology for a paper whose results were in agreement with the dominant hypothesis for their group. However, when the identical paper was used, but the results were

reversed so as to be disconfirming, an equivalent sample of referees gave it a low rating on relevance and methodology. The referees were willing to accept the studies confirming the dominant
hypothesis, but they rejected those that were disconfirming. This
type of peer review does little to advance scientific knowledge.
(Smart's study is consistent with the Mahoney experiment. An
examination of over 300 papers published in four psychological
journals found that less than 10% reported negative results.)

Armstrong, 1979, p.426

We should be interested to hear from the editor of any major established
empiricist journal who would be willing to permit this experiment to be
replicated for accounting.

Our comments so far relate only to academic journals. However there is
a knowledge dissemination process outside of journals. Popper himself refers to the research community as "the laboratories, the scientific periodicals, the congresses." Let us examine each of these in turn as a place where
ideas might be objectively evaluated.

We begin with accounting's equivalent of the laboratories. In the taught
components of doctoral studies, students are exposed only to a limited set
of what is to count as knowledge for the purpose of their doctorates and
later on, their publications (cf Zeff, 1989, on the content of most US doctoral
programs). The skills developed in students are statistical and econometric;
they do not encompass critical studies of the nature of social science and
thus of accounting. Students are thus conditioned to view econometrics and
statistics as the only appropriate field and accounting journals that publish
work using these methods as the only legitimate source of knowledge. These
students are then appointed to academic positions, and generally continue
in these beliefs, buttressed by those around them and those who appointed
them who went through the same process. The process thus becomes cycli-
cal and self-reinforcing, since these groups spawn more people in their own
image. As a result, the accounting equivalent of 'the laboratories' may well
find scholars willing to criticize the minutiae of a particular econometric
testing procedure; but they will fail to produce persons able or willing to
interrogate the grounds of knowledge production in any wider sense, because those involved will themselves be working within the same paradigm.

Turning to the accounting equivalent of "the scientific periodicals," we
find these nearly categorized into status through frequent polls, mostly of
academic members of the AAA. These apparently objective processes are
nothing of the kind. What is never clear, in the criteria for judgement of the
journals' standing, is the extent to which the knowledge claims are themselves the basis of the rankings produced (so that 'better knowledge' might
be found in JAR than in TAR, for instance) or whether it is simply the
severity of the reviewing process and the rejection rate. If it is the latter, in

which the ranking becomes nothing more than the recognition of an abusive process in which the tough survive, then the judgement is not of the substantive research content at all but rather, of the tenacity of those who succeed in appearing in its pages. In any case, such a choice of possible criteria is flawed since it ignores the social context in which the rankings operate. As argued in the previous paragraph, it is increasingly the case that, as doctoral programs are designed around journals disseminating certain worldviews, the content of this narrow range of journals becomes the legitimated content. It is scarcely surprising then when academics brought up in these beliefs subsequently judge the schools of literature in which they were trained to be superior. Just as they learned that statistical test X was more powerful than test Y, so they were taught that journal X contained better papers than journal Y. On receiving their doctorate by not questioning this, they learn not to question it.

Finally, we find Popper referring to congresses. In the US, these are also controlled by the power structure; and only a limited number of sessions are available to dissident voices.[16] No critical academic paper has ever been presented at a plenary session of the AAA. The two sections that might be considered willing to criticize established dogma, the Public Interest and Gender sections, are restricted to two sessions each out of more than 70, and with only 400 members, they are under constant threat of closure.

Finally, we may note that Popper was aware that social science— and thus business and accounting knowledge production—might not live up to his ideals. "It is true that the social sciences have not yet fully attained this method," he writes. He ascribes this partly to the influence of Aristotle and Hegel (of whom most accounting academics have scarcely heard) and partly "to their failure to make use of the social instruments of scientific objectivity. Thus they are really 'total ideologies', or, putting it differently, some social scientists are unable, or even unwilling, to speak a common language" (pp. 221–2). His solution is "the methods of trial and error, of inventing hypotheses which can be practically tested, and of submitting them to practical tests" (p.222). But, as we have already shown, it is the framing of these hypotheses and the flawed processes through which hypothesis testing proceeds, that result not in 'objective knowledge' in accounting but rather, in ideological statements. Popper's attempted program cannot operate in accounting through hypothesis testing precisely because no hypotheses will be considered, and no results accepted, that overtly threaten the interests of capitalism. Because of its libertarian language, it was not at first clear that this was just what the original WZ paper did; thus it was not rejected on ideological grounds. As we pointed out in the introductory essay, it subsequently became clear that the 1979 paper questioned capitalism's self-image, and so it fell by the wayside of mainstream accounting thought.

To sum up the above, therefore, we conclude that the gatekeeping function as it is expressed in the activities of a journal such as the *Accounting Review,* transgresses the conditions set for the creation of a world of "objective knowledge"; and it does so because of the positioning of the journal in the institutions of capitalism. We now turn to the way the immersion of an academic journal in the institutions of the capitalist state can lead to the policing of knowledge and attempt to narrow and subvert knowledge-claims on behalf of what we shall, following Althusser, refer to as the ideological state apparatus.

The Mechanisms of Reaction

In a recent paper, commenting on the "tyranny of the economically correct in academia," Martens and Stevens (1993) remark that:

> Watts and Zimmerman . . . claim that philosophical criticisms of the methodology of PAT . . . cannot be valid because they 'have failed the market test of accounting research. Referees and editors of journals have not asked researchers to alter their methodology based on these published critiques'. This comment is disingenuous in the extreme because many of the referees and editors of journals likely to publish empirical accounting research are themselves acolytes (if not founders) of Economically Correct research. Thus, we would argue that any lack of effect of the published research disproving or criticizing the PAT programme does not prove that such criticisms are invalid; rather, it may indicate the control of the Economically Correct over many academic accounting journals. (p.278)

This comment, while perceptive, requires some supplementation to be fully persuasive. We shall supplement it in three ways. First, we shall consider the positioning of *The Accounting Review* in the structures of the state. Then we shall turn to the prima facie evidence provided from the Williams and Rodgers (1992) study of oligopoly in the selection of editors and editorial boards of establishment accounting journals. Finally, we provide an elaborated analysis of the processes of knowledge-policing in its social context.

THE POSITIONING OF LIBERTARIAN ANARCHISTS IN THE STATE APPARATUS

The traditional pluralist or neo-pluralist model of the state and other institutions of a modern democracy depicts the latter as essentially separate from the former. The state is portrayed as the public sector, administered by national or local government. This is, however, to confuse content with form. A more insightful view is to understand the state through its *function*. For example, consider a country where accounting regulation is performed from within its department of commerce. If persons involved in the standard-setting process come from the technical same background and the same social and economic class as FASB persons, their activities are indistinguishable. Hence there is no substantive reason to distinguish the FASB from the US state: it is in effect part of the state. Following Althusser and Poulantzas, we may argue that the state consists of the repressive apparatus and the ideological apparatus. The former exists to repress, the latter to propagate, nurture and elaborate ideology. Examples of the latter include churches, the educational system, most political parties, the press, radio, television, and publishing. "These apparatuses belong to the state system because of their objective function of elaborating and inculcating ideology, irrespective of their formal juridical status as nationalised (public) or private." (Poulantzas, 1973, p.109). It is acknowledged that there are contradictory relations within these fractions of the state as a result of their mutual power relations. Thus we can talk of their relative autonomy. Althusser (1971) puts this clearly:

> All the State Apparatuses function both by repression and by ideology, with the difference that the (Repressive) State Apparatus functions incisively and predominantly by repression, whereas the Ideological State Apparatus functions massively and predominantly by ideology.
>
> Whereas the (Repressive) State Apparatus constitutes an organized whole whose different parts are centralised beneath a commanding unity, that of the politics of class struggle applied by the political representatives of the ruling classes in possession of state power, the Ideological State Apparatuses are multiple, distinct, 'relatively autonomous' and capable of providing an objective field to contradictions which express, in forms which may be limited or extreme, the effects of the clashes between the capitalist class struggle and the proletarian class struggle, as well as their subordinate forms.
>
> Whereas the unity of the (Repressive) State Apparatus is secured by its unified and centralised organisation under the leadership of the representatives of the classes in power executing the politics of the class struggle of the classes in power, the unity of the different Ideological State Apparatuses is secured, usually in contradictory forms, by the ruling ideology, the ideology of the ruling class. (Althusser, 1971)

The established accounting journals are, in this way, implicated in the state apparatus, notwithstanding their apparent independence in purely legalistic terms. They propagate bourgeois values (Lehman and Tinker, 1987) as these develop and change. They nurture and expand on them; and the whole corpus of empiricist research may be understood as a means of proliferating tales of economic agency and markets dominance and naturalising these for the reader. As more and more of these stories are told, they are increasingly powerful ideologically through their sheer weight, the authority structure that stands behind them, and the reward structure that underpins it all (such as tenure, reputation etc as so eloquently expressed by Watts and Zimmerman in their paper). Moreover, the system can reproduce itself, since each successive generation of accounting academics has to conform to the pattern of the old, so as to gain legitimacy.

Hence repression and ideology are both manifestations of the processes that arise to police accounting thought; ideology because constant repetition in socially constituted high-reputation journals tends to lead to acceptance of the contents as scientifically respectable and thus to be believed; repression because decisions based on acceptance by these journals can affect careers, incomes, and one's place in the social order (we elaborate on this below). This leads to double policing. There is policing as to what appears in the canon of knowledge, and policing as to who is deemed acceptable to make policing decisions. We now turn briefly to the identity of these police/gatekeepers/guardians.

IDENTIFYING THE GUARDIANS OF DISCOURSE

Commenting that an "individual must have already acquired some reputation before a discipline grants such power as a referee or editor" (p.6) Williams and Rodgers seek the elite who have fulfilled this criterion. Aware that 'reputation' is clearly inadequate—gadflies can make reputations for themselves and not be selected as editors—they analyze the memberships of editorial board of, in their view, a high prestige journal: the *Accounting Review*, from its beginning to 1991. As key indicators they select are board members' affiliations (sources of members' doctorates, their subsequent appointments, where their scholarly work was pursued) and journals in which they published. From extensive analysis, and the confluence of various criteria, they conclude that, with doctoral degree rather than affiliation as the criterion, fifteen schools have dominated the *Accounting Review*'s board for the past 24 years. They are, in order of influence, Illinois, Ohio State, Stanford, Texas, Minnesota, Washington, Rochester, Chicago, Michigan State, Michigan, Berkeley, Cornell, Carnegie Mellon, Wisconsin, and Iowa.[17] All editors during the period of analysis also came from these fifteen schools. So did 73% of AAA presidents. So had 100% of those who had been reviewers for eleven years (the maximum period found). So had 86%

of the Wildman medal winners, 100% of the Seminal contribution winners and 86% of the notable contribution winners.

We do not comment on whether this signals academic superiority in itself (whatever that might mean) since it is irrelevant to the argument. We have quoted Williams and Rodgers' results to demonstrate that there is strong evidence of a severe concentration of power over gatekeeping that accrues to a relatively small number of institutions in which socialization into particular norms was undertaken. Indeed when Williams and Rodgers later analyzed the doctoral schools of the authors of the most cited contributions to the accounting literature (data from Brown and Gardner; 1985a, 1985b) they found that *every paper listed had at least one coauthor from the fifteen schools*. This suggests, therefore, not only a concentration of affiliation but a concentration of views of the significant literature.

Helpful though this is in buttressing the suggestion of close control over the types of articles published in the *Accounting Review* (and Lehman and Tinker, 1987, demonstrate the narrow range of ideologies that the successful authors espoused) it does not provide a framework for understanding how accounting discourse comes to be under such narrow control and the significance of this narrow control. It is to this that we now turn.

THE CONTROL OF ACCOUNTING DISCOURSE

One of the insights of structuralism and poststructuralism has been the importance of language which, in the case of poststructuralism, means the ubiquity of the free-floating signifier. A key aspect of the linguistic turn has been recognition that language is not just *about* the material world, but a major part of it. Language does not act just as a communication device, but as a material moment in itself. This language—and hence the control of the signifier—opens up the debate about ideological formations.

We might suppose that the concern expressed so far has been solely about the extent to which language as it is used in accounting journals represents or misrepresents the material world. In this view—for example, under the dominant ideology thesis (cf. Abercrombie and Turner, 1978)—the journal review process is a way of both disseminating ideologies helpful to capital and censoring ideas adjudged inimical to it. Such a model is hence in danger of a number of errors; of verging on a science versus ideology positioning (cf Althusser); of treating the language of journal publication only as a means of informational dissemination; and of falling into the trap of universalism, since it would necessarily encompass all academic journals. The control of language *is*, on the contrary, control of the material world because language is itself material. Control over the knowledge-production process not only gives control over the communication media: it controls the materiality of academic accounting knowledge itself.

This is where Popper's World 3 fails spectacularly. Popper declines to appreciate the significance of language, and views it as a vehicle with the capacity to interrogate the world of ideas through experimental criticism. He takes this so much for granted that the problems of language are sidelined in his work. He objects, for example, to investigating the use of linguistic terms, in view of the potential infinite regress.[18] He rejects the Kuhnian argument for the incommensurability of languages (Popper, 1970 pp.56–7). Yet the critical processes he described can only take place through language since writing is the medium of the journals in which ideas are disseminated do so through the medium of writing.

To recognize the material nature of language is to recognize that Popper's representation of the world of knowledge cannot hold. To understand this we need to entwine two aspects of language and the project of knowledge. First, in writing for, and policing, the contents of academic journals, the academic community is manipulating some *thing,* not some depiction of a thing.[19] This raises the question of the extent to which language can be self-reflexive; that is, to the extent to which inquiries that are necessarily made through the medium of writing adequately interrogate the nature of communication through writing itself? The key point here is that what appears at first to be merely an ideological state process becomes, in its operation, part of a repressive state process. The materiality of academics' words is indistinguishable from the materiality of their working existence. Hence, to control their discourse is to control them. Pluralistic analysis might lead one to suppose that this happens at one remove; that the control of words leads to the ability of academics to achieve recognition for themselves and their ideas; and that this is then linked to their material financial rewards (since, if one is to believe Watts and Zimmerman, fame leads to increased compensation). But that "one remove" is a fiction which results from a split between the idea and the actuality, itself ideologically formulated—that is, in other words, just an immanent feature of language. To control academic discourse is to control academic life since discourse constitutes a central feature of academic life. This, of course, further penetrates into control of discourse in the world outside the process of academic knowledge production as frameworks and ideas percolate into society.

Second, the Popperian project rejects the *reader.* Understanding of reading as a creative process is a valuable contribution of poststructuralist thought (Derrida, 1972, Barthes, 1974, Cooper and Puxty, 1994). To Popper, to read scientific discourses once one is trained as a scientist (and Popper refuses to acknowledge the socialization process each scientist undergoes in learning to socially define his or her own science, and even to make sense of sense-data—cf Ravetz, 1973) is to continually reconstruct those discourses. To read Coase's 1937 paper today is different from reading that paper in 1937, in the light of its incorporation into the whole body of transaction cost theory and agency theory. Likewise to read WZ 1979 in the light of the last decade's critiques of PAT (cf Christenson, 1983; Peasnell, 1986, Whittington, 1987, Whitley, 1988, Kaplan and Ruland, 1991, Martens and Stevens, 1993, Sterling, 1990, Hines, 1989, and the responses in this volume) is to read a different paper from the one that confronted its readers in 1979. Indeed, it is different even to the manuscript reviewers; we may compare Foster's remark in the memorandum to his students that he stands by his arguments yet agrees publication was appropriate. To Foster the WZ paper, as a text in the web of subsequent texts, has become other than it was, and his recommendation to reject has become transformed into support for the paper's publication.

How, then, does the policing process operate, given this materiality of language and the relative freedom on the part of the reader? It does so through the very independence of the signifier itself. By this we do not mean that the signifier is free from the constraints of the referee, and can thus work beyond as well as through referee's socialised perceptual mechanism. Instead, we propose that the policing process recognizes the materiality and significance of the word, and acts as it does not because it is concerned with the material effects of publishing ideas unacceptable to the socialized gatekeeper but rather because it recognizes that the words used *are the things that must be controlled in and for themselves.*[20] This is consistent with, but goes beyond, both Lehman and Tinker (1987) and Cooper (forthcoming). It also means, of course, not just that the unpublished and published papers are themselves material outputs, but that the process of filtering manuscripts is as much a production process as is the refining of oil.

This however raises the question of the symbolic functions of language. It appears that, by being treated as only material, language is deprived of its function as a symbol; that by being for and of itself, it is forbidden to relate intertextually to something other. This is not so. We acknowledge that, for example, the publication of a nonmainstream paper such as Chua (1986), and "unconventional" criticism such as Christianson's (1983) in *The Accounting Review* did have a symbolic value in itself, one that signaled a potential discursive shift in the terms permitted under the journal's ideological rubric. Chua's paper does not so much criticize mainstream publications as recognize their positioning vis-à-vis other modes of thought. It recognizes, in other words, that mainstream ideologies might be treated *pari passu* with others, rather than as dominant. This is just as threatening as a critique. The isolation of these two papers and subsequent the rejection of other papers that have demonstrated a mode of reasoning at variance with the dominant mode, does indeed demonstrate the power of symbol. To publish a Chua appears to signal the freedom to think and to publish Other. To accept it in isolation is to reject its message. In this sense, as Baudrillard might argue, it is a more powerful instrument of control to publish one aberrant paper than none at all; for its very isolation points more eloquently than zero publication could, to the repressive processes at work.

Turning now to the socialization process that leads to this repression, we may return to the two conditions of academic existence that infuse all US accounting writers: their doctoral studies and their conditions of employment (both physical and psychic). Features of both shape the gatekeepers' approach. Chief among them is the monological nature of the production process of accounting PhDs. It is instructive to contrast the AAA doctoral colloquia with similar workshops for doctoral students in Europe. In the former, candidates go to hear members of the published elite instruct them on what constitutes good research, good econometric method and good publication. In the latter, although of course there is also an experienced faculty in attendance, candidates are also encouraged to present their ideas for both group and instructor criticism.[21] The tendency to one-way communication is indicative of intellectual tyranny (cf the importance Habermas has attached to undominated communication). For language as dialogue can constitute a means of inquiry, a free process in which words and ideas might develop creatively, whereas language as dictation immanently constitutes a denial of intellectual freedom. The interpellation of scientism into the inquiry process has meant that what might otherwise have been a consensual master/knowledge-seeker relationship (cf Castaneda and Nietzsche) dissolves into a handing down of the tablets. Thus the pedagogical system matches the supposed nature of the knowledge itself. Since it is presented as a set of positively-known facts, there is no room for the interrogation of those facts. If the master knows it, the only problem remaining is to ensure that the candidate also comes to know it.

THE PROCESSES OF SEMANTIC CLOSURE

Next we turn to the way the semantic closures of positivist/empiricist socialization has operated to privilege their terms of disclose. We select Kinney (1986, 1992) as an exemplar. In doing so, we do not make any claim to be exhaustive.

Kinney (1986) certain strategies for research suggested to intending researchers. It elicited a critical response from Cooper and Zeff (1992); Kinney (1992) then constituted a reply. Early in the reply Kinney makes the following statement:

> The article in question had a limited objective. It was designed efficiently to introduce beginning Ph.D. students to contemporary empirical accounting research. The focus of the article is on empirical research *planning*. I did not and do not presume to provide guidance in all possible methods of conducting scholarly inquiry

in accounting. The article does not, for example provide suggestions on how to do analytical research or historical research in
accounting. (p.93)

To begin with, Kinney is quite right to say his discourse had a limited
objective. To suggest that this was "biased" would be misleading. Its ideological import lies in its *contextualisation*. *The Accounting Review* has published no similar paper that "provide(s) suggestions on how to do analytical
research or historical research in accounting", nor on critical accounting
research, nor on judgmental studies in auditing.

Secondly, Kinney claims to restrict himself to "contemporary empirical
accounting research," by which he means the empiricism that had become
entrenched at that point. Thus there is closure on the signifier "empirical."
There is no mention of the method underlying the empirical research that
looked at the UK coal board's accounting processes (Berry et al, 1985), for
example. By excluding both this and historical research from the description, the signification used excludes them from legitimately being either
contemporary or empirical. This is the *imperialism of the signifier*. Kinney's
attachment of language *defines* contemporary and empirical through the
prescriptions he then provides.

Since neither the coal board study nor historical studies (for example,
studying the recent history of the discourses surrounding the production of
value-added statements in Burchell et al, 1985) follow these procedures, they
are excluded from being considered either contemporary or empirical. They
are something else. Alternatively, they are failed empiricism, because they
have not managed successfully to use Kinney's method.[22] Either way, they
appear not to be about the empirical world because only empirical research
can comprehend the real world. Thus they are, by exclusion, something
fanciful beyond the real world.

Kinney attempts shortly after this passage to deny this: "This is, of
course, no statement in the article that can be construed to imply that the
definitions or guidance was intended to apply to all of science or even to all
empirical research in accounting." This is reductionism of the first order. It
requires that a statement be made in order to have an effect, and says that
only explicit uncontextualised statements, have signification. This is clearly
not so. If the *Journal of Accounting and Economics* only publishes work
couched within the framework of post-Jensen and Meckling neoclassical
economics, then the editors need make no statement to the effect that lens
model studies would be unwelcome; the existing content defines the nature
of the journal to the reader without explicit guidelines. This does not deny
multiplicity of readings to the reader, but rather, demonstrates the limits of
readings that can legitimately be made. Signifiers work both in presence and
in absence. This point is elegantly furthered by Eagleton (1991):

> Someone who writes a doctoral thesis on the relations between race and social class in South Africa is by no means disinterested; why bother, for one thing, to write it in the first place? But such a piece of work normally differs from statements such as 'The white man will never surrender his heritage' in that it is open to being disproved. Indeed this is part of what we mean by a 'scientific' hypothesis, as opposed to a groan of alarm or a stream of invective. The pronouncement 'The white man will never surrender his heritage' *appears* as though it could be disproved, since it could be obtusely taken as a sociological prediction; but to take it this way would of course be wholly to miss its ideological force (p.201)

The key feature here lies in the last sentence. A statement couched in the language of description can have an illocutionary or imperative force, and we can only tell whether it is descriptive or imperative by studying the context in which it appears. To say "everyone eats Blogg's Cornflakes" in an advertisement is equivalent to "you should eat Blogg's Cornflakes." It is immaterial that the precise wording differs. In the same way, to say "contemporary empirical research operates through this method" when published in a journal to which most junior faculty aspire, written by an author who was shortly to become the journal's editor, is equivalent to writing "you should use this method." This linguistic positioning has a rhetorical force far beyond its surface neutrality.

In defending his position, Kinney later remarks:

> It seems to me that large sample studies, guided by a priori theories and using data to test the theories are, indeed, in the mainstream of contemporary accounting scholarship for a reason— they are useful and cost effective." (p.95)

Kinney has now appropriated three more signifiers: a priori theories, useful, and cost effective. Hoogvelt and Tinker (1978) also had an a priori theory about the exploitation of the peoples of Sierra Leone by "Delco", and their empirical studies bore out their hypothesis. This has been excluded from hypothesis testing in Kinney's model since it fails the "large sample studies" test. Kinney also appropriates the term "useful"; we are not told to whom or for what purpose the theories are useful. The signifier "useful" thus becomes used in the ideological wordplay, to tyrannize other research as being of unproven use. This assembly of signifiers—large sample studies, a priori theorizing, and "cost-effective", crystalizes into a discursive formation (see Pêcheux, 1982). Eagleton (1991) describes this as follows:

> A discursive formation can be seen as a set of rules which determine what can and must be said from a certain position within

> social life and expressions have meaning only by virtue of the
> discursive formations within which they occur, changing signifi-
> cance as they are transported from one to the other. A discursive
> formation thus constitutes a "matrix of meaning" or system of
> linguistic relations within which actual discursive processes are
> generated" (p.195)

Once "mainstream" accounting theorists have appropriated terms such as
'useful', these words can no longer be used beyond the context of markets
empiricism. They are embedded in the ideological formations of the apologists of markets.

The above necessarily impacts on the reviewing process evidenced in this
volume. One reviewer of Williams' paper remarks that

> it is basically an opinion piece. The reader must accept the au-
> thor(s)' interpretations and definitions to agree with their conclu-
> sions. Little substantiation for their allegations is offered.

The discursive formation within which this reviewer operates does not permit her/him to read Williams' closely-argued text (which is how the other
reviewer reads it) as anything other than opinion. This is instructive in itself;
it becomes doubly so when we realize that an opinion piece has no place in
an academic journal in this reviewer's eyes. If this were indeed an opinion
piece, then we are to understand that an opinion does not count as a contribution to the World 3 of knowledge.

The closure of signification becomes even more evident a few lines further
on in this review. We quote:

> If, in fact, the tautology does exist, it would be enlightening for
> the author(s) to consider how it could be addressed (within the
> context of the research study being reviewed). Nor do the au-
> thor(s) refer to previous research on positivism or the philosophy
> of science.

The first sentence provides evidence that the reviewer can envisage the WZ
program as the only valid one, and its purposes as the only legitimate ones.
Whereas many readers might suppose that Williams was arguing that the
whole program must fall given its mechanisms, the reviewer requires that
Williams repair (to help PAT out!) what he has argued is irreparable. The
stretching of language becomes clearer still in the next sentence. Previously
the reviewer had wanted the clear tracking of a particular empiricism: "the
author(s) do not take any one positive accounting research study and trace
its conceptual foundations through its empirical development to demonstrate where or how the tautology arises." In this sentence ("nor do the

POLICING ACCOUNTING KNOWLEDGE

author(s) refer to previous research on positivism or the philosophy of science") the reviewer wants a reference to previous studies in the philosophy of science. It is not clear how they would fulfill the reviewer's requirements since essays in these fields are also, according to the criterion offered, opinion pieces. For example, one can search through Popper's *The Logic of Scientific Discovery* or *Objective Knowledge* finding hardly a mention of particular studies, and certainly no attempt to follow a particular case through, stage by stage.[23] This makes these works opinion pieces; and we are offered no justification for the strange conclusion that an opinion piece is unacceptable, but might have been more acceptable had it referenced other opinion pieces. Yet by referring to other opinions, we are to infer, it would better justify its claim to entering World 3; and these other opinion pieces are presumably part of World 3 since they are deemed worthy of being quoted.

Conclusion

In this book we have presented evidence from debates that went on in the early days of the rise of the positivist accounting project, (the WZ submission to *The Accounting Review* dates from 1977, one year after the appearance of Jensen and Meckling) as well as debates from the 1980s. Perhaps, as we suggested in our opening essay, PAT is—in its present form—in its death throes. The ideological system from which it sprung is likely to be more resilient. We have shown in this essay the mechanisms through which it operates and the way this is expressed through the knowledge-policing process. We have done so through the argument that the supposed philosophical grounding of the project, Popper's falsificationist criterion which was developed in express opposition to the notion of the social construction of knowledge, does not hold water either as a criticism of the sociology of knowledge or in its attempt to conceive of a World 3 of objective knowledge. We have then been forced to turn back to the discursive systems of thought that buttress the policing process, to expose their appropriation of language as a necessary part of their ideological program. To expose this is not to undo its undoubted power, in particular given its program to suppress criticism as far as it can by denying its existence through the strategy of silence. However there are always political limits to the success of any project that attempts to smother disputes and struggle against a truly open society. We use this last term deliberately as an echo of Popper; for, paradoxically, it is those whose appeal to markets forms the main plank of their rhetoric, and who thus might be expected to trust the marketplace for ideas, who have undertaken political censorship through their stranglehold on academic journals and the knowledge-production process. It is, in other words, those who appeal to Popper who are most forceful in stifling open debate. As with so many other critical commentaries, this essay and this volume may not form part of a dialogue with those will not dialogue: but it provides a moment in the debates that go on in the world outside the *Accounting Review* despite its editorial board's best attempts to prevent them.

Notes

1. For an interesting discussion of the ideological roots of what is to be counted as "literature" and what is not, see Eagleton (1983).
2. This argument is weakened by the fact that researchers being at the forefront of knowledge are encouraged to read working papers in their area of expertise to discover as quickly as possible what other work is proceeding which might impact on or enrich their own; and that the rationale for conferences is to present papers to the community that they are thus expected to be aware of.
3. The brief passages in Watts and Zimmerman, 1990, do not constitute any kind of sustained response to criticism.
4. *The Open Society and Its Enemies.* The book was originally published in 1945 and its political program was not hidden by Popper: he was later to refer to it as "his war effort" (Popper, 1976 p.115). It is of interest to note Popper's hijacking of language in the later book. He refers to his program as "the critical method" which can be "generalized into what I described as the critical or rational attitude." This is, we are told, "openness to criticism—readiness to be criticized, and eagerness to criticize oneself" (ibid). As we shall see, he dismisses Marxists and sociologists of knowledge for irrationalism and dogmatism. Given the expressed and demonstrated willingness of critical theorists to undertake their investigations *through* the notion of critique, this arrogation is breathtaking. See for example the special issue of *Critical Perspectives on Accounting* on the Marx-Foucault debate as evidence of a willingness to engage in mutual criticism.
5. This conflict is elegantly explored in Abercrombie and Turner, 1978.
6. The range of subtle argument cannot be summarized here. Excellent analyses may be found in Larrain, 1979 and Eagleton, 1991.
7. In any case, it is difficult any longer to create a dividing line that clearly distinguishing Marxist from other informed critical thought.
8. Although *The Open Society* was published in 1945, Popper has permitted these passages to remain in new editions and reprints, suggesting he still fully endorses them.
9. cf Popper: "I believe that it is quite correct to insist that Marxism is, fundamentally, a method." (1945, p.84). Popper here is concentrating on what he sees as the historicist tenor of Marxism, however.
10. See the exchange of letters between Zeff and Watts and Zimmerman in this volume.
11. This should not be read as a criticism of the editor, but a comment on the structural characteristics of the system in which he and the other participants were implicated.

12. Popper of course was later to attack Kuhn's propositions concerning paradigms (cf Lakatos and Musgrave, 1973), but we see them here as well expressing the differences of approaches as between referees of the original papers and critics of it.

13. Jack, writing in the *Financial Times,* lists a series of incidents, such as a professional accountancy body (the Chartered Association of Certified Accountants) threatening a university at which there was a vocal critic that it risked de-recognition for training purposes; a partner of Price Waterhouse, named in David Cooper's then chair title, shouting down the telephone that funding would be withdrawn; a professorial interview where the vice-chancellor attempted to block an appointment because of the political views of the candidate (unnamed); and oral threats of libel proceedings when empirical evidence derived from tape data showed stock analysts in an unflattering light.

14. Thus comments tend to either question minutiae of statistical procedures or selection of data sets. This appearance of lively debate is thus doubly mystifying, for it leads to a belief that method can be the only legitimate grounds for dispute while suppressing discussions of methodology.

15. As Christenson points out, even this fails when the writers' general point is one favored by the reviewers. In WZ's 1978 paper, for example, part of the evidence points the opposite way to the hypothesis, but the paper as published neither refers to this nor, therefore, explains it. Since the paper was refereed, we must assume, carefully, that the referees were not bothered by this contrary evidence wither. Given the care with which they leap on particular questionable statements in the critiques presented in this paper, we must doubt their ability to be symmetrical in their judgements.

16. An interesting example occurred at the 1992 annual meeting when the session addressed by Briloff and Sporkin was allotted a small room, where those standing so packed the room that many could simply not enter (our empirical evidence for this is the experience of one of the authors who could not even get through the door). A symbolic gesture, perhaps, of barriers to entry?

17. There were 86 schools listed in the 1993 *Hasselback* that had offered doctoral degrees and were represented in the directory as a whole.

18. For example: "Ffor this kind of absolute precision to be demanded of a *defined* concept, it must first be demanded of the *defining* concepts, and ultimately of our *undefined,* or *primitive* terms. Yet this is impossible." (Popper, 1976 p.29). See also Gunn, 1989.

19. As a believr in the Tarskian conception of truth, Popper is obliged to view language solely (at any rate from the point of view of knowledge production and criticism) as being mappable to the physical world through something very similar to the correspondence theory of truth. In doing so he also believes the rhetorical force of language can be overcome through the community spirit of scientists. We argue in this paper that both views are mistaken.

20. This is not to deny that words do not impact on deeds, or that the material comforts of the people might not be enhanced by the judicious use of propaganda; or indeed that language cannot incite racial hatred or sexual harassment. But as part of the constellation of things-in-the-world, and especially in view of

their inter-referentiality, signifiers demand to be controlled as part of the ideological process precisely because they combine their own material and immanent consequences with such consequences for other features of capitalist society.

21. We are indebted to an exchange between Keith Robson and Nicholas Dopuch at a workshop near Manchester in June, 1992, for pointing to this contrast.

22. This arrogation of language reflects that of Jensen three years before when the expression "organization theory" had been used without one mention of the fifty years of organizational research or the hundred textbooks or thousand college courses that taught a whole body of knowledge under that title which bore no relation to Jensen's subject-matter.

23. Those who do look in great detail at particular junctures in science (Kuhn and Feyerabend) are just those philosophers who argue *against* the rationalist positivist project!

References

Abercrombie N. and Turner B. S. (1978) "The dominant ideology thesis," *British Journal of Sociology* 29,2: 149–170.

Allen V. L. (1975) *Social Analysis: A Marxist Critique and Alternative* (Longmans).

Althusser, L. (1971). *Ideology and Ideological State Apparatuses in Lenin and Philosophy and other Essays,* quoted by Callinicos, *Althusser's Marxism* (Pluto).

Armstrong J. Scott (1978) "Advocacy and objectivity in Science" *Management Science* 25,5 May: 423–428.

Arnold, Pat, and Leslie Oakes, "Hospitals in the Unites States: A Study of the Entity assumption in Accounting" *Critical Perspectives on Accounting,* (forthcoming).

Baritz, Loren, The Servants of Power: A History of The Use of Social Science in American Industry, (New York: John Wiley & Sons, 1960).

Bernstein, Richard J., Serious Play: The Ethical and Political Horizon of Jacques Derrida," a paper presented to the University of Iowa Rhetoric Seminar, March 10th, 1987.

Berry, A. J., Capps T., Cooper D., Ferguson, P., Hopper T. and Lowe T. (1985) "Management control in an area of the NCB: rationales of accounting practices in a public enterprise" *Accounting, Organizations and Society 10,1: 3–28.*

Braverman, H., LABOR AND MONOPOLY CAPITAL (New York: Monthly Review Press, 1974).

Briloff, Abraham, "Accountancy and Society: A Covenant Desecrated," *Critical Perspectives on Accounting,* Vol. 1, No. 1, March, 1990; pp. 5–30.

Brown, L. D. and J. C. Gardner (1985b) "Using citation analysis to assess the impact of journals and articles on contemporary accounting research (CAR)" *Journal of Accounting Research,* Spring 84–109.

——— (1985a) "Applying citation analysis to evaluate the research contributions of accounting faculty and doctoral programs" *The Accounting Review,* April 262–277.

Burchell S., A. G. Hopwood, and C. Clubb (1985) Accounting in its social context:

towards a history of value added in the UK *Accounting, Organizations and Society*

Christenson, C., "The Methodology of Positive Accounting" *The Accounting Review* (January) 1–22.

Cooper, C., "Ideology, Hegemony and Accounting Discourse: A Case Study of the National Union of Journalists" *Critical Perspectives on Accounting,* (forthcoming).

———— and A. Puxty (1994), "Reading accounting writing" *Accounting, Organizations and Society* 19,2 127–146.

Cooper, D. J., A. G. Puxty, K. Robson, and H. R. Willmott "The Ideology of Professional Regulation and the Markets for Accounting Labour: Three Episodes in the Recent History of the UK Accountancy Profession" *Accounting, Organizations and Society* (forthcoming).

Cooper W. W. and S. A. Zeff (1992), "Kinney's Design for Accounting Research" *Critical Perspectives on Accounting* 3,1 March 87–92.

Derrida, J. (1972), *Disseminations* (transl Athlone Press, 1981).

Dews, P., "Adorno, Post-Structuralism and the Critique of Identity," *New Left Review,* (May–June 1986) Vol. 157, pp. 28–44.

Dews, Peter, "The Nouvelle Philosophie and Foucault," *Economy and Society,* (1979) Vol. 8, p.127–171.

Dillard, J. F., and Beverly H. Burris, "Technocracy and Management Control Systems", *Accounting, Management and Information Systems Technology,* Vol.3, No. 1, 1993.

————, and R. Nehmer, "Metaphorical Marginalization," Critical Perspectives on Accounting, Vol.1, No.1, September, 1990.

————, and R. Bricker, "A Critique of Knowledge Based Systems in Auditing: The Systematic Encroachment of Technical Consciousness," *Critical Perspectives on Accounting,* Vol.3, No.3, September, 1992, pp. 205–24.

Eagleton, T. (1991), *Ideology: an Introduction* (Verso).

———— (1983), *Literary Theory: An Introduction* (Blackwell).

Edwards, R., *Contested Terrain: The Transformation of the Workplace in the Twentieth Century,* (New York: Basic Books, 1979).

Garison, B., *The Electronic Sweatshop: How Computers Are Transforming The Office of The Future Into The Factory of The Past* (New York: Simon and Schuster, 1988)

Gunn, R., "Marxism and Philosophy," *Capital & Class,* No. 37, Spring, 1989, pp. 87–116.

Hines, R. D. (1989). "Popper's Methodology of Falsificationism and Accounting Research" *The Accounting Review,* October, 657–662.

Hoogvelt A. and Tinker Tony (1978) The Role of the Colonial and Post-Colonial State in Imperialism *The Journal of African Studies* 1–13.

Kaplan S. E. and Ruland R. G. (1991) "Positive theory, rationality and accounting regulation" *Critical Perspectives on Accounting* 2,4: 361–374.

Kinney, W. R. (1986) "Empirical Accounting Research Design for Ph.D. Students" *The Accounting Review* April 338–350.

Kinney W. R. (1992) "Issues in Accounting Research Design Education" *Critical Perspectives on Accounting* 3,1 (March) 93–97.

Kuhn, T. S., The Historical Structure of Scientific Discovery, *Science,* (1962), Vol. 36. pp. 760–4.

Lakatos, I. and A. Musgrave (1973), *Criticism and the Growth of Knowledge* (Cambridge University Press).

Larrain, J. (1979), *The Concept of Ideology* (Hutchinson).

Lehman, C. and T. Tinker (1987) "The 'Real' Cultural Significance of Accounts" *Accounting, Organizations and Society* 503–522.

Lowe, E. A., A. G. Puxty and R. C. Laughlin (1983) "Simple Theories for Complex Processes: Accounting Policy and the Market for Myopia" *Journal of Accounting and Public Policy* Vol. 2 No. 1: 19–42.

Lukacs, G. (1971) *History and Class Consciousness* (Merlin Press) (originally 1923).

Martens, S. and K. T. Stevens (1993) "Positive accounting theory and the obligation for post-retirement benefits" *Critical Perspectives on Accounting* 4,3: 275–295.

Merino, B. (1989), "An analysis of the development of accounting knowledge: a pragmatic approach" *Accounting, Organizations and Society,* 18, 2/3 163–185.

Mitchell, A., and P. Sikka, "Accounting for Change: the Institutions of Accountancy," *Critical Perspectives on Accounting,* Vol. 4, No. 1, (March 1993), pp. 29–52.

Peasnell, K. V. and D. J. Williams (1986). "Ersatz academics and scholar-saints: the supply of financial accounting research" *Abacus* 22,2: 121–135.

Pêcheux, M. (1982), *Language, Semantics and Ideology* (Macmillan).

Popper, K. R. (1966), *The Open Society and its Enemies: Vol II Hegel and Marx (5th ed., Routledge).*

——— (1970), "Normal Science and its Dangers" in Lakatos and Musgrave op. cit., pp. 51–58.

———. (1976), *Unended Quest* (Fontana).

———. *Objective Knowledge: An Evolutionary Approach* (Oxford University Press).

Poulantzas N. (1973) "On Social Classes" *New Left Review,* vol. 78; reprinted in A. Giddens and D. Held *Classes, Power and Conflict: Classical and Contemporary Debates* (Macmillan, 1982).

Puxty, A. G., P. Sikka and H. C. Willmott (forthcoming) "Systems of Surveillance and the Silencing of Academic (Accounting) Labour" *British Accounting Review.*

Ravetz, J., "Ideological Commitments in the Philosophy of Science," *Radical Philosophy* (Summer 1984) pp. 5–10.

——— (1973) *Scientific knowledge and its social problems* (Penguin).

Rose, H., and S. Rose, *Science and Society,* (Harmondsworth: Penguin Books, 1969).

Shaw, M., MARXISM AND THE SOCIAL SCIENCE, (London: Pluto Press, 1975).

Spacek, L., "The Need for an Accounting Court", *The Accounting Review,* 1958, pp. 368–379.

Sporkin, S., "Accounting and Realism," in Tinker, T., (ed.) Social Accounting for Corporations: Private Enterprise Versus The Public Interest, (New York: Markus Wiener Publishing Inc., 1984).

Sterling, R. R. (1990), "Positive accounting: an assessment" *Abacus* 26: 97–135.

Sutton, Steve G., "On Audit Epistemology and Auditors' Cognitive Processing: The

Societal Impact of Information Technologies," *Advances in Accounting Information Systems,* Vol. 2, pp. 1–13, 1993 (Greenwich, CT: JAI Press, 1993).

Tinker, A. M., B. D. Merino, and M. N. Neimark (1982), "The Normative Origins of Positive Theories: Ideology and Accounting Thought" *Accounting, Organizations and Society* No. 2 pp. 167–200.

Watts, R. L. and J. L. Zimmerman (1978), "Towards a Positive Theory of the Determination of Accounting Standards" *The Accounting Review,* January, 112–134.

——— (1979), "The demand for and supply of accounting theories: the market for excuses" *The Accounting Review,* April, 273–305.

———. (1986), *Positive Accounting Theory* (Englewood Cliffs: Prentice-Hall).

Whitley R. D. (1988), "The possibility and utility of positive accounting theory" *Accounting, Organizations and Society* 13,6: 631–645.

Whittington G. (1987) "Positive accounting: a review article" *Accounting and Business Research* 17: 327–336.

Williams P. F. and J. L. Rodgers (1992), "The Accounting Review and the Production of Accounting Knowledge" unpublished working paper, North Carolina State University.

Willmott, H. C., "Serving the Public Interest? A Critical Analysis of a Professional Claim", in Cooper, D. J. and Hopper, T. M. (eds.), *Critical Accounts,* ed. D. J. Cooper and T. M. Hopper (London: Macmillan, 1989).

Willmott, Hugh, "Accountants in the Academy: A Labour Process Perspective," UMIST Manchester School of Management Working Paper, 1993.

Zeff, S. (1989) "Recent trends in accounting education and research in the USA: some implications for UK academics" *British Accounting Review,* 21,2 June pp. 159–176.

Acknowledgment

The authors and the publisher thank the following authors and publishers for supplying manuscripts, letters and other published and unpublished documents and granting permission to include them in this book.

Mr. Paul Gerhardt, and the American Accounting Asssociation, Professor Germain Boer (Vanderbilt University), Professor George Foster (Stanford University), Professor W. R. Kinney, Jr. (University of Texas at Austin), Professor Richard Laughlin (University of Sheffield), Professor Owen Moseley (Arkansas State University), Professor Tony Lowe (University of Waterloo, New Zealand), Professor Ross Watts (University of Rochester), Professor Paul Williams (North Carolina State University), Professor Stephen Zeff (Rice University), and Professor Jerold Zimmerman (University of Rochester).